7/6

THE PARISH COMMUNION

THE
PARISH COMMUNION

A BOOK OF ESSAYS

BY

W. S. BAKER	F. R. FAIRBAIRN
D. R. BLACKMAN	A. M. FARRER
J. F. BRISCOE	C. P. HANKEY
J. O. COBHAM	A. G. HEBERT
H. DE CANDOLE	M. R. NEWBOLT
GREGORY DIX	C. H. SMYTH
F. M. DOWNTON	J. F. L. SOUTHAM
E. D. TYNDALL	

Edited by A. G. HEBERT

LONDON

SOCIETY FOR PROMOTING
CHRISTIAN KNOWLEDGE
NORTHUMBERLAND AVENUE, W.C.2
NEW YORK : THE MACMILLAN COMPANY

First published 1937

MADE IN GREAT BRITAIN

PREFACE

THIS book is concerned with the Parish Eucharist, or Parish Communion, which in an increasing number of churches is celebrated every Sunday at or about 9 a.m. The central point is this: that the real question is not that of the best arrangement of the Sunday service, but rather of a deepened understanding of the meaning of the Sacrament and of the Church. This is the main thesis of the introductory essay, and the next four essays are concerned with the Redemption of Man as it is set forth in the Sacrament and in the Church: the Rev. D. R. Blackman, in a brief but weighty essay (no. II), deals with Man as the subject of redemption; the Rev. J. O. Cobham with the redemption itself, in the form of a survey of the Christian idea of Sacrifice (no. III); the Rev. Austin Farrer with the idea of the Sacrament and the Church in the New Testament, giving us a close study of the Pauline doctrine of the Mystical Body (no. IV); and the Rev. Gregory Dix, O.S.B., in essay no. V, shows how vividly this idea is realised in the ante-Nicene Liturgies.

The next four essays belong rather to the sphere of pastoral theology. In no. VI the Rev. C. P. Hankey discusses the two complementaries, Liturgical Worship and Personal Devotion; in no. VII Canon Lovel Southam speaks of Ideals for a Parish, from the point of view of the parish priest and the missioner. No. VIII, by the Rev. Denis Tyndall, is concerned with ' the liturgy outside the temple '; in one sense the offering of worship is completed when the people go out of the church door, in another it is then only ready to begin. No. IX, by the Rev. Prebendary Briscoe, is concerned with the all-important truth that no amount of attention to ways and means can be of any use if the priest himself be not living a consecrated life.

v

Then we have four essays dealing with things practical: Canon Newbolt writes on Preaching in relation to the Liturgy (no. X); to this essay is appended a List of Titles for Sundays and Holy-days and their lections, mainly taken from the Swedish Prayer-book; for this list I am responsible. In no. XI the Rev. H. de Candole gives a comprehensive outline of Instruction on the sacred actions of the Church service. No. XII, by the Rev. F. R. Fairbairn and the Rev. F. M. Downton, is mainly descriptive of a Parish Eucharist followed by a communal breakfast, in a country village; while in no. XIII the Rev. W. S. Baker does the same for a town parish, and in the light of the experience of St. John's, Newcastle, seeks to answer all the practical difficulties that we have been able to think of. Finally, to show that this book really is a unity, and does not fall apart into two halves, theological and practical, and that the details of the ordering of worship have relation to the witness that the Church is set to bear in the midst of a half-pagan world, we have the Rev. Charles Smyth's essay (no. XIV) on the Church as *Corpus Christi* in relation to the World and to the civil State.

But why this wide range of subjects? Why not include only essays dealing with the practical difficulties? The answer is that in that case we should only have been scratching the surface: for the real problem is not how to re-arrange the services, but how to reach a greatly deepened understanding of the nature of the Church. I am told that in some parishes the Parish Eucharist has been tried, and has failed. If this be so, I suspect that more often than not the reason will have been an inadequate preparation of teaching. The need for this is emphasised in several of these essays (see pp. 181, 249, 272; cf. 177–8); and it may further be illustrated from a testimony of a Belgian parish priest, quoted in *Questions Liturgiques et Paroissiales*, 1935, p. 20:

" It has been a long work; it has lasted eight years. He would be a simple man who thought that he could gain from my people an active participation in liturgical ceremonies simply by announcing from the pulpit on a

Sunday that in future this and that will be done, because
M. le curé wishes it, or even because the Pope wishes it.
There is a whole mentality to be transformed: negatively,
by demolition of prejudices, and positively, by reconstruc-
tion. The former of these is not to be done after the
manner of a bombardment or a fire, to the great scandal
of the romantically-minded devout, against criticism and
even open opposition of wounded vanities and slighted
interests, but rather by infiltration, as the water wears
away the stone by dripping upon it. If the law of growth
be disregarded, many an attempt at reform in various
spheres of pastoral activity is doomed to certain failure.
The latter work is no less slow and requires no less
patience."

Our difficulties in England differ in detail from those in
Belgium; but at bottom they are much the same. There is a
whole mentality to be transformed, if a new understanding
of the meaning of our life in the Church is to be gained.
That is why this book is compelled to include these long
essays about Sacrifice and about the idea of the Church in
the Bible and the Liturgies, before coming to deal with the
immediate problem of what the parish priest is to do.

In spite of all that we can say, no doubt there will be some
who will continue to speak of this book as 'a plea for,' or
as 'written to present the case for,' the Parish Eucharist
at 9 a.m. But no: its real aim is to set forth a conception
of the nature of the Church, which appears to compel the
adoption of the Parish Communion as its necessary expression in liturgy. It is the idea of the Church that is primary;
with regard to its expression, it is our concern more to
examine the difficulties in carrying out the Parish Eucharist
than to argue the case for it. And because the book as a
whole represents in general one consistent theological view,
it can truly be called a book with a single aim.

The authors are Catholics of the Church of England.
The crucial point here is that the Parish Communion, as we
envisage it, presupposes the observance of the Fast before
Communion, for the reasons given on pp. 23–29. But this

book is definitely addressed to our brethren in the Church as a whole, not to a party within the Church; and we have longed to be able to do something to increase and deepen the unity of the Church of England, believing that her true unity is a spiritual unity, centred round the Gospel of Redemption and the evangelical Sacraments, and that the spread of the Parish Communion will do much to further the realisation of that unity. It might seem that such an end might best have been gained by inviting representatives of all shades of opinion to contribute to a book on the Parish Communion. But we believe that such a book would have had all the unsatisfactoriness of a compromise, and would have involved such adjustments and accommodations as would have prevented the clear expression of the principles on which alone true unity is based. Hence it seemed clear that the best service that we could render to the Church was to write a book in which we could say quite plainly what we really meant; and that we must do that, and trust our brethren to understand.

For the reasons that have been given, the range of subjects covered by these essays is somewhat wide. It is inevitable that many readers will ask why such and such other subjects do not receive separate treatment. Thus, the following subjects are all more or less directly related to the Parish Communion: ' The contemporary history of the Liturgical Movement all over Christendom, and not least in the Roman Catholic Church ' (but this latter point should be handled by a Roman Catholic); ' The true principles and aims of Prayer-book revision '; ' The administration of the Sacrament of Baptism '; ' Children's worship '; ' The use of the Psalms in worship '; ' Liturgy and Evangelism '; ' Books of private prayer in the liturgical spirit '; ' Church music in relation to Liturgy '; ' Church architecture, painting and sculpture in relation to Liturgy '; ' The bearings of the Liturgical Movement on social, industrial, and economic problems '; ' The Liturgical Movement and Reunion.' But in a book of essays there are limits of size.

There are so many acknowledgments to be made, and most of them are of such a personal and informal character, that I ask to be excused from appending the usual list. I must, however, thank the Archbishop of Upsala for his courteous approval (there was no question of copyright) of the use which I have made of the Swedish Titles for Sundays and Holy-days on pp. 226–30.

I must also thank a mission-priest who wishes to remain anonymous, who in the autumn of 1935 wrote to me two letters which led to this book being undertaken. He wanted the Parish Eucharist, but not as something which " works well " or " gets people to church "; nor was he interested in ceremonial for its own sake; nor could he " encourage people to communicate without fasting." He cared for the Parish Eucharist, with its " vision of offering, communion, and fellowship " as " something at the very centre of the life of the Church which is truly according to the mind of Christ "; and of the communal breakfast he wrote: " I want to encourage priests in difficult places in town and country to make a small beginning, and be quite happy if half-a-dozen sit down to breakfast after Communion together," as a small instalment of that genuine Christian fellowship for the lack of which the world is perishing. I can truly say that, being convinced that this book was needed, I made a series of efforts to escape from the responsibility of editorship, till it was clear that it was being laid upon me as a plain duty.

A. Gabriel Hebert, S.S.M.

Kelham,
Newark.
Jan. 1937.

CONTENTS

I

THE PARISH COMMUNION IN ITS SPIRITUAL ASPECT

By The Rev. A. G. HEBERT

Of the Society of the Sacred Mission, Kelham

THE PARISH COMMUNION IN ITS
SPIRITUAL ASPECT

By 'the Parish Communion' is meant the celebration of the Holy Eucharist, with the communion of the people, in a parish church, as the chief service of the day, or, better, as the assembly of the Christian community for the worship of God; for even the phrase 'the chief service of the day' is unsatisfactory if it is understood to mean *a* service—one among several—and not *the* service—*the* divine Liturgy. While on festivals that fall on a week-day, such as Ascension Day, the hour of the Parish Communion has in most places to be quite early in the morning—7 a.m. or even 6 a.m.— on Sundays the most suitable hour will generally be not long before or after 9 a.m.[1]

It is commonly agreed that it is the ideal arrangement that the principal Eucharist should be the service of general communion; but, it is said, there are great and even insuperable difficulties in putting the ideal into practice. That the practical difficulties exist and are real cannot be denied. But it would be a fatal mistake to consider this subject only or chiefly from the practical point of view, as the problem of a convenient arrangement of parish worship. It is of cardinal importance to go deeper, and consider the underlying principles. The Holy Eucharist is the central act of worship of the Church, the People of God, God's universal spiritual family. It is the worship in spirit and in truth of which our Lord, according to St. John, ch. iv., speaks to the Samaritan woman, since it is the worship

---

[1] The observance of the Fast before Communion is assumed in the whole argument of this book; it is for this reason that it is not dealt with in a separate Essay. Since, however, it could not simply be passed over, it is dealt with in a Note appended to this Essay. See pp. 23-9.

3

of God through Christ who is the Truth, through the Spirit in whom the mystical Body of Christ lives. As the sacramental showing-forth of the one Sacrifice of Christ and of the offering-up of the members of Christ through union with Him to be a reasonable, holy, and living sacrifice to God, it sums up in itself the whole Gospel of redemption and the whole nature of the Church, Christ's Body. The subject of the Parish Communion is therefore infinite both in spiritual depth and in the range of its application, which extends to every side of the Church's life and her witness to the world.

This being so, it is clear that the subject cannot be easily or summarily dealt with. There are two dangers in particular against which it is necessary that we should be constantly on our guard; and not merely that we should guard against them, as though they had only to be named to be avoided: for they are dangers into which we are all liable to fall, and we can only rise above them by a deepened apprehension of the meaning of the Church's life in Christ.

The first is the danger of a materialistic perversion of the sacramental principle. It is only too easy to assume, as soon as it is admitted that the Parish Communion is right in principle, that the institution of a service at 9 or 9.30 a.m., labelled ' the Parish Communion ' or ' the People's Eucharist,' will prove a sort of panacea for all difficulties. If the matter is approached in this way, experience will soon prove the falsity of the assumption. The problem of the Church's worship is a spiritual problem; it is the problem of the spiritual life of each parish, of the growth of priest and people in grace and the ' fellowship of the Gospel.' And spiritual fruits are not gained except by spiritual means, by prayer and love and pastoral care and spiritual discipline. That which is born of the flesh is flesh.

Further, since each parish is the local unit of the Church, Christ's Body, and the problem is that of its spiritual life ' in Christ,' each parish presents a separate problem. Thus, if it be admitted that for many parishes 9 or 9.15 is a very suitable hour, it would be absurd to claim any special sanctity for the hour of nine. I understand that in the

Universities' Mission to Central Africa, the Parish Communion is celebrated usually about eight, before the heat of the tropical day begins. On the other hand, in the S.S.M. missions in South Africa, in which I have served, the native people have to come in long distances from the farms, and while the fast is strictly observed, it is impossible in most places to begin the service before ten or even eleven. In England, well-to-do districts, where the Sunday breakfast at 9 a.m. is firmly established, present a problem of special difficulty, which may in some cases be solved by the institution of a communal breakfast in the Parish Room. Again, in country villages, with a tripartite congregation of labourers, farmers, and the squire-family and other well-to-do people, it will often be difficult either to change customary hours of service, or to find a time when all can meet at communion. Both there and in the towns it seems that the problem of providing the people with Holy Communion can often only be solved, in special (*i.e.* exceptional) cases, by the use of the reserved sacrament for the whole and not only for the sick.[1] Yet again, it will clearly be necessary, at least for some time to come, that some churches should retain the late Sung Eucharist without communicants. This will apply especially to those which draw their congregations mainly from outside the parish.

It is a matter of the spirit, not of the letter: of the Parish Communion not as an end in itself, but as the sacramental expression of the Church's common life in Christ. The spiritual aspect of the matter must be kept steadily in view.

Secondly, since the Sacrament belongs to the Church, it would be disastrous if the Parish Communion were to become the badge of some party or group. There is in the Church of England a large diversity of ceremonial practice;

---

[1] This use of the reserved sacrament for the whole goes back to the second century; the sick, as we learn from Justin Martyr, were communicated by taking the Sacrament to them from the service (*cf.* p. 103). This use of the reserved sacrament does in fact maintain the ' family idea ' better than the provision of separate celebrations. I remember hearing a South African layman, a white man, justify to me the use of the reserved sacrament by the analogy of a family feast, with a birthday cake: when his younger son was detained on business in the city, they kept some of the cake for him to have on his return home.

B

we may regret the fact, but it exists, and a sane realism will recognise it. But the Sacrament itself matters infinitely more than the ceremonial dress in which it is clothed; and it is the Sacrament itself that is the outward and visible sign of our unity in Christ, a unity deeper than all our differences.

Therefore, those who believe that the principle of the Parish Communion is of vital importance must scrupulously avoid allowing this movement to become identified with some particular ceremonial use. It would be disastrous if, for instance, it came to be identified with the so-called English Use, as those who are zealous for that Use will be the first to recognise. Other priests and congregations are accustomed to the ' Western Use '; when they adopt the Parish Communion, there is no reason for them to give up the ' Western ' type of ceremonial. Equally, one would think, it would seem entirely natural and right to an Evangelical churchman,[1] that a Christian congregation should have, for its chief service on the Lord's day, the Memorial of the Lord's death.

In this, as in other big issues, we ought to think of what may come to pass in the course of twenty years, not of two years or five. If in the next twenty years the Parish Communion becomes something like the normal practice in English parish churches, in those places where real spiritual work is going on (not elsewhere), that fact alone will have done much to heal our party divisions. As it is by the calling and grace of God alone that we are Christians, and in Him we are one as members of His Church, so in proportion as we put the Sacrament and the Communion in the centre of our worship we shall thereby be brought to an understanding of one another far deeper than any that can be attained by Round Table Conferences. At such conferences differences are tabulated and efforts are made to reach an agreed formula; but such a formula does not express the best of what each side has to say, and it has all the unsatisfactoriness of a compromise. But in our worship of God through Christ in His Sacrament we *are* one in Him; there

[1] See the quotation on p. 12 below.

we must go to find our unity, and by that road we shall come in time to a real understanding of one another which will not be a compromise.

The movement for the establishment of the Parish Communion must not be side-tracked by being made into some sort of a ritualistic movement. It is, in fact, part of the Liturgical Movement which is going on in our day in every part of Christendom, and which is fundamentally a movement of return to the Sacraments and the Liturgy, as the sacramental expression of our redemption through Christ and of the nature of the Church as His mystical Body. Its chief danger everywhere is that this spiritual aim should be confused by some form of ritualism, by some identification of the movement with its mere externals. There is in the Church of England in certain quarters a tendency to adopt a new ritualism, as an outward expression of a humanism which sees in Communion little more than the dramatisation of a humanistic ideal of brotherhood. But the genuine Liturgical Movement presupposes the Catholic Gospel and the Catholic Creeds; it presupposes the revelation which God has made of Himself by sending His only-begotten Son, born of a Virgin, and the redemption of human nature through His death and the resurrection of His body from the grave. In this faith the Catholic and the genuine Evangelical are at one. The realisation of their unity must surely come through the Sacrament in which that faith and that unity are set forth.

The Parish Communion is a key-point of this Liturgical Movement: not, indeed, the only key-point, for we must never isolate the eucharistic Sacrament from the preaching of the Gospel and from the rest of the Church's sacramental life; in particular we must bear ever in mind the importance of Baptism, and the need of a reform in our practice with regard to that Sacrament. Yet the Parish Communion is a key-point; and it is a great and a glorious hope that it may be the appointed means by which the Church of England may come to a true understanding of herself and her calling.

2. THE NATURE OF THE CHURCH

It is generally acknowledged that the word *ecclesia* in the New Testament is taken not from the secular use of the word, as the democratic assembly of the Greek city-state, but from its Hebrew meaning in the Greek Old Testament, where it means the congregation of the Lord, the People of God, Israel. The Church of the apostolic age regarded itself as the inheritor of the Old Testament; the Church of God had, indeed, begun with Moses, if not with Abraham, but Jesus was the Messiah to whom the whole Old Testament had looked forward, and in Him Israel had been re-constituted as the Church of the New Covenant.

It follows from this meaning of *ecclesia* that the Church as a whole cannot be thought of as made up of a federation of the local communities, the churches of Jerusalem, Ephesus, Corinth, Rome, and the rest. It is the Church as a whole that is Israel; the whole is prior to the parts, and the whole is present in each part. It is clear from the way in which St. Paul addresses the Corinthians (I Cor. i. 1-3) that the assembly of the Christians at Corinth is ' Israel ' in Corinth: " Paul, an apostle of Jesus Christ . . . to the Church of God which is at Corinth."

The Church of God has been re-constituted in the person of Jesus the Messiah, by His death and resurrection. His resurrection is not one individual's survival of death, but is inclusive, so that in it the Church, which is His Body, is also raised to life: " I am the Resurrection and the Life ": " If ye be risen with Christ, seek those things that are above." Thus the Christians themselves have died and risen again: " buried with Him by baptism into death, that, like as Christ was raised up from the dead by the glory of the Father, even so we also should walk in newness of life." They have renounced at their baptism the old life of egoism and self-will, and they have been born again into the new life in Christ, in the Body of Christ, in the Israel of God.[1]

[1] A. M. Ramsey, *The Gospel and the Catholic Church* (Longmans, 1936), esp. chs. iii., iv., v.

To say that the Church is the Body of Christ is to say that the Church's essential nature is expressed in this dying and rising again. The life of the " old man " is the isolated life of self-centred man, of man in the state of Original Sin; the life of the " new man " is the life of *koinonia* in which " ye are not your own, for ye were bought with a price." The passage from the old life to the new is expressed in the baptismal rite, and it dominates the Easter liturgy, which might be said to take its key-note from the solemn baptisms anciently performed on Easter Eve.

And what do the Christians do when they meet for worship " on the first day of the week "? They meet as the Israel of God, scattered in many places all over the world, yet so that the whole is present in the part, and the unity of the whole Body is present and is expressed in the worship of the local community. Thus meet together, they confess what they corporately are by the calling and grace of God. They rehearse and set forth the mystery of the divine *agape* whereby man has been redeemed and the redeemed fellowship constituted as the Body of Christ. The central act of their worship must therefore be the act which the Lord instituted on the night that He was betrayed, as the summing-up of all His life-work: " Do this in remembrance of Me, do this for My *anamnesis*."

What is *anamnesis*? In Biblical usage it is not a subjective remembering, lest we should forget, but a concrete and objective bringing-back from the past into the present.[1] In I Kings xvii. 18, when Elijah has gone to stay with the widow woman at Zarephath, and her child dies, she cries out, " Art thou come hither to bring my sin to re-membrance (ἀναμνῆσαι) and to slay my son? " The coming of the holy man of God has caused all her sins to come back out of the past into the present in their terrible guilt and power, and they take effect in the death of the child. The eucharistic *anamnesis* is not an *anamnesis* of our sins, for these have been taken away by the death of Christ: but it is an *anamnesis* of His death and resurrection, so that we come

---

[1] I owe this exegesis of ἀνάμνησις to Fr. Gregory Dix, O.S.B. See *Theology*, Vol. XXVIII. (1934), pp. 193–5 ; also pp. 120–1 *infra*.

into the actual presence of the victorious *agape* that over-
came sin, death, and the devil. Not by a mere subjective
remembering, but by the objectivity of the sacramental
action which He gave us to do, we are at Bethlehem, adoring
with the shepherds the mystery of the Incarnation; we
are in the presence of the Exorcist who cast out devils and the
Healer who came to save men in body and soul (this is why
so many of the Sunday Gospels recount miracles of healing) ;
we are in the awful presence of Calvary, we are with Mary
Magdalen by the empty grave, we are with the Apostles
in the upper room ("the peace of the Lord be alway
with you"); we are on the Mount of Olives, and we are
in the presence of the advent with glory to judge the living
and the dead ("O Lamb of God that takest away the sins
of the world, have mercy upon us"); and we pray that as
at Pentecost the Holy Ghost may through the Communion
fill us with His grace and heavenly benediction.[1]

In the Sacrament the whole mystery of redemption is
set forth objectively, focussed in one single point. But since
that which is in itself one and simple cannot be apprehended
by us *totum simul*, it is presented to us bit by bit, line upon
line, in the course of the liturgical year from Advent to
Pentecost, by collects, epistles, gospels and other propers:
that is, almost wholly through the Scriptures. It is further
mediated to us in the Sermon, the function of which is to
act as a sort of bridge between the Liturgy and the congregation here present, to set these things out for the people in
their own familiar language, and lead them to respond by
faith and join actively in the Church's common approach
to God.

In the Liturgy there is further set forth the response of man
to the Gospel of God, in acts of confession of sin, pleading
for mercy, supplication, confession of faith, adoration and
praise. All this may be said to be summed up in the action

---

[1] Cf. the expression of this same idea by Prof. C. H. Dodd, in *The
Apostolic Preaching and its Developments* (Hodder and Stoughton, 1936),
pp. 234–5: "At each Eucharist we are *there*—we are in the night in
which He was betrayed, at Golgotha, before the empty tomb on Easter
day, and in the upper room where He appeared; *and* we are at the
moment of His coming, with angels and archangels and all the company
of heaven, in the twinkling of an eye, at the last trump."

of the Offertory, when bread and wine are presented before God in the people's name; in the ancient Church these were brought to the altar by the people themselves, and the act visibly expressed their will to offer themselves.[1] The bread and wine at the Offertory represent the whole substance of our lives, all our joys and sorrows, our plans for the future, our hopes and fears; and it is this bread and wine that becomes the matter of the Sacrament, for the *anamnesis* of the Lord's redemptive work.

The action is completed in the Communion, when that which we have offered is given back to us transformed; our lives are united with the life of Christ, united with His Sacrifice that in Him we too may be offered in sacrifice to God, united in the fellowship of His mystical Body, so that " as the Bread is one, we who are many are one Body, for we all partake of the one Bread," and we are thereby united also with one another as " the children of the Lord round the Table of the Lord " at the Lord's Supper.

Thus in the Liturgy the whole Gospel of salvation and the whole nature of the Church are sacramentally set forth. All this is done in the church service sacramentally, that those who have there been brought face to face with the real meaning of things may live their life as men redeemed to God and united in fellowship with one another, and may go about in a world which is out of joint and has lost its true centre, as men who have been called to bear witness to the Truth.

3. THE SUNDAY SERVICE

So we return to the problem of the Sunday service. Since the Church is Israel, the People of God, the Body of Christ, we cannot rightly think even about parochial arrangements except in the light of the real meaning of the Gospel and of the Church. It is hard to descend from the regions in which we have been moving to speak of things which have been soiled with controversy; and yet it is only in the light of the heavenly and spiritual significance of worship that we can rightly discuss the church service.

[1] See pp. 111-7, 305-6, *infra*; cf. also p. 277.

It has become the normal practice in Anglo-Catholic parishes for the Holy Eucharist to be solemnly celebrated with few or no communicants at 11 a.m. It being assumed that the chief service must be held in the middle of Sunday morning, it has rightly been insisted that the Holy Eucharist alone can rightly occupy this place. Yet, as everyone admits in principle, the Eucharist without the communion of the people is not the ideal. The people join in praising God and in hearing His Word; they join in the showing-forth of the Lord's death and resurrection in the act of consecration and the pleading of the sacrifice; but when it comes to the Communion, in which the benefits of His redemptive work are sacramentally imparted, they can only associate themselves with the priest in an act of spiritual communion. But that is only a second-best. To be present at the celebration of the Holy Sacrament is a less thing than to receive the Sacrament; and the parish priest knows that many regular worshippers at the Sunday Mass make their communion less often than they should.

They make their communion at an earlier service. Here again we have no desire to minimise the blessings of the quiet service in the stillness of the early morning. And yet there is an air of individualism about this ' early service.' [1] The

[1] That great C.M.S. missionary, Temple Gairdner of Cairo, writes in his exuberant way of his experiences one Easter Day in America: " Early Service on Easter morning was at 6.30 a.m., which involved early rising. . . . What do you think—it was *choral*. The choir was there in force. I felt that the processional entry, the stirring hymn, the exhilaration of both the choir and of the crowded congregation utterly smashed up that intense individualism that characterises Early Communions in England. If something were lost in quietness, greatly more, I think, was gained in joyousness and *philadelphia* and sense of triumph. A note was immediately struck that seemed to vibrate until the very end of the day. Not once, but many times, the sheer rapture of the whole thing thrilled one and well-nigh brought tears to the eyes." The continuation of the letter contains further points of interest: " The whole choir had ' favours ' of beautiful spring flowers. When I noticed it, so far from feeling it a little bit of mundane decoration, what came over one with a thrill fit to raise the hair from one's forehead was the connection between the Christian Easter and spring. Not by mere coincidence, one saw, did Christ go to Jerusalem for the spring festival, the Passover, there to enact the conquest of spiritual winter by an everlasting spring, ushering in, so to speak, an eternity of April. . . . After the service, the ladies of the congregation served breakfast to the clergy and choir in the Church Room adjoining. Here I admired

worshippers are dotted about the church singly or in little groups; there is little expression of common praise to God. Above all, this service is not the assembly of the congregation as a whole; it is not the chief service of the day, but an extra service, and the communal aspect of Holy Communion is not adequately brought out.

Everyone agrees that the ideal would be to unite the two. Very many parishes which do not as yet see their way to do this on Sundays, do it on days such as Maundy Thursday, Ascension Day, and the patronal festival, at an early hour. But ideals cannot rightly be left floating about in the air. Above all in days such as these, when the Church becomes ever more evidently face to face with a secularised world, it is important that the church service should fully set forth the nature of the Church, and the members of the Church fully know what the Church is.

4. THE MEANING OF 'COMMUNITY' IN THE CHURCH SERVICE

But there are difficulties. Many people will say that they value the quiet and peace of the service in the early morning, and fear that the noise and singing of the Parish Communion would be to them more distracting than helpful. This is far from being a superficial difficulty. It raises the whole question of 'community' in Christian worship, and of right and wrong ideas of 'corporateness.' The point is well brought out in a private letter, which I am allowed to quote:

"At the present time politicians, sociologists, educationalists, parsons, social workers, all seem to be bent on throwing us together; and they all have such watchwords as 'collective,' 'communal,' 'team-spirit,' 'corporate,' 'social and civic centres.' But the paradox is this: In these meetings there is always the impinging of 'outer' personalities on one another, the consciousness of voices, movements, brain-processes, and so on. These outer personalities are quite definitely individual, and

the place given to the human and social element; for if Easter was not the restitution of the human to its divine normal, then I fail to see what it was." *W. H. T. G. to his Friends:* Some letters of Canon Temple Gairdner of Cairo (S.P.C.K., 1930), pp. 46-7.

I think they cannot be merged into anything more than an outward friendliness. The only thing we really have in common, in equal measure and quantity, is the small portion of the ' breath of God,' or the spirit, or whatever it might be called. Real fellowship follows, I think, when spirit recognises spirit, and outer personalities are forgotten for a time. Is it hoped to foster this kind of fellowship by encouraging us to make some sort of noise together? Mightn't the spirit sometimes be given a better chance if we sometimes had a corporate silence? The Silver Jubilee, with its rejoicing and exuberance, was a great experience, but I am not sure that it was so great an experience, or that it drew people together in spiritual friendliness so closely as the Royal Funeral, with its silence and quietness.

" But this is all very difficult. The silence must be in response to some appeal-in-common, if it is to bring with it a sense of fellowship. The Church can offer opportunities for quietly sharing an experience more readily than can the politicians or sociologists or educationalists. . . . And you see, I think, our deepest reverence and silence might be called forth by the celebration of the Holy Communion, when we are before the central mystery of our faith. The quiet voice of a priest and even of a choir doesn't exactly break the silence; it provides the common appeal which ensures that we are all sharing the same experience, and there is the minimum clashing of outer personalities."

The reader will feel, I think, that this letter has said something that needed to be said. It brings before us the right ' ethos ' of Christian worship, and the meaning of our unity in the Church as something ' given,' something not dependent on the efforts of personalities to create and maintain it.

Our unity in the family is something ' given,' since out of it our own lives have sprung; hence family relationships are different in kind from those which we make with our club-mates or work-mates, as ' home ' is different in kind from the club. So it is with the nation, which similarly existed before us and gave and nourished our life; we speak of the ' home-land,' the ' motherland.' So it is with the Church, of which we were born anew in baptism; consequently we speak of the Church as our mother, our spiritual home, God's family, or again, in biblical language, as Jerusalem, the new Israel, the People of God.

In all these unities, since they are not of our making, our souls can find rest. The member of the family who is hearty in the family circle and tries to stir up a family spirit is as intolerable as the politician who lectured the boys in *Stalky and Co.* and waved the Union Jack. Similarly, since the priest in the church stands there to represent and express a unity which exists, he is required in his conduct of the service to be as far as possible impersonal. It is intolerable if he obtrudes his personality, trying unconsciously or consciously to call attention to himself and his rendering of the service; or again, if he be constantly exhorting the people to corporateness and fellowship, as though their fellowship would drop away and perish if it were not continually stimulated by his exertions. If and in so far as he does this, he is acting as though he himself were the centre of the Church's unity, and he is denying the biblical principle: " Other foundation can no man lay than that which is laid, which is Christ."

The difficulty of preaching lies in the fact that it is hard for the preacher not to obtrude his personality in some unpleasant way. Yet the invocation of the Father, Son and Holy Ghost at the beginning of the sermon forbids any attempt of the preacher to be clever or to speak as a personality in his own name. He is there to expound the word of God, not at all for his own glory but for the edification of the Church; for he is there not as a master but as a servant. When the preacher truly knows in whose name he speaks, then his word does not ' break the silence,' but rather intensifies it. He may indeed be colloquial, and he must speak to these people in language that these people understand; but there must always be the restraining consciousness that he speaks as a pastor of the Master's flock; then the sheep follow him, for they know his voice.

The same principle holds with all who take part in the church service, as readers of lessons, servers, choir, organist or congregation. In every case the obtrusion of the ego is out of place. Thus when the psalms are recited in the natural voice, as commonly at a weekday Evensong, the recitation ought to be an outward expression of the unity of Christians in Christ. Only too often each seeks to go his own pace, and the effect becomes that of a race, or a scramble. But in reality the recitation of the psalms requires as much care as the chanting of them. The magnificent rendering of the choruses in Mr. T. S. Eliot's two plays, *The Rock* and *Murder in the Cathedral* has been a revelation of what choric recitation can be. The style which is proper to the Church is, of course, different from that which suits the stage; but in the church the difference which it makes when the psalms are recited properly is almost beyond belief. The words are to be said deliberately and carefully, the pause at the half-verse being observed. Further, the recitation ought not to be a duet between priest and people —this method has its place in the responses—but antiphonal, the two sides of the church answering one another. Only so does it become quite clear that in the psalms it is the Church, *corpus Christi*, that praises God.[1]

The same applies to the sung service. Every form of obtrusion of the individual ego is out of place, whether it be that of the organist, or of the choir which thinks that it is giving a performance, or of the individual in the congregation who likes to hear the sound of his own voice; for all this signifies that these people do not know what it is to join in the common prayer and praise of the Church of God.

All this is most of all out of place at the Parish Communion. It may indeed be well for the Church of England if the Parish Communion does not spread too rapidly; for there are many priests and choirs and congregations who are so ignorant of the real meaning of the Church of God, and so tied and bound to bad traditions and habits, that their rendering of the service will only distract and annoy, and worshippers will rightly prefer the said service, where, as

[1] Unfortunately, in this matter of recitation the clergy often seem to be worse than the laity; sometimes when clergy are assembled the Office is very badly said. Is it out of place to suggest that at such gatherings the archdeacon or whoever is in charge should gently but firmly instruct the clergy in the proper manner of reciting the service?

the corporate element is less, the opportunity for its misuse is less.

Yet it is also true that the Parish Communion witnesses by its very nature against these evil habits and traditions, because the centre of the service is the pleading of the sacrifice of the Lamb of God and the participation of the people in the sacrifice. It must tend of its own nature to create a new ethos. But it cannot be said too strongly that a new ethos is needed, and not least in church music. It is not a matter only of eliminating tunes and settings which are in themselves bad and unworthy, but of finding those which truly express the spirit of the liturgy. Much that is called church music would be excellent and inspiring at an Armistice-day service or a sacred concert, but is quite unsuitable for the Parish Communion. Those who know what real plainsong is, long for the time when the people of our Church shall learn to sing and to appreciate such a setting for the *Gloria in excelsis* as no. VI in the *Ordinary of the Mass*. This is not one of the elaborate mediæval melodies; it is believed to date almost from the period of the catacombs, and nothing could well be simpler. But it is its very simplicity which makes it difficult for us, just as the simplicity of the Gospel itself is difficult for the sophisticated product of our modern education.

Here, then, is the answer to the difficulty we have been considering—that the singing at the Parish Communion will be more distracting than helpful. It is partly that those who feel the difficulty may themselves not yet have learnt the meaning of 'community' in the Church, partly that our services do not rightly express it. Certainly a new *ethos* is needed. We need to learn again that spirit of Christian community which finds so wonderful an expression in the haunting phrases of the Orthodox Eastern rite:

" In peace, and again in peace, let us pray to the Lord."
" Let us commend ourselves and one another and all our lives to Christ our God."

The unity which Christians have with one another is something *given*. The soul finds peace and rest in the bosom as of the natural so of the spiritual family, when it can repose on a unity which it has not created and which it has not to labour to maintain, but in which it can freely expand and exert its energies. The common worship of the Church is precisely the place where the Christian soul ought to find peace and spiritual joy.[1]

5. THE SPIRITUAL FACT AND ITS SACRAMENTAL EXPRESSION

But this brings us right up against an opposite difficulty, which also needs to be fairly stated and fully admitted.

Nothing could be more wrong than to treat either the gift of divine grace or our unity in the Church as if these were *dependent upon* a right ethos in the service or the right arrangement of it—as if the blessing received from the Sacrament were conditioned by the 'numinous atmosphere' of the service, or as if the unity of the Church had no real existence till enlightened persons come and establish the Parish Communion. God forbid. Every Eucharist is a Eucharist of the whole Church. Even if there are only two people present, the Christian Sacrifice is there pleaded, and we worship God with angels and archangels and in spiritual unity and communion with the whole Church of God. The reality of the unity of Christians one with another does not depend on the mere physical juxtaposition of the 'corporate communion' or on the mere multitude of worshippers. Their unity one with another is spiritual, and those who worship in countless different places are all gathered together in spirit—that is to say, really—round the heavenly altar, and all are one in Christ. Or again, when communion is given at a private celebration for the sick, or from the reserved sacrament to the sick or to the whole—as, for instance, to some hospital nurse whose duties make it impossible for her to attend the Parish Communion—we may not say that the bareness of the accessories diminishes the reality of the divine gift or of fellowship with the whole Church of God. Indeed, we can and ought to carry the principle further, and say that those who are divided from one another by the schisms of Christendom do nevertheless

[1] With this Section, cf. Essay VI, § 2, pp. 151-3 *infra*.

communicate together at the heavenly altar. In spite of the schisms, Christian unity exists as a fact; for these Christians cannot possibly be united with Christ without being united with one another in Him.

All this is of immense importance, and needs to be asserted with all possible vigour against the materialism which would identify the spiritual with its material expression, and so miss the true sacramental principle. The spiritual reality exists prior to its material expression. And yet this very point can easily be made an excuse for a practice which in effect loses sight of principle altogether, in order to provide for people's convenience. Thus the practical demand is made that the Holy Communion should be celebrated at hours convenient to everyone—at 6, 7, 8, 9.30 and 12.15 —and the result is a corrupt imitation of the Roman practice of many masses without the Roman insistence on the principle of one priest, one mass. The Eastern Orthodox principle is expressed in the rule of one celebration of the Liturgy on one day in one church. The modern Anglican practice loses sight of the principle which lies behind the Roman practice, as well as that which lies behind the Orthodox practice, and requires priests to celebrate two and three times, as a regular thing, the governing consideration being the convenience of the communicants. We ought to return to the principle, even if it involved the use of the reserved sacrament to provide communion in exceptional cases.[1]

The Parish Communion, however, does express the right principle, which we may notice is clearly intended by the Prayer Book, and was universally carried out in seventeenth-century Anglican practice. The principle is this: Because Christians are one in Christ, they ought to have an outward and visible expression of their unity in the church service. The spiritual is prior to the material, but it finds its natural expression in it. Because I am glad to meet my friend again, I shake hands with him and we go and have tea together. Our friendship does not depend on these outward things,

---

[1] I am not here demanding that there shall be one celebration only in each church on one day, but that the principle of unity shall find expression in the Parish Communion, as the chief service. In practice it will commonly be necessary to provide one or more earlier celebrations.

but it finds its natural expression in them. So, because Christians *are* one in the Church, they ought to meet Sunday by Sunday round the family altar. The communion from the reserved sacrament is the exception, and must not become the normal practice. And again, just because Christians in schism from one another are one in Christ, they must long for the time when that unity can find outward and visible expression, not indeed in occasional acts of intercommunion, which blandly ignore the fact that the schisms still go on, but in the reunion of the separated churches, of which communion together at one altar will be one among many outward signs.

6. The Unity of the Church

Here we have reached the point when we can envisage the importance of the Parish Communion for the Church of England as a whole. If by its means the people of the Church throughout the country learn a deeper sense of their spiritual unity in the Church, they will have gained a truer sense of what the Church is. As things are, we suffer seriously from a materialistic perversion of the idea of the Church, losing sight of the spiritual meaning of the Church, and identifying the spiritual reality with its outward expression, identifying the *corpus Christi* with the *corpus Christianorum*, the Body of Christ with the corporation of Christians.[1] It is almost as if the teaching of St. Paul in I Cor. xii., about the body with its various members, hand and foot, ear and eye, were to be taken as a simple description of the Church of England with its bishops, archdeacons, vicars, churchwardens, diocesan conferences, parochial church councils and mothers' meetings. All these are uninspiring, to say the least, when viewed as pieces of machinery; and the machinery, especially on its legal and its financial side, is apt to clank very unpleasantly. The bones seem at times to be very dry indeed. The ' schools of thought ' in the Church go on living uneasily side by side, tolerating one another's existence, till we are apt to assume that toleration

---

[1] This point is further developed in some of the other essays: see esp. pp. 80–87, 307, *infra*.

is in itself a Christian virtue, whereas in fact it is but the palest caricature of the love and mutual trust and inter-change of criticism which should be the mark of those who share the same sacraments. One hates to say these things about one's mother-Church, and there is very much to set on the other side; but there are many faithful sons of the Church of England who have almost given up thinking of her as a spiritual society, as she is at present. Yet she is that, or she is nothing at all. She has a true unity, and it is her unity in Christ.

There is very much that is rotten in the Church of England, very much that needs to be purged out by the fire of tribula-tion. Ought we then to pray that tribulation may come quickly? Or ought we rather to fear the things that might happen if it were to come, and the revelation of spiritual desolation that it would make? Tribulation is indeed likely to come anyhow, before many years are past; all the more urgent therefore is the need that in the time that is left to us we should stablish the things that remain, and labour to make firm the foundations of the spiritual life of clergy and people, that when that hour does come we may stand firm. This is the true mission of the liturgical movement in the Church of England.

We ought also to reflect on the meaning of the liturgical movement for the future reunion of Christendom. As we have said, Christians who are separated from communion at one another's altars on earth, are nevertheless one in Christ at the heavenly altar. The baptized are members of Christ, and every community of Christians realises in itself something of the nature of the Church, however incom-plete, fragmentary, defective that realisation may be. The members of each denomination have learnt from the Chris-tian community in which they have been brought up whatever they know of Christian faith and life; and what-ever they have learnt positively of Christ from the Scriptures and from their own orthodox tradition has been sound and true.

It is for the members of each denomination to seek to develop in themselves the community of the Christian life,

c

of necessity in isolation from other denominations, yet looking all the time towards unity, and recognising the Christians from whom they are separated to be true Christians. In thus developing their community life, as in the Quaker service, or in the Methodist class-meeting, on the basis of their own best traditions of Scriptural and orthodox Christianity, they will certainly be drawing nearer to one another.

But let them beware of those superficial attempts to make premature syntheses, which are in the air all around us: attempts to bring into one organisation Christians who have not yet learnt to understand one another and are not yet one in spirit. The falsity of these attempts lies in the same materialism that we have criticised above: in the assumption that unity lies in organisations that we can create, and not in the Church which God has made: in the assumption, again, that the present Church of England, and the other existing denominations, truly represent what God has intended them to be, and that a united Church can be formed by amalgamating these organisations together. Such a scheme as is set forth in the *Sketch of a United Church* would produce only a caricature of the Church of God.

This is not the right way. The unity of the Church exists in Christ, and it is a spiritual unity. The episcopate must be treated not as a convenient form of church organisation, but as the sacramental embodiment of the priesthood which is Christ's; there is a serious meaning in the quip that episcopacy is of the *esse* of the Church and not of its *bene esse*. Each several denomination must learn more and more in its community life the secret of its unity in Christ; so only is it preparing itself for the true Christian reunion. Reunion will come, not as the result of schemes put forth by idealists; it will come when the sense of unity in Christ which the several denominations have learnt has become so strong that it will be impossible for them any longer to remain separate. It will come at God's time, not ours. Quite probably it will not come till we have all been compelled to suffer together at the hands of a secularised state, and we have learnt in that hard school that we really are fellow-Christians. But whatever may be in store, it is for Christians of each sort to prepare for what is coming by learning in their several ways, as deeply as they may, what the Church is.

Such is the context in which we ought to think of the Parish Communion: not as a means to making a ' successful parish,' nor as if it were a panacea for our troubles and difficulties, but solely in terms of the will of God for the salvation of mankind through His Church, as the outward and visible embodiment, in the Sacrament which our Lord has instituted, of the redemption of men to God and their unity with one another in Him: that the Church may grow towards the measure of the stature of the fulness of Christ, that Christians may know what they are, and the Church be known for what she is, first in the minds and hearts of her own members, and through them by the world.

A NOTE ON THE FAST BEFORE COMMUNION

THE issue of Fasting Communion is often so presented that the choice seems to lie between a rigorism which envisages the whole matter in terms of law, and a laxity which comes near to making the comfort and convenience of the individual the primary consideration. Between this Scylla and this Charybdis we can find a way only by an appeal to principle. The Fast before Communion is, of course, a rule, and it has been the rule of the universal Church ever since the second century; but it is necessary to ask further *why* it has been the rule, and what has been the instinct in the minds of Christians that has led them to maintain the rule. The classical statement of the matter is that of St. Augustine, in the *Epistle to Januarius* (Ep. liv., ch. 6, P.L. XXXIII, col. 203) that, though at the Last Supper the Apostles were not fasting, yet " it has seemed good to the Holy Ghost that in honour of so great a sacrament the Body of the Lord should enter the mouth of a Christian before other food, and for this reason this custom is observed throughout the whole world." But there are some to whom it will not seem immediately self-evident that it is fitting that the Sacrament should be the first food of the day; and, if it were only for their sakes, it is necessary to try to probe into the matter somewhat further. But we must first give a brief sketch of the history.[1]

The first problem is to explain the transition from the non-fasting communion of the Apostles at the Last Supper and of St. Paul's Christians at Corinth, to the early and universal acceptance of fasting communion in the Church; no complete answer is possible. St. Augustine believed (*loc. cit.*) that this matter was included among St. Paul's later instructions ("the rest I will set in order when I come," I Cor. xi. 34); but, as Abbot Cabrol says, this is far from being proved. The one fact in the N.T. evidence which seems to throw light on the subject is that St. Paul at Troas celebrated the Agape in the evening, and then, having prolonged his discourse till midnight, celebrated the Eucharist apparently some time before dawn. The duration of this service thus corresponds exactly to that of the Vigil services of the ancient Church; and it is significant that the next piece of evidence is that relating to the Christians in Bithynia in the time of Pliny, who likewise celebrated the Eucharist before dawn. The Vigil Service may well contain the answer to the problem.

Certain it is that from the second century onwards (Tertullian: services before dawn, *De Corona*, 3; Sacrament

---

[1] It is not possible here to go into the evidence in detail. See Dr. Wickham Legg, *Papal Faculties allowing Food before Communion* (Church Historical Society, no. LXXXVII., S.P.C.K., 1905); where also is quoted the Faculty granted by Pope Benedict XIV in 1756 to the Old Chevalier, whom he addresses as James III, King of England, allowing him to take some small refreshment before Communion when his weak health demands it; various other Papal Faculties; an extract from the somewhat lax teaching of Zaccaria Pasqualigo, 1641, which Benedict XIV does not accept; and the letter of Pusey on the subject deprecating an extreme rigorism (*Spiritual Letters of Edward Bouverie Pusey*, ed. Johnston and Newbolt, Longmans, 1898, p. 273).

See also Abbot Cabrol in *Dictionnaire d'archéologie et de liturgie chrétienne*, s. v. Jeûne, Vol. VII., col. 2486 ff.; Fr. Puller, S.S.J.E., *Concerning the Fast before Communion* (1891); A. J. Maclean in *Liturgy and Worship*, pp. 253–6; Lacey, *The Anglo-Catholic Faith*, pp. 151–8.

received at home *ante cibum, Ad Uxorem*, ii. 5) the rule is so
universal that every real or apparent exception requires
special explanation. There is the Egyptian practice of late
evening communions on Saturdays, mentioned with dis-
approval by Socrates and Sozomen, which is apparently
the Sunday vigil service in some form (Legg, p. 14). The
evening communions on fast days (cf. the present Roman
rule that on such days Mass is celebrated after None) were
of course no breach of the rule, since the people were fasting
all day. On one day in the year, Maundy Thursday, there
was a genuine exception: in St. Augustine's time (Ep. liv.
ch. 7) the Agape and Eucharist were celebrated as a commemoration, *per modum signi*, and this practice lasted at least
to the Council in Trullo, 692. Another exception was the
custom of celebrating Mass immediately after a death, which
lasted till the thirteenth century (Legg, p. 17). The Council
of Constance (1415) repeats the rule, allowing exceptions
in the case of sickness or other necessity granted and allowed
by the Church or the canon law (quoted by Benedict XIV:
see Legg, pp. 6, 37, 65). In the Roman Church, with the
growing frequency of communion, dispensations are given
by the Pope in individual cases of necessity,[1] to priests in
special cases, to sick people, and in special circumstances
such as those of Catholics in Soviet Russia, and of the
soldiers at the front in the Great War. It is to be noted that
in each case these dispensations are not assumed by the
individual, but are given under authority; and this is a
sound principle.

No change was made in this matter at the Reformation;
in the Anglican Church, and presumably also in the Lutheran
Churches, there is little doubt that the Fast before Communion continued to be observed. " It seems very likely
that the great majority of the communions made in the
Church of England up to the end of the seventeenth century
were made fasting, because the whole of the congregation
was fasting." " In James I's time the dinner is at eleven

---

[1] Discussed in an article by Dom. J. Leclef, ' Les dispenses du jeûne
eucharistique ' in *Questions liturgiques et paroissiales* (Abbaye du Mont-
César, Louvain), no. 119, Feb. 1936.

and the supper at six " (Legg, p. 29, and see the whole
passage) : the question for the historian is, when the modern
breakfast began to come in. But, even so, the tradition of
the Fast before Communion has lasted unbroken to our own
day in certain parts of England, notably, as I have been told,
in co. Durham and Tyneside. Here is the answer to the
difficulty that is felt by many : Can an Anglican priest
rightly enjoin on his people a practice which is not mentioned in the Prayer Book? The answer is that the compilers
of the Prayer Book did not mention it, because they took it
for granted.

But here is the difficulty. In treating the matter historically, we are treating it as a rule which like all rules requires
certain exceptions. But it is always unsatisfactory when
this matter is treated merely as a rule. When we accept the
rule as binding, we seem to be guilty of a Pharisaic legalism,
and our critics remind us that " the Sabbath was made for
man, and not man for the Sabbath." If, on the other hand,
we accept their advice, and treat the Fast before Communion not as a rule but as a ' custom,' or an ' ideal,' the
result in practice will unfailingly be that each man will
do what he likes, and frail human nature will accept with
both hands the opportunity to make excuses for its laxity ;
and above all in an age when softness and self-indulgence in
small things (as, for instance, that indispensable early morning
cup of tea) have become a sin. Here is the Scylla and
Charybdis of which we spoke above; and of the two, the
wise Odysseus chose the former.

But neither legalism nor laxity is Christian; and it is a
matter of great importance to vindicate the Christian
meaning of Rule. Rule, law, is not abolished under the
Christian dispensation. What is abolished is *justification*
by observance of rules, and the notion that there is any sort
of merit to be earned by keeping rules, or indeed a moral
code of any kind. We can be justified only by faith.
Nevertheless, man in this world needs rule, not in order
that he may make the observance of precepts into a substitute for real obedience to God, but in order that by the
discipline of rule he may be saved from falling into the laxity

which is slavery to self-will. St. Augustine said, " Love God and do what you like " ; but many of us, when we do ' what we like,' show thereby how little we really love God. This was the case with St. Paul's Corinthians, who were misinterpreting evangelical freedom, somewhat thus : " All things are lawful unto me, even to eat meat in an idol temple ; for the idol is nothing and the meat is good meat " (see I Cor. viii.-x.). St. Paul accepts the principle of freedom and explains it, warning them of their own spiritual danger (x. 6-14), and concludes the discussion by laying down for them some positive rules which he expects them to keep (x. 24-29).

Such is Rule under the Christian dispensation : not a set of precepts by observance of which man is justified, nor yet a law to be blindly obeyed (see John xv. 15), but a practice embodying a principle, enjoined upon Christians to save them from falling into slothfulness, irreverence, or other sin. We have then to ask, with reference to this œcumenical rule of the Fast before Communion, What are the reasons which have led the instinct of the Church to maintain the rule that the Sacrament is to be the first food of the day?

First, surely, comes the priority of the spiritual over the physical, and the importance of spiritual discipline. Let that which is spiritual come first, and let the body's demand for food be kept waiting. It is this principle which underlies our Lord's first temptation in the wilderness. He has gone there to seek an answer to an urgent question : How is He to set about His life-work, how take in hand the bringing of the Kingdom of God to men? The first temptation—to turn stones into bread—seems to express in symbolical form the demand of the body for the satisfaction of its needs, *before* the answer to the spiritual problem has been found. Shall He admit the principle that the body must be satisfied first, and the spiritual issue be postponed to a more convenient time? No. Man shall not live by bread alone. The body must be disciplined to obey the spirit. (See J. O. F. Murray, *Studies in the Temptations of the Son of God*, Longmans, 1916, pp. 27-34; F. W. Green, *St. Matthew*

(Clarendon Bible, 1936), *ad locum*; but most commentators miss the point.)

So it is with the Fast before Communion. Spiritual things must come first. So great an act as the receiving of Holy Communion must be if possible the first act of the day, and all that precedes it be as far as possible a preparation for it. It comes first that thereby the rest of the day may be sanctified, just as the Lord's Day is the first day of the week, for the sanctification of the whole week. To come to communion at an eleven o'clock service, after a hearty breakfast and a smoke and a perusal of the Sunday paper, is a reversal of the right order.

A second point is this: The body as well as the soul needs to have its part in the preparation for Holy Communion, since it is not the soul only but the whole man that is redeemed to God. From this side, something of the principle underlying the Fast before Communion appears in the story told by Bishop King of the Lincolnshire farm-boy, who on the night before his Communion polished his boots with elaborate care and put them under his bed. A tutor at a theological college tells me that the houseboys there have on week-days a cup of tea as soon as they come down in the morning, but that on Sundays there is no cup of tea; and the abstinence from this small indulgence has direct value as an act of preparation, of looking forward to the great thing that is to happen an hour or so later. He further notes the importance of this bodily act of preparation for uneducated people, who do not readily use the theological manuals which are suitable for those of a different habit of mind. Here we see another aspect of the Fast before Communion. As a bodily act, it is a bond of union between the learned and the simple.

Every good thing has its characteristic dangers, and not least our present liberty in approaching Holy Communion. We are right to urge on people the truth that the benefit we receive does not depend on the preparation we make, but upon God's gift to us. But just because the gift is real, we receive it with reverence; and we do well to remember that in times past infrequency of Communion has not always been due solely to spiritual slackness, but, in part at least, to an intense reverence for the Sacrament and a fear of approaching it lightly.[1] There is something to be learnt from the old Presbyterian 'fencing of the Table.' We ought indeed to encourage our people to make frequent communion; but in doing so, we must not allow them to think lightly of the privilege. The observance of this simple act of bodily self-discipline, such as any healthy person can make, by way of preparation, is perhaps the most effective of all safeguards against any light estimate of the act of Communion, and is in itself a real, if elementary, act of devotion.

To sum up: The fact that the Prayer Book neither enjoins nor abrogates the Fast before Communion implies that it assumes the universal rule as a matter of course. To call it a 'laudable custom' or an 'ideal' is thoroughly unsatisfactory; we must uphold it as a rule. There are, as history and experience show, cases of necessity when the Fast cannot be kept; and here there can be little doubt that some Anglo-Catholic clergy are over-rigoristic, more rigid than the Roman Church, in refusing to recognise the existence of such cases of necessity. On the other hand, the individual ought not, in such cases of necessity, to assume a dispensation for himself, but should act under authority—that is, in the first place, the authority of the parish priest. But for the rest of us, " all that is wanted to keep the Church's rule is good-will and a resolve not to be self-indulgent." [2]

[1] In the Eastern Church to-day, communion is as a rule relatively infrequent. I am told that the ' Zoe ' movement, which encourages frequent communion (so that in some churches at Athens there are 100 or 200 communicants every Sunday), meets with some opposition from an older school, for whom communion is an act of special solemnity, to be prepared for by days of fasting and, if possible, retirement to a monastery.

[2] See Legg, p. 31 ; and cf. pp. 284-5 infra.

II

MAN, MANKIND, AND GOD

By the Rev. D. R. BLACKMAN
Vicar of St. Thomas', Keyham, Plymouth

MAN, MANKIND, AND GOD

A MAN tends to consider himself as an independent self. He can only do so by ignoring facts.

The individual is not complete in himself. His body is continuous in its change; it is part of the ebb and flow that he observes in the surrounding universe; it links him with all Nature, animate and inanimate. He continues by his subsistence upon Nature. The air he breathes, the water he drinks, and the food he eats, establish and maintain his constant solidarity with the universe that he distinguishes from himself. Climate and diet are powerful influences in the formation of his character. His body links him with the race; the colour of his skin, the shape of his skull, and other characteristics link him not only with his ancestors, but with his posterity, and they determine, very largely subconsciously, his outlook and life. Tom Jones was Jones before he was Tom, and human before he was Jones. His history not only reaches back through the embryonic to the beginning of organic life, but also forward to the posterity he alone can beget. Physically he is less an individual than he cares to think.

Mentally also he is fluid; he can attend to a very small margin of the impressions that are made upon his consciousness. He has very little control over the impressions that he receives, and his attention again is controlled by instincts and other less conscious factors that either come from his surroundings or were born in him. Mass suggestion and racial character are most powerful when not conscious. When Tom Jones studies psychology, he soon becomes bewildered by the problem of the many selves. Should he go further and dabble in metaphysics, his mind may well reel at the problems of epistemology. He may easily be lost in the labyrinth of appearance and reality, and doubt his own existence as a confirmed solipsist. At any rate he will not find a basis of reality in his own individuality.

His practical problem remains, of fitting himself into that complex which we call society, and yet retaining and developing his own personality. There seems to be an incurable habit in mankind to form societies, having as their aim the ultimate benefit of the individual. This testifies to the natural feeling of incompleteness in isolation. Man is a gregarious animal, not only by desire, but also by necessity. Morality is the study of the reaction of the individual to the communities. Ethical books are strewn with the wrecks of the attempts to solve the problem of a man's relation with a larger reality. It is a problem not so much of thought as of nature: practical as well as academic. In this region lie such constantly pressing problems as nationalism, war, and the multifarious sexual manifestations.

A man can only think of himself as a self-centred and independent reality by a process of mental abstraction and idealisation. That view of himself is a false hypothesis, untrue because it ignores facts. Civilisation, through its system of education, exalts the idea of the self-sufficient man; yet paradoxically it tends to produce as many similar men as possible; it breeds to type. It discourages any deviations from its average specimen.

Independence and isolation have the nature of sin, which is selfishness, the organisation of the self apart from the Truth. It is the primary lie, the root of sin; in fact, original sin. Men confess this sin unwillingly and unconsciously in their attempts to form associations and ideal societies. Communism is the finest confession so far in the secular sphere, of sin; the League of Nations is another magnificent confession. Communism confesses that the exaltation of merely individualistic personality is a crime against humanity that must be " liquidated." The League futilely protests against individualistic nationalism. In both, the promise of amendment is in the desire to treat mankind as a whole and as indivisible. Both, however, visualise a community that is self-sufficient. Fr. Waggett once described that vision as "a commonwealth of mutually dependent parasites." They ignore, as the world tends more and more to ignore, the relations that man has with power outside him and the universe he lives in. H. G. Wells has familiarised us with a pantheism that concedes immortality not to the individual, but to the race.

We cannot escape from the necessity of pushing the frontiers of dependence further, till we reach the conception of God, who is not only immanent in man and the universe, but also transcends it. Life must be fed from without itself. Man has testified very clearly always to his consciousness of his relation to a power not himself. Any organisation of mankind that ignores this theological necessity is as false as the others that neglect other truths about humanity. The more grandiose the conception, the more deadly; for any organism in the body of humanity that lives in it apart from the true centre, is like a malignant tumour in the human body.

The world, as we see it, is becoming a godless society of highly developed individuals. This is fundamentally sin.

Englishmen have a queer sense of detachment in their attitude towards societies, due no doubt to our strongly developed libertarianism. We think of the State as existing separately from ourselves. Readers of the recent ' Church and State Report ' probably felt as if they were studying the relations of two bodies as remote from themselves as two Greek city-states of antiquity. The State is a thing that deals with us, that takes our money, and that we can criticise without prejudice. The Church, for many Christians, is an alien corporation that exists to supply them with certain indefinite helps. It is common to approve heartily of the idea that one is a Christian first, and then a voluntary member of some Christian body. Undoubtedly *we* make the Church, and we resent any idea of a responsibility towards it. Membership sits very lightly. Baptism is a magical private act, conferring undefined benefits on an individual, without reference to any other individuals or society. Religion is not a thing that binds us together, but actually separates us. There are few who would not instantly approve the idea that it is better to pray alone than in company. It is considered possible to be a better Christian by abstaining from gathering together. Subjective prayer has a greater appeal than objective worship; in fact, it *is* prayer. Communion is an individualistic act of personal piety unrelated to anything else.

All this is based on the fundamental heresy of individualism. A voice still whispers " Ye shall be as gods," and self-expression still leads to fratricide. Self-worship and godless society are irrational attempts to solve the problems of existence. Humanity, considered either abstractly as a genus, or extensively as the sum-total of all men living or unborn, is imperfect, meaningless; it only realises its intention and purpose in relation to the created universe, and therefore to God.

The only ultimately satisfactory statement of the purpose of man's existence is, that man was created for the glory of God, not only in the sense that all other things were so created, but including the mystery of his free will. Man is to serve God with all his powers. We have the word ' love ' for that relation. Man is created for love of God. The phrase is pregnant because it is capable of expressing the reciprocity of the relation. As all men are involved in that relation, a true relation is also established between themselves. Any diminishing of the wholeness of this fact is sin. Man must love God and mankind, not out of any mere humanistic desire for the betterment of the world, for progress, or for gain, but simply because anything else is against the truth. Our Lord's statement of the divine law is God's will for humanity. It is not a mere generalisation of man's ideals, but God's expression of the true relations of God, man, and mankind. Life, as we see it now, is in opposition to this will. Sin is not a breach of fussy bye-laws, but anarchy. In Him there is no colour-bar, no nationalism, no class-war, and no sex-distinction. Without Him there is chaos.

Into this chaos the Son of God plunged Himself; He assumed humanity. He did not take upon Himself an individuality, but in the womb of Mary He took common human nature, and through this flesh and blood established a new relation between God and man. The world-anarchy broke Him upon the cross; but the sin of the world could not destroy the new bond. The resurrection is the triumph of the new bond over the old. It is the new statement, a new cosmos, a new reality, a new humanity. The risen incarnate life is the nucleus of potential restoration for fallen human beings; it is mediated by the common element of our humanity, flesh and blood.

Flesh joins, spirit divides. In re-establishing the true bond between God and man, Christ renews the bond between man and man. The Church is that new creation, not founded upon spiritual ideas, but upon the real basis of fellowship or communion. He descended from heaven and became flesh, and became food, entering into man at the lowest possible point, and thus taking hold of the whole man by taking hold of all the man. God comes to man where he is most obviously man, and not angel. The Incarnation has direct relation to man, not simply to his religious aspirations; it has its roots in the area of our real common life, the flesh, where food and sex have their place. From that level He can begin to radiate and sublimate. To get hold of love He descends to its genesis, that He may transform the seeds and the fruit.

He deals with the simplest relations of mankind; for out of them grow the highest. The love of God differs by degree, not by kind, from the love of man. God dwells in us not primarily as an idea, but in the realm of mere sustenance. The truth of the Christian revelation lies in its fulfilment of the wholeness of life; He did not take upon Him a part of human nature, nor yet an abstraction. The neglect of this truth in the interests of a supposedly higher spiritual conception has often been the cause of the weakness of the Christian Church, and a fruitful cause of both heresy and schism within it. In trying to get to the fundamentals of the Christian religion, men have often wrongly assumed that the fundamentals lie in the intellectual alone, and have ignored the simple facts of family and food, which, because they are the basis of human relations, are of course the

D

foundations of God's dealing with mankind. We become sons of God and partakers of His Table, because God so made man. To be a son is not an intellectual process, or a graduation, but a fact which we experience in the so-called lowest regions of our experience. It is at the same time a relation that transcends any possible relation achieved by treaty or agreement.

In the interests of the purely ' spiritual ' conception, the physical and materialistic basis of man's true relation with God has been decried as magical. Because Baptism and Communion are in the realm of the natural in the first place, they have been likened to the natural ceremonies by which man has attempted to realise his relations with God and man. Of course they are alike, for God has assumed common humanity; and it is not really surprising that He took hold of human instincts and ways. They were implanted. The essence of magic, however, is in its attempt to be unsocial and get outside the family and force the powers to do something not to the good of the family as a whole. Very largely we may say that magic is ' spiritual ' in its fundamental individualism and its withdrawal from common-weal; while religion, because it is social and common, is godly.

The Sacraments are of a piece with God's way with us in dealing with us, not as discarnate individuals, but as part and parcel of a great whole. Eating and drinking together in the House of God may be only the same act as eating and drinking at home; but it is also the same act as eating and drinking in heaven. In Christ the lowest of social functions is also the highest. Αὐτὸς γὰρ ἐνηνθρώπησεν ἵνα ἡμεῖς θεοποιηθῶμεν. " He became flesh that we might become God." [1]

_____
[1] St. Athanasius, *On the Incarnation of the Logos*, liv. 3.

III

THE SACRIFICE OF THE NEW COVENANT

By the Rev. JOHN O. COBHAM
Principal of the Queen's College, Birmingham

THE SACRIFICE OF THE NEW COVENANT

1. THE WORD 'SACRIFICE'

THE word 'sacrifice' in modern English usage looks back to the death of Christ upon the Cross. This is true even where the word is employed in the most secular of contexts. Thus a man is said to sacrifice his life for his country, his health for his work, his pleasure for his duty. So too a store will announce 'surplus stock for sale at huge sacrifice.' In all these instances there is implied an immediate loss willingly accepted that some further end may be achieved. The loss, the self-giving, the death—that is the sacrifice. Its type is the death of Christ " upon the Cross for our redemption," the death which, in the language of our Anglican Communion Office, is described as " a full, perfect and sufficient sacrifice, oblation and satisfaction for the sins of the whole world."

That our modern metaphorical usage of the word 'sacrifice' should be derived from the 'full, perfect and sufficient sacrifice' of Christ is theologically just. Dr. Moberly has said:

> " The Church of Christ, as exhibited in the New Testament, is priestly and sacrificial in substance, as the Church of the Old Testament was only in figure. Mosaic priesthood, with its sacrifices, was no more, on the one hand, a non-significant, than it was, on the other, a complete or substantial, thing. It sketched out, it led up to, it enacted parabolically, that which transcended itself, that in which alone its detached, external and symbolic suggestions found their unity and fullness. All priesthood, all sacrifice, is summed up in the Person of Christ." [1]

[1] R. C. Moberly, *Ministerial Priesthood*, p. 243.

Yet, theologically just as is the reference to the sacrifice of Christ, it also, unfortunately, is true that our modern, loose, metaphorical usage of the word 'sacrifice' is a positive hindrance to the understanding of the word as employed by New Testament writers. Because we know the perfect sacrifice, we tend to treat the 'Mosaic priesthood, with its sacrifices,' as a 'non-significant . . . thing.' The New Testament writers, on the other hand, interpreted the life, death and resurrection of Christ in terms of the sacrificial system that was familiar to them. It is because they did this, that we speak of 'the sacrifice of Christ.' But we shall not understand what they meant by the sacrifice of Christ, and consequently we shall not understand either the sacrifice of Christ itself or the Christian sacrifice, unless we understand the system from which the New Testament writers were drawing their symbolism, when they applied sacrificial language to Christ's life, death and resurrection, to the Christian eucharistic rite, and to the Christian way of living. Our modern association of the word 'sacrifice' with 'the loss, the self-giving, the death' will then be found to be a concentration upon what was certainly a part, an important part, of the sacrificial symbolism used by the New Testament writers, but only a part. Their sacrificial language included much that we do not ordinarily associate with sacrifice. Article XXXI contrasts "the offering of Christ once made" with "the sacrifices of Masses." It has been said that Cranmer, in the Second Prayer Book of Edward VI, "turned the Mass into a Communion." It is doubtful whether these antitheses are really true to the New Testament use of sacrificial language. That language is richer and fuller than our usage of the word 'sacrifice' would suggest. And our loss of the fulness of the Biblical meaning of the word is no trivial matter, but is, in point of fact, one aspect of the modern estrangement from the Christian faith. Men have forgotten what sacrifice is, as they have forgotten what worship is. And, as with worship, so with sacrifice, we must return to the New Testament meaning of the word, if we are to understand the revelation of God in Christ and the response that we must make to that revelation.

2. Primitive Sacrifice

If " the Church of Christ, as exhibited in the New Testament, is priestly and sacrificial in substance, as the Church of the Old Testament was only in figure," it is still true that the sacrificial language of the New Testament can only be understood in the light of the sacrificial practices of the Old. Yet even the sacrificial practices which the Old Testament enjoins or criticises, or to which it merely alludes, cannot be fully explained in terms of the religion of the Old Testament itself. These practices had already centuries of history behind them when the earliest Old Testament documents were being written. If we can sometimes discover the origin of this or that particular ceremony, the origins of sacrifice itself belong to the days before history was written, before, it may be, man even could write. The modern studies of anthropology and of comparative religion have done something towards shedding light upon the ever obscure problem of origins, and have thereby enabled us, in part at least, to understand these ceremonies as we encounter them in the Old Testament.

The object of sacrifice, it would seem, was to provide a sacred meal. The materials of sacrifice were " drawn from edible substances, and indeed from such substances as form the ordinary staple of human food." [1] If the food was flesh, the animal or bird had to be killed, but this was merely a preliminary to the sacred meal. The sacred meal was provided for the god, and normally the worshippers themselves partook of the meal. Robertson Smith has contended that sacrifice is in origin an act of communion with the god,[2] the members of the tribe partaking together of the raw flesh of the totem animal of the tribe, which, except in sacrifice, was too sacred to be slain or eaten.[3] This act established the solidarity of the members of the tribe with the god and with each other.[4] It was therefore a joyful social occasion.[5]

[1] W. Robertson Smith, *The Religion of the Semites*, 3rd Edition, p. 218.
[2] *Idem, op. cit.*, p. 240.
[3] *Idem, op. cit.*, pp. 294–5, 405.
[4] *Idem, op. cit.*, p. 263.
[5] *Idem, op. cit.*, pp. 253–4, 263–5.

In later times a sacrifice came to be thought of as a gift to the god ; [1] but still, except in the case of the whole burnt offering, the worshippers partook of the flesh of the animal with the god. In fact, it was only when they ate the flesh of the animals that had been sacrificed that men ate flesh at all.[2] The book of Deuteronomy, however, expressly permits the eating of flesh apart from sacrifice [3] when, in the history of Judah, the centralisation of worship at Jerusalem made this permission necessary if the people were to continue to eat flesh in their own homes. In early times, the sacrificial flesh was eaten raw. In later times it was roast, and it was held that the god partook of the sacrifice by smelling the odour as the smoke ascended to heaven.[4] When the animal was slain, the blood, which was thought of as the life,[5] was drained off that it might be given as a drink to the god and might be applied to the worshippers.[6]

This is a brief, but, for our purposes, a sufficient, summary of early sacrificial practices. It must be remembered that the practices and the ideas associated with them varied greatly with different types of sacrifice and at different periods in the history of sacrifice.[7] Our interest, however, is not with sacrifice as encountered in the study of anthropology, but with the rôle played by sacrifice in the story of God's dealings with man, and man's response to God.

3. The Old Covenant

That God stood, not in a blood, but in a covenant relation with His people Israel, is a fact of central importance for the understanding not only of the Old Testament, but also of the New.[8] A covenant is a treaty, the conditions of which both parties to the covenant undertake to observe. God

---

[1] G. Buchanan Gray, *Sacrifice in the Old Testament*, p. 2, 20. W. Robertson Smith, *op. cit.*, p. 396. Dr. Buchanan Gray's emphasis upon the ' gift-theory ' supplies a necessary correction to Robertson Smith's tendency to over-emphasise the communion-aspect.

[2] W. Robertson Smith, *op. cit.*, p. 241.

[3] *Idem, op. cit.*, p. 238. Deut. xii. 15, 16.

[4] *Idem, op. cit.*, p. 236. F. C. Burkitt, *Eucharist and Sacrifice*, p. 5.

[5] Lev. xvii. 11.

[6] W. Robertson Smith, *op. cit.*, pp. 233–4, 312–3, 386. Lev. xvii. 11.

[7] *Idem, op. cit.*, p. 399.   [8] *Idem, op. cit.*, p. 319, note 2.

made Israel His people on the condition that Israel would observe His law. The story of the Old Testament is the story of Israel's faithlessness. The story of the Bible is the story of the faithfulness of God.

Though the New Testament speaks of the Old Covenant of God with His people, the Old Testament records several occasions when God entered into a covenant relationship with Israel.[1] Two of these occasions are of outstanding importance. The first, to which reference is made in Gal. iii. 15–18, is the covenant of God with Abram, of which the narrative is given in Gen. xv. 7–18:

" And he said unto him, I am the Lord that brought thee out of Ur of the Chaldees, to give thee this land to inherit it. And he said, O Lord God, whereby shall I know that I shall inherit it? And he said unto him, Take me an heifer of three years old, and a she-goat of three years old, and a ram of three years old, and a turtle-dove, and a young pigeon. And he took him all these, and divided them in the midst, and laid each half over against the other: but the birds divided he not. And the birds of prey came down upon the carcases, and Abram drove them away. And when the sun was going down, a deep sleep fell upon Abram; and, lo, an horror of great darkness fell upon him . . . And it came to pass, that, when the sun went down, and it was dark, behold a smoking furnace, and a flaming torch that passed between these pieces. In that day the Lord made a covenant with Abram."

It is the story of a covenant sealed by a ceremony in which animals were slain and cut in two, and the parties to the covenant passed between the divided parts. We find traces of the survival of this ceremony in later times.[2] We need not, however, attempt to explain the ceremony, though it belongs to customs that we may probably call sacrificial,[3] for this ceremony exercised no direct influence upon the sacrificial idea which we encounter in the New Testament.

[1] A. B. Davidson, " Covenant." Hastings' *Dictionary of the Bible*, l. I.   [2] Jer. xxxiv. 18.
[3] W. Robertson Smith, *op. cit.*, pp. 312–320, 480–1, 691–2.

But the covenant to which the author of the Epistle to the Hebrews, reading the Old Testament in the light of Jeremiah xxxi, looks back (Heb. ix. 15–20), and which is to him ἡ πρώτη διαθήκη (Heb. ix. 15), the covenant that we may in consequence supremely call " the Old Covenant " (Heb. viii. 13), is the covenant which God made with His people upon the mount after the deliverance from Egypt, the covenant to which is attached the giving of the law. Of the making of this covenant, which was sealed with sacrifice, we have the narrative in Ex. xxiv. 1–11 :

" And he said unto Moses, Come up unto the Lord, thou, and Aaron, Nadab, and Abihu, and seventy of the elders of Israel ; and worship ye afar off: and Moses alone shall come near unto the Lord; but they shall not come near; neither shall the people go up with him. And Moses came and told the people all the words of the Lord, and all the judgements : and all the people answered with one voice, and said, All the words which the Lord hath spoken will we do. And Moses wrote all the words of the Lord, and rose up early in the morning, and builded an altar under the mount, and twelve pillars, according to the twelve tribes of Israel. And he sent young men of the children of Israel, which offered burnt offerings, and sacrificed peace offerings of oxen unto the Lord. And Moses took half of the blood, and put it in basons; and half of the blood he sprinkled on the altar. And he took the book of the covenant, and read in the audience of the people: and they said, All that the Lord hath spoken will we do, and be obedient. And Moses took the blood, and sprinkled it on the people, and said, Behold the blood of the covenant, which the Lord hath made with you concerning all these words. Then went up Moses, and Aaron, Nadab, and Abihu, and seventy of the elders of Israel : and they saw the God of Israel; and there was under his feet as it were a paved work of sapphire stone, and as it were the very heaven for clearness. And upon the nobles of the children of Israel he laid not his hand : and they beheld God, and did eat and drink."

By the author of the Epistle to the Hebrews, and by the New Testament writers generally, this narrative would be read as an indivisible whole. As such it moves forward to its

climax when " they beheld God, and did eat and drink."
Actually the narrative is composite. According to the usual
analysis vv. 1, 2 and 9–11 are from J., while vv. 3–8 are from
E. This fact does not, however, alter the essential character
of the sacrifice by which the covenant was sealed, for, as
Robertson Smith points out, the sprinkling of the worshippers with the blood has the same significance as the act
of communion—" the establishment of a special bond
between the god and his servant." [1]

According to the E narrative, then, Moses told the people
all the words of the Lord, and the people signified their
acceptance of the terms of the covenant. Then followed the
solemn sealing of the covenant with sacrifice. An altar
was built, and burnt offerings and peace offerings were made.
The young men slew the animals: but it was Moses himself
who manipulated the blood, sprinkling one half on the altar
and the other half on the people with the words, " Behold
the blood of the covenant, which the Lord hath made with
you upon all these conditions." Thereby the covenant was
ratified, the treaty made. God and His people had entered
into a covenant relationship. The natural result would be
rejoicing. The predominant note of this sacrifice would be
eucharistic.

In the J narrative there is no mention of the covenant.
Nor is there any mention of the preparation of the sacrifice.
The whole emphasis is on the feast, or communion, as the
climax to the sacrifice. Thus Professor S. A. Cook says,
" In Deut. xii. 7, etc., the meal is in Yahweh's presence
(cf. Driver on Ex. xviii. 12), and there is similar cautious
wording in Ex. xxiv. 10 *sq.* (carried further in the LXX);
but the prophets preserve the belief that Yahweh prepares
his feast, issues his invitations, and sends the cup round among
the guests (Isa. xxv. 6; Zeph. i. 7; Jer. xxv. 15 *sqq.*).
Similarly, Paul in 1 Cor. x. 18 *sqq.* interprets the sacred meal
as communion with the altar, *i.e.*, the Deity." [2]

[1] W. Robertson Smith, *op. cit.*, p. 344.
[2] *Idem, op. cit.*, pp. 596–7.

4. THE RELIGION OF THE COVENANT

The religion of Israel was, as we have seen, the religion of the covenant. That which God gave to His people was the law :

> " And Moses came and told the people all the words of the Lord, and all the judgements : and all the people answered with one voice, and said, All the words which the Lord hath spoken will we do " (Ex. xxiv. 3).

The law laid down the duty of man to God and man to his neighbour. The law, therefore, contained both moral ordinances and instructions concerning the ceremonial of worship. Both had their authority in one and the same law.

That the whole law as we find it in the Old Testament was thus given by God upon the mount is naturally not history. The law developed, and the stages of its development we can trace in the documents of the Pentateuch and in the book of Ezekiel. But that a covenant was made with God upon the mount and sealed with sacrifice we have no reason to doubt. And later Judaism came to regard the law as the divine ordinance given on the mount. This is clear not only from the New Testament, but also from so early a book as Deuteronomy. " The Lord our God made a covenant with us in Horeb " (Deut. v. 2). Perhaps it is an over-simplification to speak of one covenant : in Deuteronomy there are three covenants. But the essential point in Deuteronomy is that God's relationship with His people was a covenant relationship, and the author insists that God will remain faithful to His part in the bond :

> " When thou art in tribulation, and all these things are come upon thee, in the latter days thou shalt return to the Lord thy God, and harken unto his voice : for the Lord thy God is a merciful God ; he will not fail thee, neither destroy thee, nor forget the covenant of thy fathers which he sware unto them " (Deut. iv. 30–31).

Side by side with God's faithfulness stands the faithlessness of man. Even while Moses was on Mount Sinai, Israel is represented as being unfaithful in making the golden calf (Ex. xxxii.). And it was the work of the prophets to insist upon the moral demands of God, to refuse to allow any escape from these moral demands through devotion to religious exercises. In considering the prophetic condemnation of sacrifice we must not weaken the force of that condemnation. But we must also see what it was that was being condemned. The obligations of the covenant were absolute. For the unwitting transgression of the demands of God the law offered certain ways of purification through sacrifice. But the deliberate transgression of the law placed a man outside the covenant.[1] For those who through disobedience had placed themselves outside the covenant the law made no provision. The only way of return was the return through repentance to obedience. This was the way that the prophets were concerned to proclaim. But the prophets saw the people avoiding this moral demand, and satisfying their consciences by offering sacrifices—by offering sacrifices more costly to themselves, by offering sacrifices more in number. It was this escape through sacrifice from the moral demand that the prophets were concerned to condemn.

Thus we find Micah saying:

" Wherewith shall I come before the Lord, and bow myself before the high God? Shall I come before him with burnt offerings, with calves of a year old? Will the Lord be pleased with thousands of rams, or with ten thousand rivers of oil? Shall I give my firstborn for my transgression, the fruit of my body for the sin of my soul?

He hath shewed thee, O man, what is good; and what doth the Lord require of thee, but to do justly, and to love mercy, and to walk humbly with thy God " (Micah vi. 6–8).

And this offering of sacrifices rested upon the popular idea that God liked such gifts. The psalmist ridiculed any such idea:

" I will not reprove thee for thy sacrifices;
And thy burnt offerings are continually before me.
I will take no bullock out of thy house,
Nor he-goats out of thy folds.

[1] F. C. N. Hicks, *The Fullness of Sacrifice*, p. 14.

For every beast of the forest is mine,
And the cattle upon a thousand hills.
If I were hungry, I would not tell thee:
For the world is mine, and the fulness thereof.
Will I eat the flesh of bulls,
Or drink the blood of goats?
Offer unto God the sacrifice of thanksgiving;
And pay thy vows unto the Most High:
And call upon me in the day of trouble;
I will deliver thee, and thou shalt glorify me."

(Ps. l. 8–15.)

Thus we see why Jeremiah says:—

"Thus saith the Lord of hosts, the God of Israel: Add
your burnt offerings unto your sacrifices, and eat ye flesh.
For I spake not unto your fathers, nor commanded them
in the day that I brought them out of the land of Egypt,
for the sake of burnt offerings or sacrifices: but this thing
I commanded them, saying, Hearken unto my voice, and
I will be your God, and ye shall be my people: and walk
ye in all the way that I command you, that it may be well
with you.   But they hearkened not" (Jer. vii. 21–24).

It is, however, another question, and one upon which
scholars are by no means entirely agreed, as to whether this
ruthless condemnation of sacrifice as a way of escape is to
be interpreted as an equally ruthless condemnation of all
sacrifice.   In Psalm li. we have the rejection of sacrifice as a
solution of the penitent rebel's problem:

"For thou delightest not in sacrifice;
    else would I give it thee:
Thou hast no pleasure in burnt offering.
The sacrifices of God are a broken spirit:
A broken and a contrite heart, O God,
    thou wilt not despise."   (Ps. li. 16–17.)

Yet the Psalm ends:

"Do good in thy good pleasure unto Zion:
Build thou the walls of Jerusalem.
Then shalt thou delight in the sacrifices
    of righteousness, in burnt offerings and
    whole burnt offerings:
Then shall they offer bullocks upon thine altar."

(vss. 18–19)

Some would contend that this is a later addition by another hand; others disagree,[1] for the sin was rebellion against the covenant. When, however, the rebel has returned to the way of obedience, then he can make his eucharistic offering to his heavenly Father. Even earthly parents will accept the gifts of their children, useless though those gifts may be, as tokens of love. And shall a heavenly Father do less?

The prophets insisted on the moral obligations of the covenant. By so doing they emphasised man's unfaithfulness, man's sin. But the prophets had no Gospel to proclaim. They could, therefore, only bring men to the discovery that they were sinners before God, powerless to obey the law that made absolute demands upon them. It was the imperfect apprehension of the Pauline discovery that " by the works of the law shall no flesh be justified in his sight " (Rom. iii. 20). And because under the Old Covenant the people could see no other escape from their dilemma and the tension they were in, the sacrifices went on. But sacrifice did not solve the problem. So, on the threshold of the New Testament we hear the words of disillusionment. " Vanity of vanities, saith the Preacher, all is vanity."

5. The New Covenant

Within the Old Testament, however, there was one prophet who pointed forward to the solution of the problem. The Old Covenant had failed, for Israel had proved unable to keep the covenant. But God was faithful. To His people He would give a New Covenant, and with the covenant the power to observe it. Thus Jeremiah said:

" Behold, the days come, saith the Lord, that I will make a new covenant with the house of Israel, and with the house of Judah: not according to the covenant that I made with their fathers in the day that I took them by the hand to bring them out of the land of Egypt; which my covenant they brake, although I was an

[1] Professor F. C. Burkitt in *Eucharist and Sacrifice*, p. 8, says, " There is no reason whatever to regard these words as an addition by another hand." *Cf.* Professor W. E. Barnes, *The Psalms*, pp. 250, 254.

husband unto them, saith the Lord.   But this is the covenant that I will make with the house of Israel after those
days, saith the Lord; I will put my law in their inward
parts, and in their heart will I write it; and I will be
their God, and they shall be my people: and they shall
teach no more every man his neighbour, and every man
his brother, saying, Know the Lord: for they shall all
know me, from the least of them unto the greatest of them,
saith the Lord: for I will forgive their iniquity, and their
sin will I remember no more " (Jer. xxxi. 31–34).

The story of the New Testament is the story of the deliberate fulfilment by Jesus of that prophecy.   It is implied
everywhere.   But in the life of the Lord it comes out clearly
at one point only when Jesus said:

" This cup is the new covenant in my blood " (I Cor.
   xi. 25).

when at the Last Supper and upon the Cross He
established the New Covenant in His blood for them.

6. ' Son of Man ' and ' Servant '

To demonstrate the truth of that which has thus briefly
been stated will of necessity take us a little afield.   We have
to show that Jesus believed that His vocation, His service
of obedience and love, involved of necessity suffering and
death.   We have to show that He regarded this death,
which He must undergo, as redemptive, as a sacrifice.
And both points have been denied.[1]

With regard to the first, we have for example perfectly
clear foretellings of His death and resurrection in Mark ix.
31 = Matt. xvii. 22–23 = Luke ix. 44;   Mark x. 33–34 =
Matt. xx. 18–19 = Luke xviii. 31–33;   Mark viii. 31 =
Matt. xvi. 21 = Luke ix. 22.   But these foretellings are too
clear, too precise in their anticipation of events.   It has,
therefore, been contended that such passages as these are
obvious *vaticinia ex eventu*.[2]

---

[1] *e.g.* W. Bousset, *Kyrios Christos*, pp. 34, 35.
[2] *e.g.* W. Bousset, *Kyrios Christos*, p. 8.
F. J. Foakes Jackson and Kirsopp Lake, *The Beginnings of Christianity*,
Vol. I, Prolegomena, i., p. 381–2 say:—

With regard to the second point, we have clear examples
of the use of redemptive language by the Lord in the Gospels.
There is the classical passage in Mark x. 45, " to give his
life a ransom for many." But the Gospels were written
after the Pauline Epistles. Here, it is contended, is a clear
example of Pauline influence on the Gospels.[1]

To establish that Jesus during His ministry spoke of
His death as a soteriological necessity, we cannot in consequence use in the first place the prophecies we have already
quoted. Whatever their original form may have been,
in their present form they are clearly *vaticinia ex eventu*.
Instead, we must go to other material where the thought of
the death appears, but only appears incidentally.[2]

In Matt. ix. 15 = Mark ii. 19-20 = Luke v. 34-35,
we have a passage where there is but an allusion to the
death :

> " Can the sons of the bride-chamber mourn, as long
> as the bridegroom is with them? but the days will come,
> when the bridegroom will be taken away from them,
> and then they will fast."

" The prediction is explicit and precise : it could not possibly
be misunderstood by anyone. But the student of tradition—especially religious tradition—is aware that predictions are often given
explicit precision by an *ex post facto* knowledge of the event."

They, however, add :

" The records as we have them give not the *ipsissima verba* of Jesus,
but the meaning put upon them by the disciples or by the evangelists.
The recognition of this fact suggests that though Jesus did speak to
his disciples of his coming rejection by the Jewish leaders, and of
its ultimate triumph, he did not define the details of either with the
accuracy of the present documents."

[1] W. Bousset, *Kyrios Christos*, pp. 7-8, discusses this passage and finds
the original form of the saying to be " I am in your midst as the servant."
In a note on p. 8 he says that Mark has made a gloss upon the διακονῆσαι
by a reference to the sacrificial death. We shall see that, by allowing that
διακονῆσαι is original, Bousset allows the main point—the point that makes
the reference to the sacrificial death inevitable.

[2] In the whole of this section, and in the next, I am particularly
indebted to an article by Professor Gerhard Kittel, ' Jesu Worte über sein
Sterben,' which appeared in *Deutsche Theologie* for June, 1936. For a
fuller statement of the argument this article should be consulted. I have
in the main relegated to footnotes the case against which, in following
Professor Kittel, I am concerned to argue.

E

The saying is clearly Messianic. That the reference to the bridegroom shows. It also looks forward, not to continuing joy, but to coming separation and sorrow—then they will fast.[1]

Or again there are passages that show that Jesus expected to share the fate of the prophets and of John the Baptist :

"And he said unto them, Go and say to that fox, Behold I cast out devils and perform cures to-day and to-morrow, and the third day I am perfected. Howbeit I must go on my way to-day and to-morrow and the day following: for it cannot be that a prophet perish out of Jerusalem." (Luke xiii. 32–33.)

"I say unto you, that Elijah is come already, and they knew him not, but did unto him whatsoever they listed. Even so shall the Son of Man also suffer of them." [2] (Matt. xvii. 12; Mark ix. 12–13.)

But the heart of the problem is only reached when we come to the passages which speak of the Son of Man [3] as having to suffer. [4]

---

[1] W. Bousset (*Kyrios Christos*, pp. 40–41) when commenting on Mark ii. 19–20, on the other hand, argues that the whole passage 19(b)–20 is a manifest *vaticinium ex eventu*. He contends that the original saying of Jesus was simply 19(a). "Jesus thought of himself and his disciples as the guests at the marriage feast of the new age breaking in upon men— a magnificent and striking picture. It was the primitive Church that first introduced the contrast between the bridegroom and his friends and the idea of the dying bridegroom."

[2] W. Bousset, *Kyrios Christos*, p. 7, contends that Mark ix. 12b is an interpolation based on Matt. xvii. 12b, which disturbs the connection between Mark ix. 12 and 13, and that in any case the Matthean passage is secondary to the Markan. But we may note that the reference to Elijah = John the Baptist, as a prophet who has been killed, remains.

[3] Gerhard Kittel, *op. cit.*, pp. 175–82.

[4] W. Bousset, *Kyrios Christos*, p. 5, sets himself the task of proving "not that Jesus never used this title of himself, for that cannot definitely be established—but certainly that the self-designation as Son of Man in very many cases does not go back to Jesus himself, but in point of fact it arises from the tradition of the Church, and that we have before us here in the confession of Jesus as the Son of Man if anywhere the conviction of the primitive Church." Bousset sets out his case on pp. 5–21. F. J. Foakes Jackson and Kirsopp Lake in their very full discussion of the title Son of Man—*The Beginnings of Christianity*, Vol. I, pp. 368–84—say on p. 374 :

"Few things are so probable as the use of Son of Man by Jesus. It is found in his mouth in all the earlier strata of the gospels. . . . This does not prove that he applied the phrase to himself or on all the occasions on which it is attributed to him in the gospels : but it cer- tainly shows that he used it either of himself or of some one else."

" How is it written of the Son of Man, that he should suffer many things and be set at naught? " (Mark ix. 12.)

" For the Son of Man goeth, even as it is written of him." (Mark xiv. 21.)

Hebrew tradition knows the picture of the Son of Man coming on the clouds of heaven, the Son of Man of Dan. vii. 13. We find this Son of Man referred to in the Gospels (Mark xiv. 62 = Matt. xxvi. 64; Matt. xxv. 31). But Hebrew tradition knows nothing of a suffering Son of Man. And yet the Gospel asserts that it is written of the Son of Man that He should suffer. Where is it written? We know of no passage.

There is, however, in the Old Testament a picture of the suffering Servant of the Lord in Isa. liii. The early Church applied this prophecy to Jesus (Acts. iii. 13, 26; iv. 27, 30; viii. 32–35). But in the Gospels, despite the need for Old Testament prophecies of the crucifixion, we find only two passages in which Isa. liii. is clearly quoted—Luke xxii. 37 and Matt. viii. 17. Of these two passages, only one relates Isa. liii. in any wise to the crucifixion, and even then there is no mention of suffering or of dying.

Now, although there is no evidence in Judaism for a suffering Messiah, yet in the Apocalypses the language that is used in Deutero-Isaiah of the Servant is applied to the Son of Man. In Isa. liii. 1 the Servant is called " my righteous servant." In Enoch xxxviii. 2 the Son of Man is called " the righteous one." In Enoch xlvi. 3 " This is the Son of Man who hath righteousness, with whom dwelleth righteousness." In Isa. xlii. the Servant is called " my chosen." In Enoch the Son of Man is constantly called " the chosen one " [1] (Enoch xl. 5; xlix. 2; li. 5, 1; lii. 6, 9), " the righteous and chosen one " (Enoch liii. 6), " the chosen one of righteousness " (Enoch xxxix. 6). In Enoch li. 3 it is stated that " the chosen one shall in those days sit upon my throne." Professor Gerhard Kittel contends that these parallels show that, already in Judaism, there had been tendencies to unite the Son of Man of Daniel with the Servant of Deutero-

[1] In Dr. Charles' translation the allusion is apt to be missed, for Dr. Charles uses throughout the phrase " The Elect One."

Isaiah. If in this he is right, it becomes possible to reconsider the judgment on this point of the editors of *The Beginnings of Christianity*.[1] Nevertheless it remains true that it is only in the Gospels that we find the conclusion drawn that the Son of Man must suffer and die as it is written of the Servant in Isa. liii. This conclusion was drawn by Jesus Himself and is original to Him. Those, on the other hand, who, like W. Bousset, question Jesus' identification of Himself with the Son of Man, leave the Gospel story an unexplained enigma.

7. THE LAST SUPPER

How significant is this identification can be seen from two passages. The first is the story of the question of the sons of Zebedee (Mark x. 35–45 = Matt. xx. 20–28; cf. Luke xxii. 24–27), a story dominated by the expectation of the passion. This story ends:

" whosoever would be first among you, shall be servant of all. For verily the Son of Man came not to be ministered unto, but to minister, and to give his life a ransom for many."

This passage becomes intelligible the moment we see that the key word is the word ' Servant,' and that it refers back to the Servant of Isa. liii. who was to " make his soul an offering for sin " to " justify many " and " to bear their iniquities." The passage is through and through sacrificial. And it was Jesus and not St. Paul who first thought of His death in terms of sacrifice. St. Paul uses ἀντίλυτρον and ἀπολύτρωσις, but never the word used here, λύτρον.[2]

But it is in the story of the Last Supper that the most important passage occurs. Of the Last Supper we have

---

[1] F. J. Foakes Jackson and Kirsopp Lake, *op. cit.*, p. 384:

" The editors of the Gospels, or possibly the writers of their sources, used Son of Man indiscriminately as a periphrasis for the first person in the sayings of Jesus, and connected it with his predictions of suffering. Probably they had at first no passage in the Old Testament in mind. That the Messiah or the Son of Man should suffer according to the Scriptures is not a Jewish doctrine, and the fact that Jesus did suffer preceded the discovery of suitable prophecies."

[2] G. Kittel, *op. cit.*, p. 186.

four accounts: I Cor. xi. 23–26; Mark xiv. 22–25; Luke xxii. 15–18 and Matt. xxvi. 26–29. The difficulty of establishing both what were the words that Jesus used at the Last Supper and their significance is well known. And yet, however uncertain we may be about the original words, the early Church had a singularly united tradition concerning that which Jesus had done and that which He expected the Church to do.

The key word to the whole tradition would appear to be the word διαθήκη.[1] St. Paul has "This cup is the new covenant in my blood," obviously referring back to Jer. xxxi. 31–34. Jesus is initiating the New Covenant of which Jeremiah spoke and is sealing that covenant in His blood, even as the covenant upon the mount was sealed with blood. St. Mark has "This is my blood of the covenant, which is shed for many." It would seem almost certain that St. Paul has preserved the original words, and that St. Mark has tried to make the words agree with Ex. xxiv. 8: "Behold the blood of the covenant." Matthew has followed Mark: Luke in his longer account has followed St. Paul. As Professor Johannes Behm says, "The καινὴ διαθήκη is a conception correlated to βασιλεία τοῦ θεοῦ. . . . That the conception καινὴ διαθήκη is recorded but once in the mouth of Jesus, though this is certainly a decisive passage, proves as little as its rare appearance in the Old Testament apocryphal books proves against its central significance. Only from the διαθήκη-saying of Jesus can we fully understand how St. Paul and the author of the Epistle to the Hebrews have come to place the conception διαθήκη in the centre of their theological interpretation of history."[2]

In Mark the blood is shed "for many," in Matthew "for many unto remission of sins," in St. Paul the body is broken "for you." Luke in his longer version follows St. Paul. The Markan version is probably original, and is to be interpreted in the light of Mark x. 45, "to give his

[1] This section is based on the article διαθήκη by Professor Johannes Behm, in Kittel, *Theologisches Wörterbuch zum Neuen Testament.* Cf. H. Lietzmann, *Messe und Herrenmahl*, pp. 220–21.
[2] *Theologisches Wörterbuch*, Vol. ii, p. 137.

life a ransom for many," as a reference to the Servant of
Isa. liii. who made " his soul an offering for sin " to " justify
many." St. Paul, as Professor Kittel points out,[1] has here,
as often elsewhere, changed from " the objective conditioned
sphere of the third person " to the immediacy of the first
or second person. Thus, by His words at the Last Supper,
Jesus showed that He went to His death to fulfil the destiny
of the Servant of Deutero-Isaiah and to accomplish His
soteriological work.

That the bread and the cup should be given to the
disciples to eat and drink, can once again be explained in
terms of the New Covenant. " And Moses took the blood,
and sprinkled it on the people, and said, Behold the blood
of the covenant, which the Lord hath made with you . . .
and they beheld God, and did eat and drink " (Ex. xxiv. 8,
11). Further light is given by the eschatological sayings,
" I will no more drink of the fruit of the vine, until that
day when I drink it new in the kingdom of God " (Mark xiv.
25 = Matt. xxvi. 29; cf. Luke xxii. 18); " I will not eat
it, until it be fulfilled in the kingdom of God " (Luke xxii.
16). There is clear reference here to the Messianic Feast
in the Kingdom of God : " Blessed is he that shall eat bread
in the kingdom of God " (Luke xiv. 15), and perhaps
τὸν ἄρτον ἡμῶν τὸν ἐπιούσιον δὸς ἡμῖν σήμερον (Matt. vi.
11 = Luke xi. 3). It must be remembered that the Messianic Feast is likewise a sacrificial feast. The New Covenant
is established with an eschatological reference. Here and
now is set up that which will be fulfilled in the beyond.

We have not discussed whether the background of the
Last Supper was the annual Passover feast, as the Synoptists
appear to imply (Mark xiv. 12 ; Luke xxii. 15; cf. I Cor. v.
7), or the *Kiddûsh*, the weekly hallowing of the Sabbath,
which, when the Passover fell on a Sabbath, was probably
anticipated so that it became a preparation for the Passover.[2]
This question is irrelevant to the main problem. If the
meal was a *Kiddûsh*, it was a Passover *Kiddûsh*, and every

[1] G. Kittel, *op. cit.*, p. 185.
[2] W. O. E. Oesterley, *The Jewish Background of the Christian Liturgy*,
pp. 79–81, 167–77. H. Lietzmann, *op. cit.*, pp. 202–9. F. C. N. Hicks,
The Fullness of Sacrifice, pp. 215–19.

Jew would have in his mind the thought of the deliverance from Egypt, with which is associated the covenant of Ex. xxiv.

8. THE FULNESS OF THE SACRIFICE

How Jesus' words and ceremonial acts at the Last Supper were understood by the early Church can be seen by the way in which both St. Paul and the author of the Epistle to the Hebrews explain to the Christians that they are the sons of the New Covenant. Thus in Gal. iii. 15–29 St. Paul speaks of the covenant made with Abraham as having its fulfilment in Christ, and of the Christians as in consequence the heirs of the promise made to Abraham: while in Gal. iv. 21–v. 1 the theology of the two covenants is worked out in terms of the two sons of Abraham, the son of the bondwoman, the Old Covenant, and the son of the free woman, the New Covenant. That St. Paul understood the New Covenant in terms of Jer. xxxi. 31–34 is clear both from this passage and from 2 Cor. iii. 6, where he says that God hath " made us sufficient as ministers of a new covenant; not of the letter, but of the spirit; for the letter killeth, but the spirit giveth life."

The fullest exposition of the theology of the New Covenant is, however, to be found in the Epistle to the Hebrews. We cannot approach this epistle rightly except in terms of the old sacrificial system. But, if we do make this approach, we shall be able to see, both how the author of this epistle works out his analogy, and how the Lord Himself thought of His own death in terms of sacrifice. The death alone is not the sacrifice. The sacrifice includes the Last Supper and the death and the ascension and heavenly session of the Lord, the offering and the communion of the Christians, and the whole of the Christian life in the Spirit which had been given.

For a sacrifice there must be a victim. " And Isaac said, Behold the fire and the wood : but where is the lamb for a burnt offering? And Abraham said, God will provide himself the lamb for a burnt offering, my son " (Gen. xxii. 7–8). Jesus believed, as we have seen, that it belonged to the vocation of the Messiah to die as it had been written of the servant in Isa. liii. And He went forward willingly to His death. However much human flesh might shrink from death, He knew Himself to be the chosen victim and He accepted the necessity that had been laid upon Him.

Secondly, the sacrificer drew near with his victim.[1] Jesus believed that he must suffer in Jerusalem (Luke xiii. 33), and He deliberately went up to Jerusalem to die (Mark x. 32–33).

Thirdly, the sacrificer laid his hands upon the head of the victim to dedicate it to God. In the life of the Lord there may have been no corresponding ceremonial act; but, that there was the inner self-dedication, His words, and particularly His words and ceremonial acts at the Last Supper, make clear.

Fourthly, the victim must be slain. In the ancient practice it was natural that every man should slay his own victim. With the setting up of the central sanctuary at Jerusalem the slaying was gradually taken over by a special class, the Levites. It was not the work of the priests to slay the victim. In the case of the Passover, however, the offerer still slew his own victim. Certainly Jesus did not slay Himself. Perhaps we can see a theological motive coming into the words put into the mouth of St. Peter by the author of the Acts when he emphasises that it was sinners who slew Jesus. "Jesus of Nazareth . . . being delivered up by the determinate counsel and foreknowledge of God, ye by the hand of lawless men did crucify and slay" (Acts ii. 22–23). The author of the epistle to the Hebrews strongly emphasises the importance of the death (Heb. ix. 15–17).

Fifthly, the blood was splashed by the priests upon the altar, and in the early days upon the people too (Ex. xxiv. 6–8).

The author of the epistle to the Hebrews emphasises the fact that " even the first covenant hath not been dedicated without blood " (Heb. ix. 18). In I Cor. xi. 25, we read, " This cup is the new covenant in my blood." In the

[1] G. Buchanan Gray, *op. cit.*, pp. 17–18.

Epistle to the Hebrews we have such phrases as " the blood of the covenant " (x. 29), " the blood of the eternal covenant " (xiii. 20), " to Jesus the mediator of a new covenant, and to the blood of sprinkling that speaketh better than that of Abel " (xii. 24), " Jesus also, that he might sanctify the people through his own blood " (xiii. 12). The death has liberated the blood, and the purifying power of the blood of Christ is strongly emphasised in Heb. ix. 11–14 and x. 19–20.

Dr. Buchanan Gray says, " None but a priest could manipulate the blood, whether in applying it to the altar or to the worshipper." [1] This is in part at least why the author of the Epistle to the Hebrews emphasises that Christ is not only victim, but also priest. But he is careful to insist that Christ is priest after the order of Melchizedek (vii. 17). The mysterious figure of Melchizedek stands outside the First Covenant, for Abraham paid tithes to him (vii. 4). He is the eternal priest, appearing in the Old Testament. To insist that Christ is " a priest for ever after the order of Melchizedek," is to insist on the newness and finality of that which Christ wrought (Heb. vi. 20–vii. 17).

Sixthly, the flesh was offered to God, usually by being burnt by fire. The Hebrew word ôlah, which was used to describe the whole burnt offering, means, according to the generally accepted etymology, " that which goes up from the altar in smoke." [2] Christ once for all offered up Himself (Heb. vii. 26–27; x. 14).

The seventh moment in sacrifice is not man's but God's. God accepts—or it may be refuses—the gift that man has sent up to Him. The technical word in the Old Testament for doing this means literally " to smell an odour that quiets the anger of the Lord." [3] Thus in Gen. viii. 21, when after the flood Noah offered his burnt offering, we read that " the Lord smelled the sweet savour; and the Lord said in his heart, I will not again curse the ground any more for man's sake." In Lev. xxvi. 31 on the other hand, the Lord threatens that He " will not smell the savour of your sweet odours."

[1] G. Buchanan Gray, *op. cit.*, p. 200.
[2] *Idem, op. cit.*, p. 7.   [3] *Idem, op. cit.*, p. 77.

For the New Testament writers the token that God has accepted the sacrifice of Christ is that He raised Him from the dead. In the Epistle to the Hebrews it is the heavenly session of the Lord. "But he, when he had offered one sacrifice for sins for ever, sat down on the right hand of God" (Heb. x. 12; cf. viii. 1–2; ix. 25–28). But the Christians remain upon earth in the midst of the conflict. Hence His continual intercession (vii. 25).

In the ancient sacrificial system, the sacrifice was normally completed by priest and people partaking of the flesh of the victim. To this generalisation a number of very important exceptions must be made. Certain sacrifices were considered so holy that the whole of the victim was given to God, the whole was consumed by fire. In the sin offerings only the priests dared to partake, for the later Jewish theology emphasised the point that the sinners on whose behalf the sin-offering was offered might not themselves partake.[1] This explains why on the Day of Atonement no one partook of the sacrifice. But normally peace-offerings, burnt-offerings and sin-offerings would be made simultaneously, and in this sense the act of partaking, of communion, belongs to the full cycle of sacrificial practices and ideas.[2] Thus St. Paul says, "Behold Israel after the flesh: have not they which eat the sacrifices communion with the altar?" (I Cor. x. 18). So at the Last Supper we read, "And as they were eating he took bread, and when he had blessed, he brake it, and gave to them, and said, 'Take ye: this is my body'" (Mark xiv. 22). St. Paul records the command to repeat that which at the Last Supper the Lord did, "This do, as oft as ye drink it, in remembrance of me"; and he adds, "For as often as ye eat this bread, and drink this cup, ye proclaim the Lord's death till he come" (I Cor. xi. 25–26). That the early Christians did continue "the breaking of the bread" we have abundant evidence.[3] It is to this that the author of the Epistle to the Hebrews refers when he says, "We have an altar, whereof they have no right to eat which serve the tabernacle" (Heb. xiii. 10).

[1] F. C. N. Hicks, *op. cit.*, p. 13.   [2] *Idem, op. cit.*, p. 20.
[3] Acts ii. 42, 46; xx. 7; I Cor. x. 16; xi. 20.

But the sacrifice of the New Covenant does not stop here. It comprehends the whole life of the Christians. In Jer. xxxi. the nature of the New Covenant is set forth: " I will put my law in their inward parts, and in their hearts will I write it; and . . . they shall all know me . . . for I will forgive their iniquity, and their sin will I remember no more." Thus St. Paul, in the passage in which he is discussing the two covenants, Gal. iii. 15–v. 1, points to the fact that the prophecy of Jer. xxxi. has been fulfilled:

" But when the fulness of time came, God sent forth his Son, born of a woman, born under the law, that he might redeem them which were under the law, that we might receive the adoption of sons. And because ye are sons, God sent forth the Spirit of his Son into our hearts, crying, Abba, Father. So that thou art no longer a bondservant, but a son; and if a son, then an heir through God " (Gal. iv. 4–7).

The gift of the Spirit is the sign that Jeremiah xxxi. has been fulfilled. The Gentiles too, who once were " strangers from the covenants of the promise," have now been " made nigh in the blood of Christ." " The middle wall of partition " between Jew and Gentile has been broken down " that he might create in himself of the twain one new man . . . and might reconcile them both in one body unto God through the cross." The Gentiles, therefore, " are no more strangers," but " fellow citizens with the saints, and of the household of God, being built upon the foundation of the apostles and prophets, Jesus Christ himself being the chief corner stone; in whom each several building, fitly framed together, groweth into a holy temple in the Lord; in whom ye also builded together for a habitation of God in the Spirit " (Eph. ii. 11–22).

To the members of this Church of the New Covenant which is one new man in Christ and a habitation of God in the Spirit, St. Paul, can write, " I beseech you therefore, brethren, by the mercies of God, to present your bodies a living sacrifice, holy, acceptable to God, which is your reasonable service " (Rom. xii. 1). The Church's whole life becomes a life of self-oblation in Christ, so that St. Paul can speak of the gifts of the Philippians to himself as " an odour of a sweet smell, a sacrifice acceptable, well pleasing to God " (Phil. iv. 18) : or the author of the Epistle to the Hebrews can say, " Through him then let us offer up a sacrifice of praise to God continually, that is, the fruit of lips which make confession to his name. But to do good and to communicate forget not; for with such sacrifices God is well pleased. Obey them that have the rule over you " (Heb. xiii. 15–17). The members of the Church upon earth have to live so that through the Spirit they may become that which the Church of the New Covenant eschatologically already is.

Thus does the sacrifice of the New Covenant fulfil, and by fulfilling overthrow, the ancient sacrificial ceremonies. " In that he saith, a new covenant, he hath made the first old. But that which is becoming old and waxeth aged is nigh unto vanishing away " (Heb. viii. 13).

9. The Eucharist

We turn now to the Christian rite, the Eucharist. On the one hand we have the strong assertions in the Epistle to the Hebrews of the uniqueness of that which Christ did. On the other hand we have the use of sacrificial language with regard to that which the Christians were in the rite required to do. How did the Church relate these two aspects of the sacrifice of the New Covenant?

The best way to come to an understanding of this is to examine the language of the Christian rite itself. The difficulty of this task arises from the diversity of liturgies in East and West, and from the varying interpretations that have been put upon the rite in Patristic, Scholastic, Reformation and modern times. Yet, if we consider the main structure of the Anaphora or Canon, we discover, despite a wide range of variations, a certain unity of form. The Anaphora of the 'Apostolic Tradition of Hippolytus' would appear to provide us with a primitive Anaphora from which both the Anaphoras of the Antiochene group of liturgies and the Canon of the Roman Mass may be said to be descended.[1]

---

[1] H. Lietzmann, *Messe und Herrenmahl*, p. 174.

The Anaphora of the 'Apostolic Tradition of Hippo-lytus'[1] opens with the *dialogue*. This is followed at once by a *thanksgiving*, in which eucharist is made for the work of Christ, His incarnation, His obedience to the Father's will, His voluntary passion, the whole ending with a record of that which the Lord did at the Last Supper (the *institution*), the record that supplies the authority for the Christian rite.[2]

Then, mindful of His death and resurrection[3] (the *anamnesis*), the Church proceeds to offer (the *anaphora*, in the most restricted sense of the term) the bread and the cup,[4] and to ask that God will give to the communicants in the act of partaking His holy Spirit for fulfilment and for the confirmation of faith in truth[5] (*epiclesis* and *communion*).

This rite is clearly sacrificial. There is the act of offering, there is the communion upon that which has been offered. But all besides that belongs to a sacrifice has already taken place: the voluntary death of Christ the victim, the resurrection or acceptance of the sacrifice. The Church repeats the rite because Christ commanded this. Yet what the Church does is done having in memory what Christ did, and particularly His death and resurrection. And the whole moves forward to its climax of which the communion is the means—the filling of the communicants with the holy Spirit.[6]

---

[1] Hauler, *Didascaliæ Apostolorum Fragmenta Veronensia Latina*, pp. 106–7. Cabrol-Leclercq, *Dictionnaire d'Archéologie Chrétienne et de Liturgie*, Vol. XI, Pt. I, Cols. 582–3. The text is quoted, pp. 101–3 *infra*.

[2] quando hoc facitis, meam commemorationem facitis.

[3] Memores igitur mortis et resurrectionis ejus.

[4] offerimus tibi panem et calicem.

[5] Et petimus ut *mittas spiritum tuum sanctum in oblationem sanctæ ecclesiæ*; in unum congregans des omnibus qui percipiunt sanctis in repletionem spiritus sancti ad confirmationem fidei in veritate ut te laudemus et glorificemus.

Fr. Gregory Dix, 'The Origin of the Epiclesis,' Part I, in *Theology*, March 1934, contends (p. 132) that the words above put in italics are an interpolation into the original text of Hippolytus. This strengthens our contention that the original purpose of the *epiclesis* was for the holy Spirit to come upon the communicants, and that the *epiclesis* for the holy Spirit to change the elements is a later development.

[6] Throughout I have used a small " h " for holy in the phrase " the holy Spirit " to suggest that the Spirit was not yet clearly thought of as the Third Person of the Holy Trinity, but rather as the equivalent of the " grace " of God. This point becomes important when we come to the Roman rite.

It is this climax that suggests the significance of the whole rite. The token that the prophecy of Jer. xxxi. had been fulfilled was that the holy Spirit had been given. That which Christ did at the Last Supper and upon the Cross was to establish the New Covenant in His blood. Here there is no direct mention of the New Covenant. And yet the rite as a whole is the Sacrifice of the New Covenant. It looks back to, it depends upon, that which Christ did. And the rite, by re-presenting that which Christ did, implements the purpose of the New Covenant, the filling of the Church with the holy Spirit of God.

The historic Eastern rites developed considerably the simple structure of the Anaphora of Hippolytus. The *thanksgiving* came to include not only the work of Christ in redemption, but, in some cases, the whole history of God's dealings with man from the creation up to the work of Christ. The story of the *institution* of the Eucharist is given at greater length. The majority of the Liturgies, when they come to the cup, repeat the Pauline words concerning the blood of the New Covenant.[1] The *anamnesis*

---

[1] *The Liturgy of the 8th Book of the Apostolic Constitutions* (Lietzmann, p. 25):

λαβὼν ἄρτον . . . τοῦτο τὸ μυστήριον τῆς καινῆς διαθήκης.

The Liturgy of St. Basil (Lietzmann, p. 27):
τοῦτο ἐστί τὸ αἷμά μου τὸ τῆς καινῆς διαθήκης.

Brightman, who follows the Codex Grottaferrata, has (p. 328):
τοῦτό μου ἐστὶν τὸ αἷμα τὸ ὑπὲρ ὑμῶν.

The Liturgy of St. John Chrysostom (Lietzmann, p. 29):
τοῦτ' ἐστὶν τὸ αἷμά μου τὸ τῆς καινῆς διαθήκης.

The Greek Liturgy of St. James (Lietzmann, p. 30):
τοῦτό μου ἐστὶ τὸ αἷμα τὸ τῆς καινῆς διαθήκης.

Serapion (Lietzmann, p. 36):
πίετε, τοῦτο ἐστὶν ἡ καινὴ διαθήκη, ὅ ἐστιν τὸ αἷμά μου.

St. Mark (Lietzmann, p. 40):
τοῦτό ἐστι τὸ αἷμά μου τὸ τῆς καινῆς διαθήκης.

Hippolytus (Lietzmann, p. 42):
Hic est sanguis meus, qui pro vobis effunditur.
de sacramentis (Lietzmann, p. 44):
hic est enim sanguis meus.
Roman (Lietzmann, p. 45):
hic est enim calix sanguinis mei, novi et æterni testamenti, mysterium fidei, qui pro vobis et pro multis effundetur in remissionem peccatorum.

is expanded to include the passion, death, resurrection, and second coming.[1] With the *anaphora* there is sometimes more hesitation about making the offering. It is done on the authority of Christ's institution. It is remembered that God stands in need of nought. And yet God is asked graciously to accept the offered gifts for the honour of Christ.[2] The *epiclesis* becomes a request that God will send His holy Spirit upon the sacrifice [3] to change the gifts, as well as that those who in *communion* partake of them, may be filled with the holy Spirit.[4] This petition is developed, articulating the blessings of the New Covenant, though there is but seldom direct reference to it.[5] The blessings sought come rather out of the inner needs of the Christian life, than from any direct literary dependence on Jer. xxxi. The same is true of the blessings sought in Heb. xiii. 20–21. And yet the blessings sought are the blessings of the sons of the New Covenant. These blessings in Jer. xxxi. are:

" I will put my law in their inward parts, and in their hearts will I write it; and I will be their God, and they shall be my people: and they shall teach no more every man his neighbour . . . saying, Know the Lord: for they shall all know me . . . for I will forgive their iniquity, and their sin will I remember no more."

Mozarabic (Lietzmann, p. 48):
  Miss Moz. F.
    Hic calix novum testamentum in meo sanguine.
  Lib. ordin. B.
    Hic calix novum testamentum est.
  Editio Leslie.
    Hic est calix novi testamenti in meo sanguine.
[1] H. Lietzmann, *op. cit.*, pp. 50–68.
[2] *Idem op. cit.*, pp. 50–68.   [3] *Idem, op. cit.*, pp. 68–81.
Cf. the O.T. idea of the descent of the fire of the Lord from heaven upon the sacrifice, Lev. ix. 24; vi. 13; Judges vi. 21; II Chron. vii. 1, and I Kings xviii. 38.
[4] H. Lietzmann, *op. cit.*, pp. 68–81.
[5] St. Mark has (Brightman, p. 134; Lietzmann, pp. 77–78):

ἔπιδε ἐφ' ἡμᾶς καὶ (ἐξαπόστειλον) ἐπὶ τοὺς ἄρτους τούτους καὶ ἐπὶ τὰ ποτήρια ταῦτα τὸ Πνεῦμά σου τὸ Ἅγιον ἵνα αὐτὰ ἁγιάσῃ καὶ τελειώσῃ ὡς παντοδύναμος Θεός καὶ ποιήσῃ τὸν μὲν ἄρτον σῶμα τὸ δὲ ποτήριον αἷμα τῆς καινῆς διαθήκης αὐτοῦ τοῦ κυρίου. . . .

In this prayer that the Holy Spirit may make the cup the blood of the New Covenant, St. Mark is followed, with minor variations, by most of the Alexandrian liturgies.

In Hebrews xiii. 21 they are :

" make you perfect in every good thing to do his will, working in us that which is well-pleasing in his sight."

In the ' Apostolic Constitutions ' they are:

> " that all who partake thereof
> may be confirmed in piety,
> may receive remission of their sins,
> may be delivered from the devil and his wiles,
> may be filled with the Holy Ghost,
> may become worthy of thy Christ,
> and may obtain eternal life,
> Thou, O Almighty God, being reconciled to them."

The Roman Canon is derived, according to Lietzmann, from an Anaphora (to use the word in its wider sense) similar in structure to that of the ' Apostolic Tradition of Hippolytus.' [1] Comparing the Roman Canon with the Anaphora of the ' Apostolic Tradition,' we see that there is in the Roman Canon, after the *Sanctus* and the *Benedictus*, no thanksgiving for the life and work of Christ.[2] All that remains of this is an elaborate narrative of the *institution*. The *institution*, which Western tradition fixed on as containing the moment of *consecration*, is followed, however, quite normally by an *anamnesis*, and an *anaphora* (using the word in its most restricted sense). That which is offered is " a pure sacrifice, a holy sacrifice, an immaculate sacrifice, the holy bread of eternal life, and the chalice of everlasting salvation." And the *anaphora* goes on to ask that God will accept the gifts as He accepted the gifts of Abel and the sacrifices of Abraham and Melchizedek. The request that the gifts may be carried up to the altar on high, presents to the historian of liturgy a difficult and obscure problem.[3] But in its present context this prayer is another form of the request to God to accept the gifts.

We should now expect an *epiclesis*, and there is indeed a request that the communicants may be filled with all heavenly benediction and grace. This request is very

[1] H. Lietzmann, *op. cit.*, p. 262.
[2] *Idem, op. cit.*, p. 173.   [3] *Idem, op. cit.*, pp. 119–20.

similar to that in the ' Apostolic Tradition ' where it is asked
that God would send His holy Spirit upon the oblation that
the communicants might be filled with the holy Spirit.
The "holy Spirit" of the ' Apostolic Tradition ' probably
means much the same as "the heavenly benediction and
grace " of the Roman Canon. Whether the Roman Canon
contains a true *epiclesis*, and, if so, which of the petitions is
to be regarded as the *epiclesis*,[1] is a controversial question
into which we need not enter. But it would certainly
seem that the Roman Canon has preserved a petition for
the filling of the communicants with the holy Spirit or grace,
more primitive in form than the developed *epiclesis* of the
classical Eastern liturgies. That which the Roman Canon
has preserved is, we suggest, the original purpose of the
epiclesis, a prayer for the benefits and blessings of the New
Covenant.

It follows from what has been said that the Roman Canon
is weak in that it has lost the *thanksgiving* for the life and work
of Christ leading up to His crucifixion and resurrection.
The result of this omission is a tendency to throw too much
emphasis upon the eucharistic gifts, and an inadequate
relating of that which is done in the rite, to that which Christ
once did through His life, death and resurrection. The
rendering of διαθήκη by ' testamentum ' too is unfortunate.[2]
And yet the *anamnesis* does preserve the classical allusion to
the passion, resurrection and ascension of the Lord.

10. The Anglican Communion Office

The first English Prayer Book of Edward VI, the Prayer of
Consecration of which is based upon the Roman Canon, does
therefore go some way towards restoring the ancient proportion by emphasising the work of Christ, that He suffered
" death upon the crosse for our redempcion " and that He
" made there (by his one oblacion once offered) a full,
perfect, and sufficient sacrifyce, oblacion, and satysfaccyon,
for the sinnes of the whole worlde." The *Quam oblationem*

---

[1] H. Lietzmann, *op. cit.*, pp. 117–22.
[2] This rendering is common to Western rites.

F

of the Roman Canon has been developed into a definite
epiclesis.[1] The *institution* follows. The words over the cup
become " this is my bloude of the newe Testament," a
development from the Latin " testamentum " which
further loses the original association of the words with " the
blood of the New Covenant." The authority of the
institution is quoted for that which the Church does in
celebrating with the holy gifts the memorial Christ commanded. Then follows the *anamnesis* and the request that
God will accept the sacrifice (*anaphora*). The sacrifice is
defined as " our Sacrifice of praise and thankes geuing," an
allusion to Rom. xii. 1. With this is associated another and
very definite *anaphora*, " And here wee offre and present unto
thee (O Lorde) oure selfe, oure soules, and bodies, to be a
reasonable, holy, and liuely sacrifice unto thee." Here a
deliberate change of emphasis has taken place. The Roman
anaphora, *offerimus* . . . *Hostiam*, was understood to be an
offering of Christ in His eucharistic gifts. The Reformers
were concerned to emphasise that that which Christ did
was done once and was complete. They sought to follow
closely the argument of the author of the Epistle to the
Hebrews. The Church, they contended, could not add to
what Christ had done. " Wherefore the sacrifices of Masses,
in the which it was commonly said, that the Priest did
offer Christ for the quick and the dead . . . were blas-
phemous fables, and dangerous deceits " (Article XXXI.).
And yet they had a theology of the eucharistic sacrifice.
They were Augustinians and they went back to Augustine.
St. Augustine taught, " If you wish to understand the body
of Christ hear the Apostle speaking to the faithful ' Now ye
are the body and members of Christ.' If you then are the
body and members of Christ, your mystery is laid on the
Table of the Lord, your mystery you receive " (Ep. cclxxii.).
And again, " This is the sacrifice of Christians—' the many
one body in Christ '; which also the Church solemnises
by the sacrament of the altar, known to the faithful, where it
is shewn to her that in the very thing that she offers she

---

[1] F. E. Brightman, ' The New Prayer Book Examined,' in *Church
Quarterly Review*, July 1927, pp. 240–2.

herself is offered " (*De Civitate Dei*, ix. 6). The eucharistic sacrifice of the Prayer Book of 1549 is the offering of the Church herself, whose head is Christ, " hauyng in remembraunce his blessed passion, mightie resurreccyon, and gloryous ascencion." And so there follows the petition that the communicants " maye worthely receiue the most precious body and bloude of thy sonne Jesus Christe : and bee fulfilled with thy grace and heauenly benediccion, and made one bodye with thy sonne Jesu Christe, that he maye dwell in them, and they in hym." Quite logically it insists that " Christ our Pascall lambe is offred up for us, once for al . . . wherefore let us kepe a ioyful and holy feast with the Lorde," and this, so long as we remember that the feast is a partaking of the sacrifice, is very good theology.

It would take too long to work historically through the subsequent Anglican revisions. The important change, however, was made in 1552, whereby the *communion* has been inserted into the very centre of the service. This change has been retained ever since. It can be contended that by this change something has been lost. But at least let us seek to understand the significance of the change. It, too, is thoroughly Augustinian. That which Christ did He did once for all. The *consecration* (the *institution*) is the showing-forth of this one sacrif e of Christ. In the *communion* Christ gives to us His Body and His Blood, and by so doing unites us with Himself. In our humanity we cannot offer ourselves to God ; it were Pelagianism to imagine that we could. But as those who in *communion* have had our membership of His Body renewed in us, we can offer ourselves in Him (*anaphora*) ; for it is Christ who has united us with His sacrifice, and who now offers us up with Himself as members of His Body.

11. SUMMARY

Upon the mount was sealed with sacrifice the Old Covenant between God and His people. To that covenant the people of God proved unfaithful. So the prophet foretold a New Covenant. It was this New Covenant that Christ sealed with sacrifice, the sacrifice of Himself. At the

Last Supper Christ offered Himself, and made His disciples partakers of His Body broken for them and His Blood out-poured for them.   Upon the cross He died.   And the Church, in offering her sacrifice, offers that which com-pletely depends upon, and yet complements, that which Christ did.   Of that sacrifice we partake, and the fruits of the New Covenant appear in our lives through the Spirit who has been given.   This is the Sacrifice of the New Covenant—not Christ's unrepeatable death alone, nor the Church's offering alone, but the offering of Christ expounded by rite and act at the Last Supper, actualised in His death and resurrection and ascension and heavenly session, realised in the Church which is His Body, and yet not fully realised here upon earth—anticipated now, but fulfilled only in the Church Triumphant, when Christ shall indeed be " head over all things to the church, which is his body, the fulness of him that filleth all in all " (Eph. i. 22–3).

IV

EUCHARIST AND CHURCH IN THE NEW TESTAMENT

By the Rev. AUSTIN M. FARRER
Fellow of Trinity College, Oxford

EUCHARIST AND CHURCH IN THE NEW TESTAMENT

1. ORIGINS

THE purpose of this Essay is to show how the content of the New Testament Gospel is expressed, summed and mediated by the Eucharist in the Church. Our business is primarily to exhibit a connection of Biblical thoughts; and this we shall do by tracing the links which lead one thought on into another, but without implying that the order we choose was historically the order first followed by our Lord or the primitive community. We will start, then, from the *eucharistia*, the thanksgiving for bread and for wine.

The Jewish piety of that age attached importance to this solemn grace before meat. The proper way to fit the gifts of God for human use, and derive from them the blessing God intended, was to acknowledge Him as their Giver and His Covenant as the terms on which they were given.[1] Not only is God acknowledged as Creator and Sustainer of the whole world and of mankind: the order of Grace is also involved, as Deuteronomy reminds us.[2] It is the God of the Exodus who has given His chosen people the fruits of the Promised Land.

But now the Israelite of a later day could not fail to reflect that his possession of the Land and its blessings was incomplete; and in his Messianic hopes the country of corn, wine and oil held a prominent place. Not only would the Messianic Kingdom give him undisturbed ownership of it; but a miraculous enhancement of its fertility would belong to the glory of those days. Thus the thanksgiving over

---

[1] A summary of the Jewish doctrine and practice can be found in *Liturgy and Worship* (Gavin), p. 85. I Tim. iv. 4–5 expresses the ordinary Jewish view. [2] Deut. xxvi. 1–11.

bread and wine received a new character. To the age of
Deuteronomy it was a pledge of the present kingdom in
Canaan: to the age of Christ, it could be a pledge also of
that kingdom as it should be restored and glorified.[1]

Our Lord is a Jew, when at the Supper, making the
thanksgiving for wine, He looks forward to that ' new '
wine of the glorified Canaan [2] of which Apocalyptic spoke
such marvels.[3] To Him, perhaps, not more than a symbol
for the fellowship of that future joy, as in those parables
which develop the symbolism of the Messianic Feast. Or
perhaps we ought to say that He accepted the miraculous
fruits as scriptural, while placing elsewhere the essence of a
divine Kingdom which is not food and drink. An old
Rabbinic list [4] enumerates outward blessings of the Age to
Come, and couples with fruitfulness of earth and brightness
of luminaries the restoration of man to Adamic stature and
glory. For all we, having sinned, forfeit with Adam the
Shekinah of God,[5] as St. Paul reminds us: but that radiance
of the divine presence shall return in the Kingdom of the
Resurrection, when Spirit shall dominate flesh, and, in the
words of the Gospel, they shall neither marry nor be given
in marriage, but be as the angels of God.

St. Paul and the Primitive Church saw in this new-
creation of man the essential blessing of the Kingdom of

[1] The grace of the Sanctification of the Sabbath was explicitly
Deuteronomic, referring to the election of Israel and the joyful feasts
of Canaan. That for Passover-tide adds the redemption from Egypt, a
prototype of Messianic deliverance. Cf. Oesterley, *Jewish Background
of the Christian Liturgy*, pp. 81 and 170 ff.

[2] Mark xiv. 25.

[3] Apoc. Baruch, XXIX. 5; Ethiopic Enoch, X. 19; Papias ap.
Irenæus, V. 33.

[4] At the Fall, Man lost six things: ' life ' (immortality), height of
stature, radiance (' glory '), fruitfulness of ground, fruitfulness of trees,
brightness of heavenly luminaries; all of which return with the Messianic
Age. Strack-Billerbeck, *Kommentar*, Vol. I, p. 19. Apparently this
list of six things was a hallowed formula to the Rabbis of the later third
century.

[5] Rom. iii. 23. R.V. renders " fall short of the glory of God," but
that " *go* short of " is the true rendering will be seen by anyone who con-
siders the contemporary use of the verb, the Rabbinic parallels (as above)
and the parallel of Rom. v. 12 ff., where it equally a question of how all
sharing the Fall, share its consequences—in ch. 5, loss, not of ' glory,'
but of ' life.'

God: and at the Supper our Lord had Himself thrust this
very thing into the place of the fruits of Canaan. Of those
fruits, the present bread and wine were pledges to thankful
partakers; but the present human substance of the Messiah
given over to death was the pledge of the Resurrection-life
to men who had fellowship with Him. As often as they did
this, made their Eucharist, they would give thanks indeed
for the fatherly Providence which gives daily bread, the
token of a care supporting man through this world into that
which is to come; but still more thankfully acknowledge
the gift and sacrifice of the Christ's manhood, in which
their present partaking through the Spirit was the token of
their Resurrection-being.

This is not the place to demonstrate, were that possible,
that our Lord's conscious intention at the Supper was such
as we have outlined. It is enough to show how the Apostolic Church understood Him to have acted; and that their
interpretation contains no intrinsic historical improbability.
Indeed, if we cannot accept the Christ whom the New
Testament Church knew, it is foolish for us to imagine that
any critical sleight of hand will find us another behind all
evidence.

It will immediately occur to everyone to say, that the
bread of the Jewish ' Eucharist ' was no sacrament, and
that in suggesting this line of thought we are reducing our
Lord's Institution to the merest token of a reality yet to
come. The answer to such an objection does not lie in a
mere emphasis on the literal sense of " Hoc est corpus
meum." Rather we need to point out the essential difference between the Jewish and Christian views of the relation
existing between anticipation and fulfilment. To the Jew
the Messianic Kingdom, the restored Canaan, simply was in
no sense present: the produce of the unredeemed earth was
not the Kingdom's produce, but a quite separate and
external thing, at most its token and its pledge. But the
novelty in our Lord's teaching was that it made the powers
of the World to Come already active: the sun of the Kingdom, though still itself behind the horizon, threw its beams
before, to penetrate the world: where Christ by the finger

of God cast out devils, there the Kingdom of God was upon them,[1] exercising its force: and men who had the force to do so, grasped it.[2]   This meant a new reality in anticipations of the Kingdom: for in them not a token only of the thing, but the thing itself could be seized: though not in the revelation of glory, yet in the essence of power and the security of possession.   Hence the possibility of a Sacrament. The new-created manhood of the age to come was actual in the Christ, though hidden, and could be spiritually received along with the token of it.

2. THE BODY

The Resurrection and Enthronement of Christ meant that one representative, and He the chief, of the redeemed and spiritualised Israel, was already there, in the fulness of glory and the finality of completion, its King, its Head, its Firstfruits, its Corner-Stone; the last day would but raise the faithful to the same state of being that the Lord's manhood already enjoyed: would but add the courses of masonry to the Corner-Stone, the full harvest to the Firstfruits and His brethren to their King.   But meanwhile the Resurrection-being, the spiritual mode of embodiment, was possessed in actuality by Christ alone: the faithful might indeed walk in newness of spirit, but must groan still in expectation of their body's redemption,[3] that is, a manner of embodiment that would express and obey those aspirations of the Spirit which are its proper nature: which in this house of clay remain largely hidden even from ourselves, being heard only in groanings past utterance.[4]

But we shall never understand St. Paul's doctrine of the Body, nor therefore of the Sacrament, if we fall into making too sharp a division between the spiritual new self we already

---

[1] Luke xi. 20 (= Matt. xii. 28).

[2] Matt. xi. 12 (= Luke xvi. 16).   The interpretation here given follows Otto, *Reich Gottes u. Menschensohn*, p. 84: which gives the ordinary sense to βιάζεται, explains how Matthew could have understood the saying in its context, and Luke (or his source) paraphrased it as he did.   It expresses the paradox of salvation—the Kingdom forces its own way: yet the individual must be a man of force, and seize it like a robber seizing his booty.

[3] Romans viii. 23.   [4] Rom. viii. 26.

have,[1] and the new embodiment as yet denied us, but laid up for us in heaven with God.[2] We are inclined to say: Here are two elements: Spirit or mind, which thinks, desires and rules; and Resurrection-body, its mere vehicle or instrument. The former Christians already have; the latter they have not. The last day will but add the second to the first.

That is a misunderstanding. Spirit and body are not thus separable. The full gift of the Spirit is only possible in and with that of the body. That body is its home, as the sun is the home of the sunlight: yet it can shine abroad —outward in the dimension of space, from our Lord's Glorified Body to our mortal bodies: backward in the dimension of time, from our true and ultimate being to what we now are. Those two participations—in what Our Lord already is, and in what we ourselves are to become —are themselves complementary and inseparable. The receptacle, as it were, in which we receive the substance of glory derived from Christ, is the nascent body of glory in ourselves; even though it as yet only exists as a spiritual anticipation, it is the sole vessel we possess that will hold that marvellous life: we can only receive what belongs to the world to come, in so far as we are made part of it.[3] The Spirit is not separate from the Resurrection mode of embodiment, but can shine beyond it into that which is to become it.[4]

[1] II Cor. iv. 16.   [2] II Cor. v. 1.

[3] II Cor. iv. 7 ff. The incompetence of the earthen vessels makes it evident that they are not the true containers of the ' exceeding greatness of the power,' but that that belongs to the Resurrection world (vv. 10 and 14). According to II Cor. v. 14–17, Gal. vi. 14–15, the ' man in Christ ' belongs to the new creation which ushers in the World to Come.

[4] Hence called ' firstfruits ' (Rom. viii. 23): ' earnest ' (II Cor. i. 22, etc.). It is so much a matter of course that the full possession of our true spiritual being has its home in the body, that we are unclothed, naked without it, and it is necessary seriously to consider whether it is better to be absent from the body and present with the Lord (in an intermediate state), or absent from the Lord but present with the (still unredeemed) body (II Cor. v. 1–8). And though St. Paul prefers the first, evidently it is only the promise of the Resurrection-body *some day* (v. 1) which makes that alternative even a possible conception. Phil. 1. 20–23 uses the conclusion of the debate in II Cor. v. without troubling to repeat the considerations on which it then rested.

If such be the manner of our association with our Risen Lord, St. Paul's doctrine of the Body of Christ begins to be intelligible. His Mystical Body, the Church, is the overflow of His Glorious Body. It is the overflow upon us of the powers and Spirit of that Risen Manhood, by which we are made the members of Him who is our Head. It has been often noticed that St. Paul does not distinguish between the Mystical Body and the Glorified Body; and that becomes natural enough, when we remember that the Glorified Body is the centre, substance and source of the other. If St. Paul uses the word σῶμα indifferently for either, that is exactly parallel to his double use of χριστός. Usually ' Christ ' stands for Him alone who is the Head; but can also stand for the whole ' mystical person ' made up of Head and members together: for " as the body is one and has many members, so *is Christ* : for with one Spirit we were all baptised into one Body." [1] Here the Spirit is the element or power whereby the Glorified Body or Person of Jesus is present to us and inflows upon us: while the Body is the organic structure of the divine Society into which we are incorporated by the Spirit's action. And the whole is called ' Christ '; for in so far as we are members of the Body, we are nothing but Christ: it is not we that live, but He that lives in us, and is the substance of our redeemed existence.

For the double use of σῶμα we may take the very curious instance of Col. ii. 17 and 19. " Let no one judge you in matters of meat or drink—which are a *shadow* of the things to come, whereas the *body* of them is Christ's. Let no one condemn you at his whim over a question of . . . angel-worship, vainly puffed up by his unregenerate mind, and not keeping fast hold of the Head, from whom the whole body is supplied and knit together through the channel of its joints and bands, and so grows with a growth that is of God." Here we have two contrasts. First, the ordinances of the ancient law are condemned as a mere symbolic shadow of the World to Come, whereas Christ's Body—His

---

[1] I Cor. xii. 12. Cf. also Ephes. i. 10 and the phrase ἐν χριστῷ; also II Cor. i. 21: " He that stablishes us into the Anointed and hath anointed us, is God " (χριστόν and χρίσας).

Glorified Person—is the very substance of it—is, indeed, the body that cast that shadow.[1] Second, the angels are set aside, because all that is essential, in order to be in the Mystical Body of the Messiah, the redeemed community, is that we should hold fast by the Head, from whom the divine life of that Body flows. In the first case, Christ's Glorified Body is the substance of the World to Come; in the second, this substance becomes, even in this world, the Head of the Mystical Body which it forms and animates by overflowing into it.

We can now understand I Cor. x. 16, 17: " The cup of blessing which we bless, is it not a partaking in the Blood of Christ? The bread which we break, is it not a partaking in the Body of Christ? Because there is one bread (loaf), we all of us are one body, for we all share in the one bread." Here the parallel with the first sentence shows that the ' body ' in which the communicants partake is the Glorified Body—which was once the suffering body—of Jesus; and this it is which is present in the bread, or in the blessing, breaking and partaking of the bread. But, on the logic of the passage from Colossians just discussed, it goes without saying that those who partake of the Glorified Body—who receive the overflow of its heavenly substance—are knit thereby into one Mystical Body by their common dependence on the one Source, and (therefore) their common organisation or embodiment round one Head. Because there is one bread (typifying the one Body or Person of Christ), therefore we many partakers form one Body (since we are the organic extension which that Body or Person, by overflowing into us, makes for itself).

The logic of this passage is: ' Were it not for our real partaking in the one Glorified Body, our forming one

---

[1] It will not do, however, to take σῶμα here as bearing the sense of ' reality ' simply. For as well as being contrasted with ' shadow,' it is above (vv. 9–11) contrasted with the ' fleshly body.' The *bodily* indwelling of (the manhood of) Christ by the fulness of Deity gives Him a new mode of ' bodiliness ' in virtue of which He is able to dispense with and ' strip off ' (vv. 11, 15) the fleshly body in the death of the cross. And we participate both in the stripping off of the one, and in the ' being filled ' with the other (v. 10), though at present in a ' hidden ' anticipatory way (iii. 3, 4).

Mystical Body would be inexplicable, for it would lack its cause of unity.' For the Apostle is emphasising here the reality of the Christian's communion with Christ, a communion which excludes ' communion with devils ' in the heathen sacrifices. Such a communion we have in the Eucharist—of course we have! For how else explain that spiritual union in one Mystical Body, which we all admit? He argues from the one Mystical Body to the one Glorified Body as the cause of its unity; but, as we began by saying, without any clear division made between the two applications of the word ' body.' Rather, we are in face of one of those ' mystical identifications ' which, none the less, involve a difference.

According to the doctrine of Colossians,[1] the whole of the divine purpose for the creation was implicit in Christ. He, to borrow scholastic language, contained the reality of it all in ' a more eminent manner,' in a higher mode of being; as the reality of the broken lights cast on ruffled waters might be said to be contained in the pure and single light of the sun that radiates them. And, when the created world had gone astray, God poured all this fulness into one Creature—the Humanity of Jesus [2]—thereby making this Creature, the Glorified Body or Humanity, a head or focus which had power in it to gather the whole creation [3] round

[1] Col. i. 15–20.

[2] The distinction here made between God the Son and the manhood of Jesus as a creature belongs of course to later theology, not to St. Paul. And yet that distinction was made with the object of enabling two classes of N.T. texts to be intelligibly stated side by side; and unless we suppose that St. Paul, if he could have been made to understand the issue, would gratefully have accepted the distinction, we shall have to suppose that full-blown Gnosticism was the intention of the Apostle—a subordinate hypostasis, Jesus, whom God used to create the world, and into whom He afterwards poured the *pleroma*, for the work of redemption.

Of course, the distinction between Christ according to His deity and His humanity is relevant to the verses referring to Creation itself. How far is St. Paul thinking of a divine archetype, after the manner of Logos-doctrine: how far of a (predestined) perfect Creature, for whom, and so in whom (regarded as a purpose), the world is made; on the analogy of the Rabbinic doctrine that the world was made for, and built upon, Israel?

[3] There is no reason to suppose that St. Paul has been converted to universalism: cf. in the same Epistle, iii. 6 and 25. He means that redemption has power to embrace every type of being. That some do not receive it effectively is another matter.

itself as a unified body partaking of its own redeemed and glorified being.

Since, then, the whole reality of the redeemed society resides in Christ, who is both its focus, its cause, and its higher archetype, and who, by the predestinating Grace of God, must spread abroad His being to embrace all beings within it, we see what the mystical identification means: The Glorified Body *is* the Mystical Body—that is, the second has no reality that is not the reality of the first; just as in the sentence ἐμοὶ τὸ ζῆν χριστός [1] the sense is ' The life I have, deserving of the name, has no reality that is not Christ's.' And what the Eucharist means is the creation of the Mystical Body by partaking in the Glorified Body —not yet in the fulness of Resurrection-being, but in that spiritual anticipation of it that we have tried to set forth above. Though now, in the light of our later exposition, we can add the essential qualification—there is no such partaking in the Head which is not communion with the members: the separation of the two aspects is unthinkable.

3. THE CHURCH AND THE CHURCHES

For St. Paul, this inseparability would need no proof. It follows directly from the fact that the sacramental fellowship is an anticipation of the Kingdom of God. The End—the *eschaton* of eschatological hope—was the restored and glorified Israel of God, a community gathered round its King and Christ; and to have a part in the World to Come was to have a part in such a fellowship. But now the Church of God is the anticipation of this community, in the Spirit; and is perpetually new-created as such by communion with her Head in the Eucharist.

" Because the bread is one, therefore we many partakers are one body." The congregation of communicants, then, typifies—we should prefer to say ' is mystically identical with '—the Israel of God, the whole company of faithful in all the world, in Heaven and in Earth, who draw their participation in the Resurrection-life from the one glorified Person of our Lord. It is inevitable here that the con-

[1] Phil. i. 21.

ception of the Church's ' presence ' in this place or that
should follow the conception of Christ's presence, since
Christ is the whole reality of the Church, in the manner
we have set forth.　The Church is the Bride of Christ,[1] His
complement and counterpart, and will be thought of as
being present in the world just so many ways as Christ is
thought to be present.

Now, there are, in fact, many ' loaves,' in spite of St. Paul's
asseveration, for the Eucharist is celebrated in many places
at once.　Yet Christ is not thereby either multiplied or
divided, but is effectively present in each place in the
fulness of His Glorified Person, to create the fellowship and
unity of the Church in that place.　So with the Church:
as there is one Head, there is but one Body, as the teaching
of Colossians abundantly shows: one not only in the elect
of human kind, but in the whole spiritual universe—the
very angels, and whatever other creatures are capable of
God, are to find their place in it.[2]　And yet as the one
Person of Christ is effectively present in many Eucharists,
in undivided reality, so the mystical ' person ' or ' body '
which is His Bride has many incarnations and is real in each
sacramental fellowship.　And so the local congregation is
for St. Paul, as his language shows, *the* Church of God, not a
mere part of it.[3]

In accordance with this way of thinking, there was a
usage in New Testament times of calling the original Jerusalem congregation ' the Church ' simply:[4] as though,
when other communities arose outside it, the Church has
not so much spread as become re-incarnate elsewhere,
while in her first embodiment remaining with undiminished
fulness what she was.

Such a conception of the one Church's many sacramental

---

[1] In II Cor. xi. 2–3, the local church is the Bride of Christ, and the
antitype of Eve; in Eph. v. 23, the universal Church has both these
attributes.

[2] Col. i. 20; Phil. ii. 10; Rom. viii. 19–22; Eph. iii. 10.

[3] Cf. p. 8, *supra.*

[4] *The* Church, Acts xviii. 22; *the* Saints, I Cor. xvi. 1; II Cor. viii.
4; ix. 1 and 12; Rom. xv. 25, 31 (but cf. v. 26).—No doubt one can
compare the Jewish usage: *the* council, *the* elders at Jerusalem; and
then the local synagogal organisations elsewhere.

' presences ' is inevitable, if we are to be able to say (as we must) that actual fellowship in ἀγάπη is the very essence of the Church; for such fellowship can, under the conditions of this life, be realised only in one place and in a limited number. In this matter as in others, the key to understanding lies in that consummation of which the Church on earth is but the fragmentary anticipation. For, however little we may think so, the New Testament knows that the end is more intelligible than the beginning.

We try to understand Heaven by Earth, as an extension and complement of these hard and sensuous realities that our hands can grasp: but Scripture as often as not interprets Earth by Heaven, as a confused and splintered image and anticipation of an intelligible unity. It is in this way that we should understand the text of St. John concerning the Sacrament: when our Lord meets the complaints of His disciples against the hardness of His claim to be the Bread from Heaven that must be eaten if men are to live, " Does this scandalise you? " He says. " What then if ye shall see the Son of Man ascending where He was before? It is the Spirit that giveth life: flesh profiteth nothing." From the vision of the fulfilment, of Christ in Heaven, they are to understand the earthly counterpart: to realise that the Sacrament is not the unredeemed flesh and blood of man, but the earthly presence, in spiritual anticipation, of the Heavenly, Glorified Person of the Christ.[1]

So here with the Church. The very essence of her heavenly fulfilment, in all the pictures drawn of it, is the co-existence of fellowship and universality. The limitations of time and space are annihilated, in order that all the

---

[1] John vi. 61–3. No doubt the true comment on these two verses is the Farewell Discourse, where the presence of Christ in the Spirit is in juxtaposition to His removal to the Father's side, and is consequent upon the latter. The whole of ch. vi. is a homily on v. 31b, "He gave them bread from heaven to eat." It must be shown (a) that Christ is true Bread, (b) that He came down from the true Heaven, whereas the manna was earthly bread from the visible sky. The two propositions are treated as equivalent: the miraculous feeding is the ' sign ' for one, the miraculous Coming (v. 25) for the other; and here the Ascent is to be the proof of the Descent, as in Eph. iv. 9. But the Ascent does not remove what descended; there remains a presence of it ' in Spirit,' when indeed it first takes on its full character of ' true manna.'

G

blessed may be found in the immediate presence of God
and of one another.

> Qui scientem cuncta sciunt, quid nescire nequeunt,
> Nam et pectoris arcana penetrant alterutrum:
> Unum volunt, unum nolunt; unitas est mentium.

> Licet cuiquam sit diversum pro labore meritum,
> Caritas hoc facit suum quod amat in altero;
> Proprium sic singulorum fit commune omnium.[1]

So writes St. Peter Damian after St. Augustine,[2] philosophising
most movingly that biblical picture of one worshipping
fellowship before the throne of one Almighty Lord.

But in this world, where human intercourse is limited to
the gross instrumentality of flesh and blood, the fellowship
of the Church and her universality must fall apart: as
universal she is one in all the earth; as fellowship she is
multiplied. And since fellowship is as essential to her as
universality, the Church is as really *the* Church in every
congregation, as really incarnate there in her full being, as
she is in the world-wide Catholic society. And if we find it
hard to hold together these two aspects of her existence, we
must remember that spiritual realities become unintelligible
in so far as they are expressed in an unredeemed universe:
for their explanation we must look to their end and
consummation.

If we turn back now to our original statement, that the
many ' presences ' of the Church are to be thought of as
strictly analogous and complementary to the many sacramental presences of Christ, we shall find it necessary to
qualify. Christ is absolutely identical and personally the
same in every presence, being but one real Person. But
while the Church is in each of her presences identical so
far as she is the Church, she is different in so far as she is

---

[1] Full text, *Hundred Best Latin Hymns* (ed. Phillimore), pp. 45-7.
Here is a doggerel version:

> All must they know, who know the Omniscient:
> The secret each of other's heart doth find;
> One thing they will and will not, one's their mind.

> Though to each labour different wages fall,
> What's in another loved, love makes her own,
> And one's possession is the wealth of all.

[2] *De Civ. Dei*, XVIII. 17-18.

incarnate in different men, who are her real personal constituents. The difference of one loaf from another makes
no relevant or spiritual difference in the presences of the
one Christ: the content of *what* is present is not affected.
The eucharistic Christ of Corinth, Philippi, and Ephesus
being summed together, is nothing but the one Christ whole
in each; but the eucharistic congregations being summed
are not identical with each single congregation taken alone,
but form a fresh sum: and not a mere sum in the sense of
an aggregate, but an organism, in which the interconnexion
and mutual necessity of all the several members may not
be evident now, but will be in the Heavenly Israel. Clearly,
then, we cannot say that the whole Church is present
in every local community, with such completeness as we
believe the one Christ whole in each Eucharist.

It is this aspect that makes congregationalism, in the
strict sense of the term, a travesty of the truth: the Apostolic
ministry must bind together the many congregations, in
order that the universality of the Church may find both
sacramental expression and active force; and the dependence
of the local ministry on the Apostolic expresses the union
of the two sides. For the Church is universality as well as
fellowship.

To pursue that line of thought would take us into a different
discussion; we are concerned here with the Parish Eucharist,
the local fellowship, which has stepped into the place of the
ancient Episcopal Eucharist as the effective unit. And the
question to be asked is this: How can the ' One bread,
therefore one body ' find true expression, unless week by
week something like a representative congregation of the
local church both assembles round the altar together, and
together partakes from it? Doubtless, ' where two or three
are gathered together,' there the one Church as well as the one
Christ is effectively present; and a congregation which
knows the Catholic unity of the whole Church, and is served
by a multitude of small Masses, has what is essential; and
yet the obvious and potent symbolism of St. Paul's Eucharist
is sadly hidden. However much we believe that the reality
of the Sacrament is present and received in every valid

Eucharist, its moral effect on the soul depends on whether it be received in charity; and it is in the presence of the community that charity is expressed. We may venture to wonder whether we can congratulate ourselves on the status and numbers of the Diaconate to-day,[1] if the effect is to make us prefer many small Masses, for convenience of administration.

4. THE BLOOD

All that has been written so far might seem to have advanced nothing against the simple solution—Communion in one kind—for all has been concerned with the two words Body and Bread. It is time now to readjust the balance by thinking of another pair: Blood, and Death. Why did our Lord institute the Sacrament—for we see no cogency in the arguments to deny that He did [2]—in two species? If we are speaking of the conscious human intent of Jesus, it is no doubt abundantly sufficient to reply that graces for bread and wine were those actually offered at a solemn Jewish feast, and it was natural that One who loved a double parable should have allowed established custom to guide Him into a double Sacrament; in which, as in the twofold similes of the Gospel,[3] one and the same thing was conveyed —His human substance, given over to death, to win life for others, through winning it Himself.

Certainly Blood was not added to Body because these two are complementary constituents of one substance; that would have required Flesh rather than Body.[4] Rather, the

---

[1] See p. 286, *infra*.

[2] *e.g.* Lietzmann's *Messe und Herrenmahl*, pp. 240–8: controverted by Hugo Huber, *Herrenmahl im N.T.*, 1929.

[3] Mustard-seed and Leaven; Lost Sheep and Lost Coin; Hid Treasure and Pearl of Price; Bread-stone and Fish-scorpion, etc.

[4] Which actually appears, for this very reason, in John vi. 51, 53, 54. But this was not our Lord's language at the Institution, nor is it St. Paul's. The Fourth Gospel is here developing the idea that Christ, as in the Sacrament, is the true Manna, true sustenance: which no one supposes to be the root idea of the Eucharist, though a natural enough reflection on the Eucharist once established. But to bread and wine (= complete sustenance), flesh and blood (= complete Person) naturally correspond. Then the Blood loses any special or separate sense. As in v. 51 σάρξ stands alone for the sacrament, so perhaps does αἷμα alone in xix. 34 and I John v. 6–8.

two suggest different trains of thought about the one substance—Body the wholeness and the reality of the person, and its continuity here and hereafter: [1] Blood the sacrificial death, that which is poured out, given, and not recovered, the discontinuity and the break—for the death remains death, in itself real passion and loss, however happy its consequence: as we see by comparing the possibility that man had not sinned, and Christ could have led him to a like glory and Kingdom not through death. And, in suggesting the death of the Sacrifice, blood suggested also the Covenant.

Another line of interpretation which has won recent acceptance,[2] that Blood meant not death but life—appears to be anachronistic. No doubt there had been a time when the taking of the blood from the sacrificial victim had meant the setting free of its vital power for the benefit of the worshippers, or even for the benefit of the god, that, so vitalised, he might be strong to aid his devotees. But such ideas belonged to a distant past. In Isaiah the blood-soul of the servant is simply spilt, " poured out unto death." [3] In the New Testament the Blood of Christ is a ransom-price, a means of purging, the element to ratify a solemn covenant; but the explanation offered for all these ideas—the communication of life—is never stated, but has to be read in.

It is by no means enough to remind us that the early Church read in Leviticus the verse,[4] " The soul (life) of the flesh is in the blood . . . the blood maketh atonement by reason of the soul"; because there is no suggestion that atonement is affected by a positive charge of life which

[1] This is not so for St. Paul only (I Cor. xv.). It is common scriptural tradition, from Isa. xxvi. 19 onwards; and involved in the very idea of resurrection.

[2] It is not possible here to take to pieces in detail the web of construction in the Bishop of Lincoln's *Fullness of Sacrifice*. We must be content with the single observation that he produces no positive evidence for sacrifice having been so understood from the time of Leviticus to that of the New Testament. Of course he has the texts from St. John, for which see above. The Bishop of Lincoln refers to W. Milligan, *Resurrection of our Lord*, pp. 274–304, where the unconvincingness of the case, so far as the N.T. is concerned, may be conveniently studied.

[3] Isa. liii. 12. [4] Lev. xvii. 11.

drives out the negative charge of impurity: rather 'a life forfeit for a life' is the suggestion made.[1] As for the touching of things with the blood,[2] no particular conclusion can be drawn from that; it is just the application of its atoning efficacy, however that efficacy may be conceived. The smearing of things with holy substances in order to hallow them is too general a custom to allow of particular inferences.

In the whole matter we must guard against the too common mistake of assuming that ritual is bound always to bear the significance which, many centuries before, had guided its formation. Nothing could be further from the facts.

Yet the view here criticised does represent a partial truth. The New Testament does not separate death and resurrection, atonement and redemption, as was done by some less discreet expressions of Calvinist doctrine; and if the main object of the sponsors of this view is to deny that the death can be taken by itself alone, then they are theologically right, though historically wrong in their interpretation of the New Testament term, Blood. But if they are attempting to identify blood with life *simply*, to the exclusion of the death through which it has passed, they are theologically wrong too. It is indeed significant that the New Testament often does speak of the death alone, even though the second aspect of life may always be taken to be implied.

Blood, then, expresses death on its sacrificial side, and not life; and whether our Lord used little premeditation or much in adding the cup to the loaf in His institution, it was precisely this emphasis on death which gave it separate value for the Church, according to the foreordaining providence of God. It is this element which forbids us to forget that not only do we communicate with the Lord's Glorious Body in the sacrament, but equally we declare the Lord's death, until He come.[3]

---

[1] *Loc. cit.* 'I have given it to you upon the altar to make atonement for *your souls*; for it is the blood that maketh atonement by reason of the soul' (in it).

[2] *E.g.* in the Day of Atonement ritual (Lev. xvi.).

[3] It would be a mistake to draw any particular conclusions from the

It is not merely that our Lord passed through death once, in order to obtain that glorious state and being in which it is now our privilege to communicate with Him. That we might well remember, if we had only the bread. No: it is that we communicate precisely with His death: the wine of blood-shedding makes us see that: " This is My blood of the New Covenant." And it is the blood that we receive, so that the covenant-status—another description of the Mystical Body—is only entered, as a consequence of our present communion with the Victim's death. And this is just as true as the symbolism of the Bread—that the covenant-status consists in a continued communion with the Victor's life.[1]

To embrace life and to suffer death are not two things, but one and the same. We are in a world where the Re-surrection-life can be possessed only by anticipation, only in the Spirit, and in such manner that the old life of the flesh continues alongside of it and in strife against it. Even, perhaps, were we sinless as our Lord, our fleshly being would continue to make inordinate claims, even though, like Him, we never conceded them; and so we should still find the death-pains of the flesh to be the continual growing-pains of the spirit. But fleshliness or unregeneracy is en-trenched not only in our own body, but in the whole world, and above all in human society: it imposes on us bonds of unregenerate association, which make up in large measure our social existence, and that is a great part of our self—

---

fact that the wine was *drunk*. Some have inferred that the cup at the Eucharist cannot be primitive, as no Jew could think of drinking blood: others, that there is a conscious reversal of Jewish sacrificial tradition. We ought to begin from the other end: the drinking of the ' cup of blessing ' was an established fact, and our Lord must fit the new signi-ficance to it as best He may. No doubt St. Paul is accurate, when he says the *drinking of* the cup is a *communion with* the blood. The com-munion with the blood took the form of drinking the wine, because that is what one does with wine. It is not what one does with blood. One also pours libations of wine, but that would not have expressed ' com-munion with.' It remained for the Fourth Gospel to emphasise the drinking of blood (*vide supra*, p. 88), but *not* in a sacrificial context: Christ is set forth rather as the true meat and drink of man.

[1] The parallelism is worked out explicitly in reference to the other Gospel Sacrament: Rom. vi. 4–11; Col. ii. 12.

one has only to remember St. Paul's standing in the Jewish community, a share in a conspiracy of pride. And here the death-struggle with unregenerate flesh may be a struggle against other men, who, actuated by fleshly motives, attack us through our flesh. Our flesh goes over to the enemy, whether by responding to persecution with fear, to contempt with injured pride, or to enticement with selfish pleasure. Thus struggle against temptation within and against persecution without are for St. Paul not different in their essence: in both we are denying flesh its claim, and starving it to death.[1] In our Lord's case this meant actual death; and so it may for any of His followers, as He sufficiently warned them.

For anyone in contact with the Resurrection-life, through and in Christ, there are only two possibilities: either, continuing to identify himself with flesh, he is part of the life that is warring against, killing, Christ; or, accepting Christ and the Resurrection-being, he is inflicting death on flesh—primarily on his own. And since the acceptance of Resurrection and of Christ is, in this world, process and not completion, a daily dying to the flesh is always the other side of it.

5. THE SOCIAL EUCHARIST

This is so wherever and however Christ is present to us; and must be equally so in the Eucharist, as I Cor. xi. teaches. If the communicant fails to receive the Bread as the Body of the Lord, as the substance of the new and spiritual world, he is among the forces of flesh that are stabbing that Body to death.[2] Either he is allowing that Glorious Body to overflow into him and make him a member, an organic part, of the Mystical Body; or else he is a foreign and hostile substance intruded into the vitals of the body to wound both members and Head.

To live in Christ is to die to flesh and self: but it is also to live for the members in the body; and it was failure to do this in the feast accompanying the primitive Eucharist

---

[1] Compare the νέκρωσις of II Cor. iv. 10–11 with that of Col. iii. 5 (θανάτωσις in Rom. viii. 13).   [2] I Cor. xi. 27.

that drew St. Paul's sharpest censure and gravest warning. It was not the Lord's Supper but their own supper,[1] because it was not received and eaten in the life of the Lord's Mystical Body—in the Lord, to use St. Paul's shorter phrase— but according to the dictates of private and fleshly appetite. Some of these people were hungry, and they began first.[2] But suppose they had been in a hurry to leave, because they wanted to catch a bus and go out for the day, would St. Paul have thought that so very different? And suppose they had a priest ready to consecrate a separate Mass for them first, as quickly as possible, without exposition of God's Word, or singing to His praise, would the Apostle have thought that a laudable solution?

Then there was the scandal of divisions and parties in the congregation. How much pleasanter it would have been if they had thought of celebrating several Eucharists at different hours: for then personally antipathetic members could have avoided communicating together, and doctrinal factions might have had their several tastes catered for by an accommodating clergy. Yet one wonders again whether St. Paul would have been pleased with this way of managing it: for he had written " There must be factions among you, in order that the true Christians (οἱ δόκιμοι) may become manifest among you " [3]—i.e. those who show themselves superior to faction, who die to it as to a form of fleshliness. It is better then, on his view, for things to be so arranged that people are put to the test of their willingness to forego faction, by the necessity of a common Eucharist, rather than that the issue should be tactfully avoided.

It would be well, then, if there were one principal

---

[1] I Cor. xi. 20–1.

[2] Did they take inordinate *pregustationes* out of their own provisions before grace had been said for the common meal, at what was officially its chief course? Allowance is made for *pregustatio*, and the question of its relation to the grace discussed in Mishna, *Berakhoth*.

[3] v. 19. By saying ' must ' St. Paul probably means that it is prophesied. There are two lines of such prophecy: Isa. viii. 14 (the Stone of Stumbling) taken up in Luke xvii. 1 = Matt. xviii. 7 (it is impossible but that stumbling-blocks should arise); and Micah vi. (division in families), taken up in Luke xii. 51–53 = Matt. x. 34–5. In Matt. xxiv. 10 the two are run together. In Rom. ix. the Isaiah text is applied; perhaps the Micah text would be more appropriate here.

Eucharist which clearly expressed the truth that life to Christ and death to self is a rebirth into the community.

It is often and rightly said that the adoration of God is the first purpose of worship. And yet if we think that we can climb into Heaven by our own strength, to spy upon Divine Majesty, we are doubtless doomed to disappointment or delusion. We see and know God in His actions upon us, and most in the greatest of them: the highest reception and commemoration of grace is the highest opportunity of worship. And if the ancient Jew joined in one act the blessing of bread for use and the blessing of God for the gift, there need surely not be less of adoring thankfulness in the Christian Eucharist, merely because the gift is greater.

Some have contended that God should be adored for what He is, and not for what He gives, while others have denounced the presumption that pretends to know anything of God save in His acts of blessing.[1] Where the gifts concerned are natural bread and wine, there is perhaps some meaning in this quarrel: but where the blessing is God's gift of Himself, there is nothing left to quarrel about. To adore God in the giving of Himself is to adore God simply, so far as He wills to be known; and we shall hardly pretend to go beyond that.

The Pauline Eucharist, therefore, is not only death, life, fellowship, and the possession of the world to come: not though we add, communion with the Risen Christ: it is also thanksgiving to God. For the eucharistic action cannot begin till gratitude to God the Father has released it: for it is by thanks given for His promise and institution that the Body of Christ is consecrated for our reception, which reception redounds again in eucharist to God.

Christianity is whole and indivisible: where Christ is present to us, there are of necessity together all those things of which we have spoken. If the Eucharist is the presence of Christ, it cannot be an aspect of department of our religion, but the whole of it, so far as that whole can be in worship at all: for our religion is Christ, and Christ is not divided.

[1] For the ' Pure Love ' controversy, see Kirk *Vision of God*, pp. 450 ff.

V

THE IDEA OF 'THE CHURCH' IN THE PRIMITIVE LITURGIES

By The Rev. GREGORY DIX, O.S.B.
Nashdom Abbey

THE IDEA OF 'THE CHURCH' IN THE PRIMITIVE LITURGIES

THE mystery of the Church is the mystery of " Christ in us, the hope of glory," and this indwelling is in them that " eat His Flesh and drink His Blood " and so " have eternal life." There is a necessary, intimate and obvious relation between the doctrines concerning the Mystical and the Sacramental Body of the One Christ, which finds its profoundest expression in the Liturgy. In the eucharistic rite of the pre-Nicene Church when its outlines were still uncomplicated by the later decorative additions of piety, that relation was expressed with a classic simplicity and truth, not only in the formulæ, but in the very substance and structure of the Liturgy.

In the primitive view the *raison d'être* both of the Church and Eucharist is ultimately one thing only—λατρεία, worship, offered to God. That " God *seeketh* " worshippers " in spirit and in truth " is the Divinely-given reason for the Incarnation, which holds good of its extensions in the Church and the Eucharist. This worship is both the result of and a participation in a Divine action, into which the Church and its human action are taken up. The Church's worship is effective, it absolutely glorifies God, because the Church " is one with (ἀνακεκραμένη) Jesus Christ as Jesus Christ is with the Father." [1] The primitive writer significantly continues: " Let none deceive himself. If any man be outside the place of sacrifice (θυσιαστηρίον), *he lacketh the bread*." There is a whole realm of sacramental theology behind that abrupt description of the self-willed schismatic. It is in virtue of the Church's indissoluble union with Jesus

---

[1] Ignatius, *Eph.* v. 1.

Christ, because the whole Church is "accepted in the Beloved," that "prayer and the Eucharistic thanksgiving in the Church must be offered through Christ Jesus the universal (*catholicum*) priest of the Father."[1] It is because each one of her members has "put on Christ" in Baptism, and has been endowed with His Spirit (*i.e.* that by which He is anointed as Messiah) in Confirmation, that the Church can effectually offer the *anamnesis* (lit. re-calling) of the atoning and latreutic sacrifice of Christ's Passion and Resurrection by and with her Lord. And that sacrifice the Church not only offers but she *is*, as the Priest and victim of Calvary are one and the same. And by that sacrifice of herself to God the Church lives, as He that lost His life for ever saved it. In and by that *anamnesis* of the death and resurrection the Church ever receives anew in each of her members that Spirit of the Son "whereby we cry, Abba, Father"; is ever conjoined afresh by faith to Him who is "the Truth" in which we worship. All this is contained in the primitive eucharistic liturgy.

I. The Primitive Eucharistic Rite

The eucharistic rite as it is now found throughout historic Christendom is a fusion of two services originally distinct, the *Synaxis* and the *Eucharist* proper, later distinguished by the somewhat unfortunate names of the 'Mass of the Catechumens' and the 'Mass of the Faithful.' The former was, as its name states, simply a 'public meeting' into which any one, Jew, pagan, catechumen or believer might make his way. It answers (very roughly) to our 'ante-communion' service, and we are not here concerned with it, but with the Eucharist, from which it continued to be distinct in theory down to the end of the fourth century. Ultimately it came to be fused with the Eucharist, because it normally preceded it, but so late as the sixth century the typical Eucharist of the year, the Maundy Thursday 'Mass of the Sacrament' in the evening, began without it at the Offertory.[2]

---

[1] Tertullian, *adv. Marc.* iv. 9.
[2] Martène, *De Ant. Eccl. Rit.* iv., cap. xxii.; vi. 5; cf. the Gelasian Sacramentary, Maundy Thursday, ed. Wilson, p. 72.

A. *The Prayers of the Faithful*

Many, but not all, pre-Nicene accounts of the Eucharist begin with the Intercessory 'Prayers of the Faithful,' in which none but those confirmed might take part. But there is good evidence that these prayers strictly belonged to the end of the preceding *Synaxis* and were not part of the Eucharist itself. The Catechumens and the unbaptized were expelled before these prayers, not because they had any integral connection with the Eucharist, which might or might not follow,[1] but because the solemn prayer of the 'Holy Church' was in itself an august thing. It is nothing less than a function of the Church's priestly life in union with "Christ Jesus the universal Priest," a part of that "worship in spirit and in truth" in which those who had not yet received the Spirit or been incorporated in Him who is "the Truth" could have no part. But from their generally immediately preceding the Eucharist at the end of the *Synaxis*, and from their being attended only by those admitted to the Eucharist itself, these intercessory prayers came early to be confounded in it, and became a source of complication in later rites, duplicating the intercessions which developed out of the final clauses of the Canon. Though not an integral part of the Eucharist they partook of its markedly corporate and collective character, inasmuch as these prayers really were *the People's* prayers. The president gave out a subject, the people prayed together in silence on bended knees for a while, and the president concluded by summing up their prayers in a brief public collect, often of a single sentence, after which he announced another subject. The part of the clergy was thus limited to ordering the prayer of the assembly. What was important, what formed the prayer itself, was the prayer of the *whole Church*.

B. *The Eucharist*

Stripped of these introductory intercessions, which are not an integral part of the rite but an early addition to it,

---

[1] When the Eucharist did *not* follow, the Synaxis still ended with 'Prayers of the Faithful' before which the unconfirmed were expelled.

the pre-Nicene Eucharist has a clear-cut outline of the most austere simplicity. It has four *momenta* only—Offertory, Thanksgiving Prayer (Canon, Anaphora), Fraction, Communion—and nothing else. It thus reproduces exactly the " took bread—gave thanks—brake—gave " of the Gospels. The following account is based chiefly on the *Apostolic Tradition* of St. Hippolytus [1] which certainly represents the practice of Rome in his own youth *c.* A.D. 180, and probably of a period much earlier. Other pre-Nicene information is also used where available, but I have not thought it necessary to give references except on one or two points.

1. *Arrangement of the Church*

The celebrant-bishop has his throne, covered with a white linen cloth, *behind* the altar. He sits facing the people and will celebrate still facing them across the altar. On either side of him in a semi-circle sits the Sanhedrin of presbyters who will concelebrate with him. Close to him on either side stand the archdeacon and another deacon who will minister to him as his personal assistants. The altar, generally of wood, and a cube of perhaps 3 feet each way, stands between the clergy and the people. The latter, men in front and women behind, stand facing the altar and the clergy. In a cleared space between the altar and the people stand the remainder of the deacons and perhaps the sub-deacons.

2. *Offertory*

Two deacons spread a linen cloth upon the altar. The bishop begins by greeting the Church with the words " Peace be unto you." All give the kiss of peace, the bishop to the clergy, and among the people laymen to laymen and women to women. Each of the laity has brought for him or herself a piece of bread (? and/or a little flask of wine.) These are now collected by the deacons who "bring them up " (ἀναφέρειν is the technical word) to the altar, arrange them upon it from the people's side, and retire.

---

[1] The text is that prepared for my new critical edition in which certain questions are discussed which are here taken as settled.

3. *The Prayer*

The bishop and presbyters now advance to the altar from the opposite side and stand facing the silent people. In silence they together lay their hands upon the " oblation " (προσφόρα) of the ' Holy Church.' Some of the presbyters stand with the bishop around the altar; others stand further off in a semicircle around him, each one having a portion of the oblation held before him in a glass paten by a deacon.

The *Eucharistia* or Prayer of Thanksgiving begins with a dialogue.

> *Bishop.* ℣ " The Lord be with you."
> ℟ " And with thy spirit."
> ℣ " Let your hearts be on high."
> ℟ " We have ⟨*them*⟩ unto the Lord."
> ℣ " Let us make eucharist [*give thanks*] unto the Lord."
> ℟ " ⟨*It is*⟩ meet and right."

" And forthwith he shall continue thus:

a. " We render thanks unto thee, O God, through thy Beloved Child (παῖς—the ' Servant ') Jesus Christ, whom at the end of the ages (ἐπ' ἐσχατῶν χρονῶν) thou didst send to us ⟨*to be*⟩ a Saviour and Redeemer and the Messenger of thy counsel; Who is thy Word inseparable, through whom thou madest all things and in whom thou wast well-pleased;

b. " ⟨*Whom*⟩ thou didst send from heaven into the Virgin's womb and who conceived within her was made flesh and demonstrated to be thy Son, born of Holy Spirit and a Virgin;

c. " Who fulfilling thy will and preparing for thee a holy people stretched forth his hands for the Passion that he might release from passions them that have believed in thee;

d. " Who when he was betrayed to his voluntary Passion, that he might abolish death and rend the bonds of the devil and tread down hell and enlighten the righteous and establish the ordinance (ὅρος) and demonstrate the resurrection;

H

e. " Taking bread and making eucharist [giving thanks] to thee said: ' Take, eat: this is my Body which is broken for you.' Likewise also the cup, saying: ' This is my Blood which is shed for you. When ye do this ye do the *anamnesis* of me.'

f. " Doing therefore the *anamnesis* of His death and resurrection, we offer to thee the bread and the cup, making eucharist to thee because thou hast bidden us [*or* found us worthy, κατηξίωσας] to stand before thee and minister as priests [ἱερατεύειν] to thee.

g. " And we pray thee [*that thou wouldest send thy Holy Spirit upon the oblation of thy Holy Church* [1]] that thou wouldest grant to all thy holy ones who partake to be made one [*with thee* [2]] that they may be fulfilled with the Holy Spirit for the confirmation of ⟨*their*⟩ faith in truth,

h. " That we may praise thee and glorify thee, through thy Child Jesus Christ,

i. " Through whom glory and honour be unto thee with ⟨*the*⟩ Holy Spirit in the Holy Church now and for ever and world without end."

All. " Amen."

4. *The Fraction*

The bishop " breaks the bread " [3] with the cry Τὰ ἅγια τοῖς ἁγίοις (" Holy things for the holy ones.")[4] " The presbyters also shall break the bread." [5] " The deacons also break the bread " while the bishop gives communion.[6]

---

[1] I have stated elsewhere (*Theology*, xxviii. p. 127 *sq.*) the purely textual grounds for regarding this clause as a later interpolation in the original text, and have discussed the point at length in my edition. Here I can only take it as settled.

[2] These two words are found only in the Syriac, and though at first sight required, seem to be an interpolation.

[3] *Ap. Trad.*, xxxiii. 5.

[4] This formula is found in all the post-Nicene rites at this point except in the Roman. But Hippolytus Περὶ τοῦ Πάσχα iii. rebuking those who do not prepare seriously for communion ὅτι μὴ ἁγίως τῷ ἁγίῳ προσίασι " because they do not come holily to the holy thing " appears to refer to it. Presumably it disappeared from the Roman rite in the fourth century when the *Pax* was transferred to this point and replaced it.

[5] *Ap. Trad.*, xxiv. 2.

[6] *Ap Trad.*, xxiv. 1.

5. *The Communion*

The people, like the celebrant at the present day, stood to receive communion. " On the first day of the week the bishop if it be possible shall with his own hand deliver to all the people. On other days they shall deliver as the bishop shall direct." [1] " And when the bishop breaks the bread, in distributing to each a fragment he shall say: ' The bread of heaven in Christ Jesus '; and he who receives shall answer : ' Amen.' And the presbyters—but if they are not enough the deacons also—shall hold the chalices . . . first he that holdeth the water, the second he who holds the milk and honey, the third he who holds the wine. And they who partake shall taste of each, thrice, he who gives it saying : ' In God the Father Almighty,' and he who receives shall say : ' Amen.' ' And in the Lord Jesus Christ '; and he shall say, ' Amen.' ' And in the Holy Spirit in (*sic*) the Holy Church '; and he shall say, ' Amen.' [2]

A deacon dismisses the assembly.[3]

Deacons carry away the Sacrament to the absent, the sick, and those who are in prison for the faith; the faithful carry away other portions (of Bread only), with which to make their daily communions at home on days when there is no liturgy or when they cannot attend. Portions are sent from the bishop's eucharist to be placed in the chalice at all other eucharists celebrated under his jurisdiction elsewhere in the city.

6. *Later Additions*

Such was the primitive eucharist—this and no more. No *Sanctus*, no *Pater Noster*, no Thanksgiving or final Blessing. Some of these additions are, however, found fairly early.

[1] *Ap. Trad.*, xxiv. 1, 3.
[2] *Ibid.*, xxiii. 7 *sq.* The chalices of water and milk and honey were given only at the Baptismal Mass and then, apparently, only to the neophytes. We do not know what the words of administration for the Chalice were at the ordinary Mass, whether this threefold formula was used or another.
[3] I know of no positive statement in pre-Nicene sources that this was done by the deacon, but the dismissal is universally assigned to him in the fourth and fifth centuries. That there was a dismissal, cf. Tertullian, *de Anima*, 9.

The first certain evidence of the use of the *Sanctus* comes from Jerusalem in the fourth century, and its use spread very rapidly. The *Pater* at the end of the Canon is likewise first attested in St. Cyril of Jerusalem's *Catecheses* (A.D. 348) though it was still not in use at Antioch or in Egypt a generation later. Early in the fifth century St. Augustine tells us [1] that "almost the whole church" now concludes the Canon with this prayer. The exception he probably has in mind is Rome, always slow to accept liturgical novelties, which only adopted the *Pater* at the end of the Canon under St. Gregory the Great (*c*. A.D. 595.) In the fourth century the custom of making a brief public thanksgiving after communion becomes common, but some of the pre-Nicene texts are explicit that communion ended the rite.[2] The celebrant's final blessing is, in the West, an early mediæval accretion; some of the Eastern rites have never accepted it at all.

None of these things, now so familiar, are any more an integral part of the Eucharist than is the custom of saying Ps. 42 *Judica me* at the altar step before the liturgy begins. They are part of that steady process of accumulating devotional 'extras' around the rite which has gone on ever since the fourth century and which continues even to-day.[3] The primitive core of the rite is one clear swift action in four scriptural movements, a steady ascent from Offertory to Communion, which ends at its climax. The primitive custom of the silent taking of the Ablutions immediately after the Communion now survives in the Roman rite alone.[4]

---

[1] *Ep.*, 59.

[2] *E.g.*, St. Cyprian, *de Lapsis* xxv. The communion takes place *solemnibus adimpletis*. There is no mention of a thanksgiving anywhere in pre-Nicene writers.

[3] *E.g.* the addition of the "Pope's Prayers" after low Mass by Leo XIII in the Roman rite, or the modern custom of singing a hymn after the blessing in Anglican churches, etc.

[4] In the Eastern rites it has now been transferred to after the thanksgiving. In the fourth century Antiochene rite the Sacrament was removed to the Sacristy *before* the thanksgiving (? for purposes of reservation). In the seventh century the Constantinopolitan rite still placed the ablutions before the thanksgiving (*Chron. Paschale*, A.D. 624) where they still remained in the ninth century (*Typicon* of Nicephorus, *ap*. Pitra. *Mon.* ii. 341).

It serves admirably to mark off the completion of the vital eucharistic action from its merely decorative accompaniments.

Before embarking on a detailed commentary it is well to insist here on the fundamental characteristic of the primitive rite. The Eucharist is unmistakeably the action and the offering, not of the celebrant, but *of the whole Church* in its hierarchic unity. As *e.g.* St. Hippolytus describes it, it *requires* the co-operation of all, laity, deacons, the presbyterate (of which the bishop from one point of view is only one member) and the bishop, in that order, and it finally unites *all*, in the reverse order, in communion. So strong was the sense of the necessity for the corporate offering of the Eucharist that the Church was prepared to take risks to secure it. St. Cyprian can lay it down [1] that when only a single presbyter can be smuggled into the imperial prisons to celebrate for the confessors awaiting martyrdom, he should still be accompanied by a deacon.

II. The Meaning of the Rite

A. *The Character of the Primitive Eucharist*

1. *The Sacrificial Action*

First and foremost, the Eucharist is essentially an " oblation " ($\pi\rho o\sigma\phi o\rho\acute{a}$) and a " sacrifice " ($\theta v\sigma\acute{\iota}a$), something offered to God. For St. Clement in the first century the especial function of those who have the $\dot{\epsilon}\pi\iota\sigma\kappa o\pi\acute{\eta}$, the " episcopate," is to " offer the gifts " ($\pi\rho o\sigma\phi\acute{\epsilon}\rho\epsilon\iota\nu\ \tau\grave{a}\ \delta\hat{\omega}\rho a$),[2] precisely as it is for St. Hippolytus a century later. For St. Ignatius the eucharistic assembly of the Church is " the place of sacrifice " ($\theta v\sigma\iota a\sigma\tau\eta\rho\acute{\iota}o\nu$). The Eucharist is a sacrifice. On this point Justin, Irenæus, Clement of Alexandria, Tertullian, Hippolytus, Origen, Cyprian, the *Didascalia*, are at one in their positive statements with their predecessors the Apostolic Fathers, and even with such abnormal documents as the *Didache*. If there were any great doubt as to the implications of the New Testament evidence

[1] *Ep.* 5.   [2] 1 *Clem.* 44, 4.

on the Eucharist (and I do not think there is to-day any real dispute about this in the field of scientific history) the unbroken unanimity of the early Christian understanding of the rite would suffice to dispel it. The early terminology is exclusively sacrificial; words like κοινωνία (communion) as descriptions of the *rite* are conspicuous by their absence.

It must be remembered that this sacrificial language was then endowed with a vividness of meaning which it cannot have to-day. To us it is no more than a metaphor and one, moreover, which raises no clear mental picture. Few modern Christians have ever seen a bloody sacrifice. But for those who first used this language sacrifice—in its crude and bloody reality—was an every-day spectacle. For many of them it had been the very heart of religion for half a life-time before they ever heard of the Eucharist. It is very significant that while these same writers are never tired of ridiculing the sacrificial cultus of paganism and depreciating the effectiveness of the ' typical ' sacrifices of the Old Testament, their reaction against the sacrificial systems they had discarded never led them to avoid such language about the Eucharist. Accordingly, when they use it, it must be given its full meaning.

2. *The Twofold Oblation*

Secondly (and this is more complicated) what is " offered " in the Eucharist is a *twofold* thing. First, it is the oblation of bread and wine, " the gifts of thy Holy Church." [1] Secondly, and more important, it is the Passion and Resurrection of Christ (viewed in combination as a single event) which constitutes the Christian Paschal sacrifice. "Holy was that victim " (θῦμα), says St. Hippolytus, speaking of the Passover lamb, " because it was the type of the true Lamb. But our victim is holy because true; being given up to death and slaughter by the ignorance of wicked men, being accepted by the will of God for an holy sacrifice, and by His own will being offered as an oblation to the Father. For, the Scripture says, the Father gave up His own Son

[1] *Ap. Trad.*, iii. 5.

for us, and Christ ' offered Himself' to the Father for the Church ' as an oblation and sacrifice for an odour of sweetness.' " [1]

Put simply, the thought of the first part of Hippolytus' Canon runs thus: The Word of God is His eternal agent in creation. The Word was " made Flesh " that He might offer that passible Flesh as a Paschal Victim,[2] thereby to *create* a new ' People of God ' out of all nations to worship God, as the old ' People of God ' had been created out of Egyptian bondage to worship God through the death of the typical Paschal Victim. That Paschal sacrifice was offered in the Passion and Resurrection viewed as a single event.[3] Before it was offered our Lord had taken bread and wine and ' made eucharist,' declaring " This is my sacrificed Body and Blood," and commanded that thus should be made the *anamnesis* (lit : ' re-calling,' an important word of which more hereafter) of his sacrifice. This the Church does when she ' makes eucharist.'

But it is important to observe that the duality of the offer-

----

[1] Περὶ τοῦ Πάσχα, ii.

[2] With the wording of Hippolytus' Canon and the passage from the Περὶ τοῦ Πάσχα cited above cf. " The word *is* that Flesh which was offered as a sacrificial gift (προσενεχθεῖσα δῶρον) by the Word of the Father, which was taken of Holy Spirit and a Virgin, being shewn to be the perfect Son of God. It is clear therefore that He Himself offered Himself to the Father." Hippolytus, *Contra Noëtum*, 4.

[3] Cf. § *d* of the Canon. It must be remembered that the pre-Nicene Paschal feast was literally a Christian " Passover " (πάσχα). It was, like the Jewish Passover, a nocturnal feast, celebrated on the Jewish date in Asia, on the night of the following Saturday–Sunday elsewhere. It was *not* the feast of the Resurrection, but of the *Redemption*, *i.e.* of the Passion, Resurrection and Ascension in one. The idea of the separate celebration of the Passion on Friday and the Resurrection on Sunday is an innovation of the fourth-century Church of Jerusalem, which was not accepted everywhere until the late fifth or sixth century. The pre-Nicene Paschal Gospel lection began with the trial of Jesus and continued to the end of the account of the Resurrection. The evidence for these facts will be found in a pamphlet on " The Mass of the Pre-Sanctified " (Ch. Lit. Ass.) reprinted from *Laudate*, xiii. The following passage from Hippolytus' Περὶ τοῦ Πάσχα, vi., sufficiently illustrates the Paschal significance of § *d* of his Canon: " O new festival of all renewed creation . . . whereby the darkness of death was done away, and life was poured out upon all things, and the gates of heaven were swung wide, and the God-man was manifested and the man-God ascended, by whom the gates of hell were shattered and the adamantine fetters loosed."

ing by the Church and by Christ is not lost even in their identification. "Making therefore the *anamnesis* of His death and resurrection (*i.e.* His offering), *we* offer to thee *the bread and the cup* because thou hast bidden *us* . . . *to minister to thee as priests.*" It is still ' the bread and the cup,' the oblation made by the Church at the offertory, and it does not lose that character even though it has been taken up into and identified with the offering of Christ by Himself to the Father. The Canon concludes with a petition and doxology which will require further examination.

It seems necessary to emphasise at once those apparent opposites, the permanent duality of the eucharistic offering and also its unity, because it has a close relation to the doctrine of the Church expressed in the liturgy.

The Church's oblation of bread and wine is a permanent thing, even though as St. Irenæus puts it : " The cup and the bread receives the Logos of God and *becomes* (γίνεται) the Body and Blood of Christ." [1] As he states the facts more clearly elsewhere : "The bread from the earth receiving the invocation of God is no more common bread but ' eucharist,' *consisting of two realities, an earthly and a heavenly.*" [2] Irenæus is a writer whose belief in the real and substantial presence of the Body and Blood of Christ in the elements it would be hard to over-state. He affirms it again and again, and even makes it the basis of arguments to prove the reality and substantiality of the physical Body of the Incarnation against the Gnostics. Yet Irenæus is the writer of all the pre-Nicenes who has treated most fully and beautifully of the reality of the Church's oblation of bread and wine as a sacrifice *in its own right.* Similarly, for Hippolytus the reserved sacrament is simply σῶμα χριστοῦ, " the Body of Christ," *tout court.*[3] Yet Hippolytus can also speak of the bread and wine as being " eucharistised into the *likeness* (ὁμοίωμα) and *antitype* (ἀντίτυπος) of the Body and Blood," words which like the similar expression *figura* in Tertullian are found frequently in the older liturgies.[4] There is here

[1] *Haer.*, v. 2, 3.
[2] ἐκ δύο πραγμάτων συνεστηκυῖα ἐπιγείου τε καὶ οὐρανίου, *ibid.*, iv. 18, 4.
[3] *Ap. Trad.*, xxxii. 2.
[4] *Ibid.*, xxiii. 1. Cf. the old Roman canon *ap. De Sacramentis*, Serapion, Lit. of St. Basil, etc.

no contradiction. These writers believed with all the vigour of St. Justin that " the food made eucharist *is* (εἶναι, no word could be stronger) the Flesh and Blood of that Jesus who was made Flesh." [1]   It is simply that though the sacrifice of the Church is made one with that of Christ it also persists in itself, and as such can rightly be described as ' antitype ' and ' likeness.' It cannot be too much insisted on, that though the early centuries were very well aware of the ' Real Presence,' their thought is wholly different from that which finds its focus in the ideas of ' Presence ' and ' Communion.' It is concentrated wholly on *Sacrifice*. What the early centuries believed in was the ' Real Sacrifice ' rather than the ' Real Presence,' though, of course, this postulated a ' Real Victim ' as well as a ' Real Priest.'

So much for the moment for the duality of the Eucharist. Now as to its *unity*.

The Church's oblation of bread and wine is itself the fulfilment of a Divine command.   " For giving His disciples the precept to offer to God the first-fruits of His own creation—not that God had need but that they themselves should be neither unfruitful nor ungrateful—He took of that bread which cometh of creation and gave thanks, saying : This is My Body.   And likewise the cup, which cometh of creation like ourselves, He acknowledged for His own Blood, and *taught the new oblation of the new covenant* : which the Church receiving from the Apostles now offereth in all the world to God, bringing the first-fruits of His own gifts in the new covenant unto Him that provideth food for us." [2]   The Church's oblation considered in itself is a sacrifice of first-fruits.

But it does not stand apart from, it is *directed to* Christ's sacrifice in the Passion and Resurrection by the terms of the very command which institutes it.   The oblation of bread and wine by the Church at the offertory stands to the offering of the Passion and Resurrection by Christ Himself as the eternal High Priest, precisely as the Institution at the Last Supper stands to Calvary and Easter in the Gospel Story.   It is its basis, its prophetic symbol, its

[1] I. *Ap.*, 66.   [2] Irenæus, *Haer.*, iv. 17, 5.

pledge. That which unites the two oblations in the Euchar-ist is that which unites the Last Supper with the Passion in the Gospel, the formal statement of our Lord Himself, 'This is my Body, This is my Blood,' offered in sacrifice for you. That is why the narrative of the Institution is absolutely central in the primitive canon, coming always *out of* its historical order *after* the thanksgiving for our Lord's sacrifice. It sums up all that precedes: "Who when He was betrayed to His voluntary Passion" ("voluntary" to emphasise its sacrificial character); it is linked with all that follows by the connection of the command and its fulfilment: "Do this for the *anamnesis* . . . Doing the *anamnesis* . . . *we* make eucharist. . . ."

B. *The Structure of the Primitive Rite*

1. *The Offertory*

We have therefore to consider the offertory as an element of the primitive eucharist in its own right and not, as with us, merely as a necessary utilitarian preparation for consecration.

1. The offertory opens with the greeting of the Risen Lord to His own: "Peace be unto you." In symbol of that peace which is hers, "but not as the world giveth," the whole Church gives the kiss of mutual charity before making its oblation at the altar. The harmony of the members is a necessary condition of the oblation of the Body. Extraordinary pains were taken to insist that this was no formality. The deacon's cry, Μή τις κατά τινος, "Let none keep rancour against another," at this point in the Eastern liturgies is at least as ancient as the middle of the third-century, and the bishop and presbyters sat to arbitrate on differences and reconcile the parties before the Eucharist.[1] The *Didache* declares that "if a man having his dispute with his fellow join your assembly before they have been reconciled, your sacrifice is defiled."[2] The fathers are quick, too, to quote in this connection Mat. v. 23 *sq*. "If thou offerest thy gift (προσφέρῃς τὸ δῶρον) before the altar and thy brother hath aught against thee. . . ."

---

[1] *Didascalia*, ii. 54. [2] *Didache*, xiv. 2.

2. There follows the offertory proper, each communicant for himself or herself making oblation of bread and wine into the hands of the deacons before the altar. The collected gifts are arranged on the altar by the deacons. The classic text on this is St. Irenæus, *Adv. Haer.*, iv. 18, a chapter too long to cite in full, but of which some extracts will give an idea.

" Sacrifices sanctify not a man, for God hath no need of sacrifice. But his good conscience that offereth sanctifieth his sacrifice. Wherefore since the Church offereth in singleness of heart, rightly is her oblation esteemed of God a pure sacrifice. . . . We must make oblation to God in a sound belief and a faith unfeigned, a firm hope and a fervent charity, offering to Him the first-fruits of that which is His, His creation. This pure oblation the Church alone offers to the Creator . . . the Jews offer it not, for their hands are full of blood, for they received not the Word (by) [1] Which (it) is offered. Nor do all the assemblies of the heretics . . . for how shall that bread which has been ' eucharistised ' be known to them for the Body of their Lord, and the Chalice of His Blood, if they confess Him not as the Son of the (world's) Creator, who is His Word, by Whom the tree fruits and the fountains flow and the earth yields first the blade and then the ear and then the full corn in the ear? . . . Thus did the Word Himself bid the people offer oblations—not that He had need of them but that they might learn to serve God. Thus also He wills that we in our turn should offer oblation at the altar often and without intermission. For there is an altar in heaven ; for thither are our prayers and oblations directed."

With this authentically primitive language in mind, I ask attention for the words of the Roman Canon taken as they stand. It opens by praying the Father " through Jesus Christ thy Son our Lord that thou wouldest accept and bless these gifts, these offerings (*munera*), these holy and unspotted sacrifices . . ."—neuter plurals all of them, clearly the people's oblations of bread and wine now upon the altar. " *This oblation* of us thy servants . . . do thou be pleased to accept . . . *which oblation* do thou all together (*in omnibus*,

[1] There is a doubt about the text here, some MSS. reading *Verbum per quod offertur*, others *Verbum quod offertur*.

in all the separate oblations) graciously make blessed, ratified, reasonable (from Rom. xii. 1) and accepted, that it may become unto us [1] the Body and Blood of thy well-beloved Son Jesus Christ, who on the day before He suffered. . . ." Here follows the Institution (Consecration).

But even after the Consecration the Church's oblation is not lost sight of: " Wherefore, O Lord, making the *anamnesis* of (*memores*) His most glorious passion and resurrection from the dead and ascension into heaven, we offer unto thee *this* immaculate *victim, this holy bread and cup of eternal life*." [2] The one offering is here two things in apposition, the heavenly victim, and the earthly bread and the cup offered by the Church. Yet by the union of the two offerings the latter has become, in Johannine fashion, the vehicle of ' eternal life,' even while remaining the Church's offering. " And we beseech and pray that thou wouldest receive this oblation at thine altar on high, by the hands of thine holy angels as thou wast pleased to receive the offerings (*munera*) of thy righteous servant Abel and the sacrifice of our patriarch Abraham and that which thine High Priest Melchizedech offered unto Thee." It is still—after Consecration—the Church's own offering, strictly comparable to those of the Old Testament, which is in question, here as in Irenæus. At this point the text of *de Sacramentis* fails us, but in the (somewhat re-arranged) sixth century Gelasian text and ever since the prayer ends thus: " That as many of us as by this partaking of the altar shall receive the most holy Body and Blood of thy Son may be filled with all heavenly benediction and grace, through the same Jesus Christ our Lord." . In this prayer it is by the union of the earthly sacrifice of the Church in bread and wine with that which is ever pleaded at the heavenly altar where stands the " Lamb as it had been slain "—by the union of the *sacrifices*—that the

---

[1] *ut fiat nobis*. In the earlier text of *de Sacramentis*:—*quod est figura corporis*, " which is the figure of the Body." In early times such a phrase would not be misconstrued.

[2] I use here, so far as it is extant, the text of this prayer as found in the late fourth or fifth century *de Sacramentis* : (P.L. xvi. 462 *sq*.), where it is still without the decorative repetitions introduced by St. Leo the Great, *c.* A.D. 450. The current text is the same in all essentials.

communion of each of the receivers with the Lord is effected. Can we ask, then, Does the ' Real Sacrifice ' of primitive conceptions take place at the heavenly or the earthly altar? I do not think it would have occurred to a primitive writer to have put the question quite in that way. The earthly oblation is *identified with* the heavenly victim by the words ' This is my Body.' And the Eucharist, like the Church, was viewed essentially as an eschatological rather than a purely temporal fact. To this last point we shall have to return briefly.

3. But it would be much too superficial to suppose that the Church viewed the offertory and her own oblation merely as an " offering of first fruits," a weekly acknowledgement of the material bounty of God, even though that is an important aspect of it. Let Irenæus again speak for the pre-Nicene fathers. " The rite of oblation has not been reproved. There were oblations then (in the O.T.) and there are oblations now; there were sacrifices among the People, and there are sacrifices in the Church. But the kind of oblation has been changed, for that it is now no more offered by slaves but by free men. For the Lord is one and the same, but the nature of the servile offering is proper to itself, and proper also that of the free . . . for they had only the tithe of their possessions consecrate, but we that have obtained freedom set apart all that is ours for the Lord's uses . . . that poor widow the Church in the oblation casts in *all her life* (πάντα τὸν βίον, Lk. xxi. 4) into the treasury of God." [1]

That is the essential meaning of the offertory. It is no mere ceremony, but the supreme expression by each individual of the faithful separately for himself of a whole life lived to God. And the Church was zealous to see that it did not become a formality. The penalty of grave postbaptismal sin was that the sinner was " forbidden to *offer*." [2] This carried with it the refusal of communion, because in the primitive notion the layman's communion, like the

---

[1] *Haer.*, iv. 18.
[2] *E.g.* St. Cyprian, *Ep.*, 16,14, of those lapsed in persecution, *interim prohibeantur offerre.*

modern priest's, is simply the consummation of his offering of the sacrifice. It is some lingering memory of this deep meaning of the primitive offertory which leads the later liturgies so often to use St. Paul's phrase λογικὴ λατρεία, the "rational worship" of free sovereign creatures,[1] of what had become a mere ceremonial action, the placing of bread and wine upon the altar performed by the clergy alone. St. Augustine puts the primitive doctrine admirably when he tells the neophytes: "After the sanctification of the sacrifice of God, because He has willed that we also should be His sacrifice—which was signified when it was first placed upon the altar, *i.e.* that we also are His sacrifice and it (the oblation) is only the symbol of what we really are—we say the Lord's Prayer."[2] And more tersely still—"There *you* are upon the table; there *you* are in the chalice."[3]

The Offertory is, then, the most striking expression of that common priesthood which is shared by the laity, whereby singly and collectively they offer to God a real sacrifice of "themselves, their souls and bodies" to become the Body of His Son. The offerings of the people were "brought up" (ἀναφέρειν) by the deacons and placed upon the altar; the celebrant on the further side of the altar intervened not at all in the oblation; it was the collective action of the Church. This *anaphora*, the act of "bringing up" and offering the oblation of the Church, remained the characteristic ministry of the deacon for centuries before either the singing of the Gospel or the custody of the Chalice were exclusively committed to him.

Even in the fourth century this conception of the Offertory was vanishing in many rites, as we shall see. But it survived in the Roman rite, and above all in the Papal liturgy of the Stations, right down to the Captivity at Avignon in the fourteenth century.[4] It is true that by the seventh century the Pope had come to have a part in the collecting of the Offertory, advancing to the rails with his deacons after the Gospel to receive the people's breads in a silver dish called

---

[1] Rom. xii. 1.   [2] *Serm.*, 227. P.L. 38, 1101.
[3] *Ibid.*, 229. *ibid.*, 1103.
[4] It finally disappears, I think, in *Ordo Rom.*, xiv., written by Jacopo Caietano *c.* A.D. 1340.

the *offertorium*. But at Rome tradition was always a little stiff. The Pope did not offer the oblation. He surrendered the *offertorium* to two deacons who placed it on the altar and disposed its contents, while the Pope returned to his throne behind the altar for the *lavabo*. The only bread and wine offered by the Pope were his own personal *prosphora* and a little cruet of wine poured into the chalice already containing the people's offerings.[1] There is no better expression of the spirit of the primitive offertory than that of a prayer still found in the Roman Missal:

" Be gracious, O Lord, unto our supplications, and of thy goodness receive these oblations of thy servants and hand-maids: that what each has offered to the honour of thy Name may avail for the salvation of all; through . . ." [2] This is of Roman origin, and ancient. When we compare it with the invariable prayer at the offering of the Com-munion breads in the Ordinary of the Mass, we become aware of a contrast. " Receive, Holy Father, this immacu-late victim which *I* thy unworthy servant offer . . . *for all who stand around* . . ." This prayer is an intrusion into the Roman rite from later Gallican sources. Here ' clericalism ' has invaded the sanctuary. The sacrifice has become some-thing done *by* the clergy *for* the people. Yet the Roman rite still insists on the collective nature of the sacrifice. At every Mass the celebrant before approaching the ' action ' of the Canon turns to the people to say: " Pray brethren that this my sacrifice and yours may be acceptable to God the Father Almighty." And the people answer: " The Lord receive this sacrifice at thy hands . . . to our use and that of all His holy Church." This response is an integral part of the rite. Alone of all the responses at Mass it must be said by the celebrant himself (changing ' thy ' to ' my ') if there be no one else present with enough Latin to say it.

4. *Substitutes for the Offertory.* This oblation ' of the people by the people ' was anciently universal. In the East it had

---

[1] This looks like a primitive survival, but I do not know of any pre-Nicene evidence. It certainly touchingly illustrates the primitive idea.

[2] *ut quod singuli obtulerunt . . . cunctis proficiat ad salutem.* Secreta of the fifth Sunday after Pentecost.

disappeared by the fifth century.[1] At Rome it vanished only with the mediæval decline of general communion, keeping its place even then for a while on the rare occasions when the people did communicate. At Milan Cathedral it has survived in a ceremonial form right down to the present day in the *Vecchioni*, or guild of *Vetuli* and *Vetulae*, six old men and six old women who still present bread and wine at the offertory of the Capitular Mass.[2] But most of the Gallican Churches early abolished it in favour of the Byzantine substitute, the 'Great Entrance,' or 'Procession of the Elements,' as it was called in the West. In this the elements became no longer the substance of sacrifice rendered by the priestly people to God, but a hieratic object brought in a pompous procession by the clergy from the sacristy where it had been privately prepared beforehand. The part of the laity was no longer to offer themselves in the oblation of the Church, but merely to look on, and also to pay to the unconsecrated sacramental elements that strange worship then and now rendered among the Byzantines at the Great Entrance.[3] The contrast of the offertory when it had become a clerical ceremony with what it had meant, *e.g.* for St. Irenæus, is striking. But this meaningless custom was further removed from all connection with the primitive rite when it began to be transferred from its place and to be performed during the Kyries, Gloria or Gradual, in fact whenever fancy suggested, or a passage of music offered the opportunity for a clerical parade. At a few places in Gaul where Roman influence was strong, *e.g.* Cluny,[4] the ancient offertory survived the Middle Ages and lasted into the eighteenth century. In England the primitive offertory,

---

[1] Cf. *e.g.* Theodore of Mopsuestia, *Catecheses* V. ed. Mingana. Woodbrooke Studies, vi. *p.* 85 *sq.*

[2] Some of the wine, but not the hosts, are used at the Mass.

[3] Cf. Gregory of Tours, *de Gloria Martyrum*, I. 86.

[4] " A l'offertoire le Célebrant descend quelques degrez au bas de l'autel, et là il reçoit les hosties de ceux qui doivent communier, qui mettent chacun la sienne sur la patène, dont ils baisent le bord interieur . . . le Diacre tient le calice à costé du Célebrant, et le Préchantre vient mettre du vin dans le calice, le Diacre y met l'eau . . . ." *Voyages Liturgiques en France*, by le Sieur de Moleon, Paris, 1718, p. 149. At Cluny communion was still received under both kinds by the ministers at the Conventual Mass on Sundays down to the Revolution.

introduced from Rome by St. Augustine, is known to have been the general Anglo-Saxon custom. After the Norman Conquest a good deal of the ornate Norman–French ceremonial, including the ' Procession of the Elements,' was introduced by the new foreign prelates. The " Use of Sarum," in its extant form a compilation of these French customs made soon after the middle of the thirteenth century, directly or indirectly ousted the old English usages almost everywhere in the later Middle Ages, though they lingered on in some places, chiefly in houses of Black Benedictines.[1] But England still possesses one survival of the primitive offertory in its full significance, which is probably now unique in Christendom. At the coronation of an English King, the monarch newly anointed and crowned comes to the altar step, and kneeling presents the bread and wine for his own communion.[2]

2. The Eucharistic Prayer

We have dealt sufficiently with one element of the primitive eucharistic offering, the Church's oblation of bread and wine. We return now to Hippolytus' Liturgy to consider the second, the offering of the Paschal sacrifice of Christ.

1. *The Dialogue.* The silent imposition of hands by the bishop and the concelebrating presbytery upon the oblation is connected not with the offertory but with the prayer that follows. There may be some connection with the *Semik'ah*, the O.T. ' laying on ' of the offerer's hands on the head of the victim before it is slain in sacrifice, but there is no evidence for this. A more probable comparison would be with that silent imposition of hands by all the bishops present on the head of the bishop-elect, described by Hippolytus, before one bishop alone (with another imposition of hands) says the prayer which actually consecrates to the episcopate.[3] Such a parallel suggests that this is in some

---

[1] An English *offertorium* plate said to have come from Chertsey Abbey is still preserved at S. Kensington.

[2] He comes *within* the sanctuary to make his offertory, as did the Byzantine and Holy Roman Emperors.

[3] *Ap. Trad.*, ii. 5. Cf. also, perhaps, the imposition of hands (but with vocal prayer) before baptism (*ibid.*, xx. 8) and confirmation (xxii. 1).

I

sense a setting apart for the infusion of 'the Spirit.' This we shall see better further on.

The dialogue which follows is part of the Eucharistic Prayer. "He shall say giving thanks, 'The Lord be with you,'" says Hippolytus.[1] This quotation from Ruth ii. 4 was in use in pre-christian times among the Jews to recall a man's companions to remembrance of the Law, according to the Talmud.[2] The response, with its direct reference to the bishop's sacramental endowment with the Spirit, is not Jewish but Christian. "In saying 'And unto thy Spirit,' they do not refer to his soul but to the grace of the Holy Spirit . . . by which he drew nigh unto priesthood."[3] No Jewish origin has been found for the next ℣. and ℟. either, and they seem to be thoroughly Christian. St. Augustine excellently comments: "You are bidden 'Lift your hearts on high.' This befits the members of Christ. For the members have a Head. 'The third day He rose again and ascended into heaven and sat at the right hand of God the Father.' If the Head had not led the way the members could not follow. Therefore you answer, 'We have them with the Lord.'" The ℣. which follows is nothing less than the old Jewish "invitation to kiddûsh," the solemn grace at a religious meal, "when more than 100 persons are present." In view of this restriction it may not have been used at the Last Supper, but it must come down from the earliest Jewish-Christian Church of the Upper Room with its "120 persons." The ℟ "Meet and right" has no ascertainable Jewish precedent, though its Semitic parallelism seems obvious.

"Having," as James of Edessa puts it, "given them direction, and they having given him their consent and pronounced his intention to be right, they with him and he with them have been made one body of Christ, and of one mind."[5] The whole purpose of this dialogue between the bishop and the Church which is "a royal priesthood," is to emphasise the fact that the eucharistic prayer which

---

[1] Ap. Trad., iv. 2.   [2] Berakoth, T. vii. 23.
[3] Theodore of Mopsuestia, Catecheses, vi. ed. cit., p. 91.
[4] Berakoth, M. vii. 5.   [5] Assemani, Bib. Or., 1, 480.

follows, though spoken by the bishop alone, is the prayer and
' action ' of the whole Church. " Let *us* ' make eucharist ' "
and the church assents, " It is meet and right." Only
then can the bishop begin : " We render thanks. . . ."

2. *The ' Eucharistia.'* The ' Eucharistia,' the Eucharistic
Thanksgiving is simply ἡ εὐχή, ' *the* prayer,' for many early
Greek writers, as it is simply *prex*, ' *the* prayer ' for later
Roman ones.[1] Its structure is derived directly from the
Jewish ' prayer of benediction,' the *barakah*, to the rules of
which it originally conformed with strictness. The principle
of the *barakah* was this : It fell into three parts, a blessing
and a petition followed by a doxology. In the first part God
was ' blessed ' or ' thanked '[2] for one or more past mercies
which have a bearing on the petition now to be offered.
The petition prays for a repetition of such mercies now.
In other words the ' blessings ' of God are the excuse or
justification for the petition they introduce. These petitions
are often introduced by the words " Now therefore. . . ."
The whole concludes with a ' glorifying of the Name ' of
God, without which the prayer was held not to be a *barakah*
at all.[3] An excellent specimen of a *barakah* (but without the
phrase ' now therefore ') will be found *e.g.* at 1 Maccabees
iv. 30–34. A still more striking example is that at Nehemiah
ix. 4 sq., according to the LXX. text. The Levites begin with

---

[1] The term *Canon* in the modern sense seems to be found first in
St. Gregory I. The parallel eastern term *Anaphora* is also comparatively
late. In pre-Nicene times ἀναφέρειν is the function of deacons, προσ-
φερεῖν of bishops, *e.g.* in Serapion's Sacramentary the bishop's prayer
is Εὐχὴ προσφόρου not ἀναφορᾶς. Cf. also the succeeding rubric, μετὰ
τὴν εὐχήν . . . ' After *the* prayer the fraction, and at the fraction *a* prayer.'
[2] These are synonyms, just as εὐλογεῖν and εὐχαριστεῖν are synonyms
in the New Testament accounts of the Eucharist, *e.g.* Mark xiv. 22
and 23.
[3] The Eucharistic prayer is often held to be derived from the *berakoth*
used by the Jews at table, which were a specialised form of *barakah*. In
these God was blessed *for* the food, etc., which was held to bless the food
itself. But in fact no Christian *eucharistia* blesses God *for* the bread and
wine. The prayers of *Didache* x., which do so, are now known to be
for the ' Agape,' not the Eucharist proper, which is dealt with separately in
Did., xiv. (cf. *D.A.C.L.*, xi. 539 *sq.*, to which other evidence can be added).
The ' Eucharistic ' prayer of the Mass is in fact only one of a whole
class of similar Christian ' eucharistiæ,' for the Chrism, the Font, the
Paschal Candle, Virgins, Bishops, etc., which have no connection with
the Jewish table *berakoth*.

the cry "Stand up": (cf. the Alexandrian deacon's cry, Ἀνάστητε, before the anaphora) "Let us bless the Lord our God. . . ." And then Ezra begins his 'eucharistia' alone, like the Christian bishop, with a hymn of praise for the creative work of God:

> "Thou alone art the true Lord; thou madest the heaven and the heaven of heavens and all their array, the earth and all things that are therein, the seas and all things in them; and thou quickenest all things and the hosts of heaven worship thee."

Had Ezra added here, "saying, Holy, Holy, Holy," and ascribed creation to the Word of God, it is the perfect opening for a Christian eucharistic prayer of the fourth century type. But Ezra has no *Sanctus*, as Hippolytus has none, and as I venture to think no Christian canon originally had one. Ezra continues: "Thou art the Lord God who didst choose Abraham . . .," and there follows a magnificent recital of the innumerable mercies whereby God had *made* Israel into a people to serve Him, just as Hippolytus' canon more briefly recites how God had 'prepared a holy people' for Himself in the Church. Only at verse 32 does Ezra reach his petition, with the words, "*Now therefore*, O our God . . . who keepest covenant and mercy, let not all the trouble seem little in thy sight which has come upon us," which introduce a prayer for deliverance after backsliding— a petition *justified* by the preceding 'blessings' for previous deliverances after similar backslidings.

We have already outlined the thought of the first half of Hippolytus' *eucharistia*. Here is one more reason why the narrative of the Institution is so emphasised and placed after the 'blessing' for the Passion. The virtual promise it contains is the supreme *justification* for the petition for communion which is to follow.

3. *The Anamnesis*. The eucharistic sacrifice in the early writings and liturgies hinges upon the word *anamnesis*, which is not easy to translate adequately. Words like 'memorial,' 'remembrance' have in English a connotation of something which is itself 'absent.' Ἀνάμνησις has, on the contrary, the

sense of ' re-calling,' of making a past thing ' present ' again, so that it is here and now *operative by its effects*. Thus the widow of Sarepta reproaches Elijah (I Kings, xvii. 18) with being come " to re-call my iniquity " (ἀναμνῆσαι ἀδικίας μου), and *therefore* her son has now died. Similarly, the sacrifice of the wife accused of adultery (Num. v. 15) is a " sacrifice re-calling sin " (θυσία ἀναμιμνήσκουσα ἁμαρτίαν) which if she was guilty in the past will *now* make it public. It is as the *anamnesis*, in this active sense, of the Paschal Sacrifice of Christ, as the ' *re-calling* ' of it before God and man so that it is *here and now operative by its effects*, that the Eucharist is the effectual offering by the Church of the Sacrifice of Calvary, the " solemn proclamation of the Lord's death till He come." [1] St. Cyprian speaks for the whole Church when he says: " We celebrate the Lord's resurrection in the morning. And because we make mention of His passion in all our sacrifices—for the passion is the Lord's sacrifice which we offer—we ought to do nothing else than what He did (at the last supper)." [2]

4. *The Petition for Communion.* We come now to the petition: " And we pray thee that thou wouldest grant to all thy saints who partake to be made one, that they may be fulfilled with the Holy Spirit for the confirmation of ⟨*their*⟩ faith in truth, in order that we may praise thee . . ."

The communicants are ' the Saints,' the " holy people " gathered in the arms stretched out upon the Cross (*cf.* §*c*). They *are* " Saints " in virtue of their membership in the Holy Church, not in virtue of the Communion they are about to receive. It is not that their merits are their own; these are drawn entirely from the Passion and Resurrection (§ *c*, *d*) into which they have been baptised. But there is here a serene confidence in the sanctifying power of Christ to ' regenerate ' His own, in the holiness of the mystical Body of Christ because it *is* His Body. This is totally unlike that language of ' fear ' which begins to be found in Eastern rites (it never entered the Western rites) concerning communion as early as the fourth century, and which is now echoed among ourselves in such language as " we are not worthy

[1] I Cor., xi. 26.   [2] *Ep.*, 63, 16.

so much as to gather up the crumbs under thy table." The
primitive Church had a strong grasp of the fact that by
entrance into the 'new covenant' man had been *made
worthy* to do so (cf. §*f* of Hippolytus' canon). The redeemed,
by the fact of redemption, are the priestly people of God.
As St. Cyprian expresses it: [1] " Because Christ bore us all
Who bore our sins, we see that by the water (of the mixed
chalice) the people is to be understood, but in the wine is
shewn forth the Blood of Christ [2] . . . That commixture can
never be separated again. Wherefore nothing whatever
will be able to separate the Church—that is, the people
brought together in the Church and faithfully and firmly
continuing in that which they have believed—from Christ,
so that their mutual love should not ever cleave together and
remain undivided."

Next, the communicants receive " that they may be made
one " (with one another). The unity of the Mystical Body
derives from the unity of the Sacramental Body. The
Eucharist is *not*—as has been so unscripturally said by a
succession of Lambeth Conferences—the " expression " of
the Church's unity. (That is to make the Church a mere
human association.) It is its *cause*. " The Bread which we
break, is it not a partaking of the Body of Christ? *Because*
(ὅτι) the Bread is one, we being many are one Body. For we
all partake of the one Bread." [3] Breach of communion,
excommunication, does not register a breach already made in
the Church's unity; it *is* that breach, though not the reason
for it. The unity of the Glorified Body of Christ constitutes
the unity of His Sacramental Body, and it is by the unity of
communion in that one Sacramental Body that the Church
is one. She has no being at all save as the fruit of His
sacrifice, [4] and the Eucharist is the *anamnesis* of that sacrifice,
making it operative in her by its effects. In the New

---

[1] *Ep.*, 63, 13.
[2] This idea passed into the liturgies. Cf., *e.g.* the ancient Irish
rubrics at the mixing of the Chalice " Water, first, into the chalice . . .
that is the figure of the people poured forth into the Church . . . wine,
then, for water into the chalice, that is Christ's Godhead for His manhood
and for the people at the time of His begetting." *ap. The Stowe Missal,*
H.B.S., Vol. ii., p. 40.
[3] I Cor., x. 16.   [4] Eph. v. 25.

Testament it is by the sacraments that that sacrifice energises in the Church. It is into ' the death and resurrection ' that souls are baptised.[1] It is because Jesus is now " glorified " that the Spirit is now given [2] in Confirmation and Order. It is because Jesus " gave Himself for " the Church that He can, after the cleansing of Baptism, " present it to Himself " in the Eucharist " a glorious Church, holy and without blemish." The communicants are " made one " for a purpose—" that they may be fulfilled with Holy Spirit for the confirmation of faith in truth."

Here it has to be remembered that the baptismal creed in Hippolytus' day ran, " Dost thou believe in the Holy Spirit in (sic) the Holy Church? " [3] with which is to be compared Hippolytus' doxology and the words of administration for the third chalice. A passage from Hippolytus' Περὶ τοῦ Πάσχα, lii. will explain what is in his mind in his canon. " They incur the guilt of impiety who do not prepare their bodies for the commingling (ἀνάκρισιν)[4] with His Body, which He has given unto us that being united to It (πρὸς αὐτὸ κιρνάμενοι) we might be united to the Holy Spirit. Since it was for this reason that the Word of God gave Himself altogether into a body (ὅλως εἰς σῶμα ἔδωκεν ἑαυτόν) and was made Flesh, as the Gospel says, in order that since we could not partake of Him as Word we might partake of Him as Flesh, making our flesh fitting for His spiritual Flesh and our spirit to His Spirit so far as we can, that we might be established as likenesses of Christ, becoming ' temples of the Spirit,' as saith the Apostle. And again he says, ' know ye not that your bodies are the temple of the Holy Spirit? ' And by the commingling with the Holy Spirit our bodies become part of the [mystical] Body of Christ, so that we should cherish them in sanctity as members of Christ."

We must beware of interpreting pre-Nicene writers too rigidly in terms of developed fourth century theology. Hippolytus distinguishes somewhat vaguely as a rule between the heavenly Christ, whom he frequently styles

---

[1] Rom. vi. 3.   [2] John vii. 39.   [3] Ap. Trad., xxi. 17.
[4] This is the word he uses in his Contra Noëtum of the union of Godhead and manhood in the Incarnation.

πνεῦμα (Spirit), and the Third Person of the Trinity. It is quite possible that he is here thinking rather of the " Second Adam who was made a quickening Spirit" rather than strictly of the Third Person of the Trinity. If I may adopt a phrase from another essay in this book which I have been permitted to read, " The Spirit is the element or power whereby the glorified Body or Person of Jesus is present to us and inflows upon us," [1] expresses very exactly the somewhat impersonal notion of " Holy Spirit " here.[2]

In any case, by receiving of the Spirit the communicants are to be " led into all truth." As St. John puts it in a eucharistic passage: " He that *believeth* hath everlasting life " [3]—the " everlasting life " that comes by " eating the Flesh and drinking the Blood of the Son of Man." [4] This seems to be the implication of Hippolytus' petition " for the confirmation of their faith in truth."

And the purpose of it all is the purpose of the whole Christian economy—" *worship* " in that " Spirit " and " Truth " which the communicants have received: " That

---

[1] Obviously this has a bearing on the origins of the epiclesis. It may help to justify my entire neglect of this question elsewhere in this essay to add a note on the matter here. If I understand it rightly, the theory of the epiclesis is that by the illapse of the Spirit on the elements the communicants receive the Body and Blood of Christ, which unites them to the mystical Body, whereby they receive the fruits of communion. This seems to me to reverse the idea of Hippolytus, that by receiving the Body and Blood of Christ in the elements *the communicants* receive the illapse of the Spirit, which unites them to the mystical Body, whereby they receive the fruits of communion. The consecratory epiclesis in the current Eastern sense first certainly appears in Syria in the fourth century. I subjoin three passages from fourth century Syrian writers who *used* a consecratory epiclesis of the Spirit. (1) St. Ephraem, speaking of the last Supper: " He called the Bread His living Body and filled it with Himself *and with the Holy Spirit.* . . . This is my Body, and whoever eats it with faith *eats with it the fire of the Divine Spirit* " (*Opp.*, ed. Lamy, iv. 173). (2) Theodore of Mopsuestia, *Catecheses*, vi.: " This food is holy and immortal as it is the Body and Blood of our Lord and is replete of holiness *on account of the Holy Spirit who dwells in it* (ed. Mingana, p. 108). (3) Liturgy of St. James, narrative of the Institution: " . . . He took the cup . . . and blessed and *filled it with Holy Spirit* and gave . . ." (εὐλογήσας, πλήσας Πνεύματος ἁγίου ἔδωκε . . .). It seems to me that we have here traces of an older language which agrees exactly with that of Hippolytus, but which is not fully adjusted to the later theory of the epiclesis. Regarded in this light the historical question of the epiclesis loses a good deal of its interest.

[2] P. 80, *supra*.   [3] John vi. 47.   [4] *Ibid.*, vi. 54.

we may praise Thee through thy Child Jesus Christ." And so the anaphora comes to its doxology, the old Jewish "glorifying of the Name of God" in the fulness of the new Christian revelation of God's Being—the doxology without which Rabbi Judah the Saint once declared no *barakah* could be held to bless, and which Hippolytus himself elsewhere declares is the essential ending of every Christian *eucharistia*.[1]

3. *The Fraction*

There follows the Fraction. Here it must again be emphasised how little there is of a ' celebrant ' about Hippolytus' bishop. The fraction, in which some fifteenth-century theologians saw the priestly mactation of the victim and a sacerdotal act, is here shared not only with the presbyters but with the deacons also. And the deacons continued to have this right in the Papal Mass—though not apparently in other Masses—right down to the eleventh or twelfth century at Rome, so strong was the force of primitive tradition there.

The cry " Holy things unto the holy " is well illustrated by St. John Chrysostom, who says that " all sacrifices are called holy, and the proper meaning of holy is a thing offered to God." [2] Once again it emphasises the " holiness " of " the Saints " simply as the ' People of God ' and members of Christ, the insistence of the primitive Church on the efficacy of the fact of baptismal redemption. It was not that the Church overlooked the defects of her individual members. Early writers are full enough of denunciations of shortcomings and much-needed exhortations to " walk worthy of the vocation wherewith ye are called." But the baptised and confirmed *as such* are " in the communion (κοινωνία) of His Son Jesus Christ our Lord." Procopius of Gaza puts it: " even when people are impious but are set apart, for some particular service (λειτουργία), they are called holy, as Zephaniah (i. 7) shews." [3] It is the very spirit which led

---

[1] *Ap. Trad.*, vi. 4.   [2] *In Joan.*, 82, 1.
[3] On *Deut.*, xxii. 9, cited G. L. Prestige, *God in Patristic Thought*, 1936, p. 21.

St. Paul to write to that factious and quarrelling congregation of Corinthian rebels as " the Church of God which is at Corinth, them that are sanctified in Christ Jesus, elect saints," [1] for all their drunken communions and sins " not so much as named among the Gentiles."

4. *The Communion.*

The words of administration in Hippolytus, " The Bread of Heaven in Christ Jesus " and the threefold credal formula at the chalices, are somewhat unexpected. We know from his contemporary Tertullian that in Africa they were simply " The Body of Christ," " The Blood of Christ," to which the communicant answered " Amen." It is probable that Hippolytus' form is more primitive and has a special meaning. Clement of Alexandria supplies a commentary: " He is ' heavenly bread ' and ' spiritual food,' furnishing food by life and knowledge; and the ' light of man,' that is, of the Church. ' And my Flesh is the bread that I will give,' He says; that is, to those whose flesh is nourished by the Eucharist. Or, better still, the ' Flesh ' is His Body, ' which is the Church.' The ' heavenly bread ' is a ' blessed assembly.' " [2] So too St. Cyprian: " In the very sacrament our people is exhibited in its absolute unity, that we may know that as many grains collected and ground and mingled make one bread, so in Christ who is the Bread of Heaven our Body is all one, for in Him is conjoined all our multitude in Him united." [3] Thus even in the very act of communion were the faithful reminded that the Christian does not come to God like the pagan, as " the alone to the Alone," but as the member of the Body of Christ. Even there, in what we are accustomed to consider the most sacred moment of personal religion, the fact that only in the Church and through the Church do we reach Jesus was brought to the mind of Christians.

The triple formula for the three chalices may have been proper to the Baptismal Mass, when the neophytes received

[1] I Cor., i. 2.
[2] *Exc. ex Theodoto*, 13, a passage which is a comment by Clement on a Gnostic extract.   [3] *Ep.*, 63, 13.

the special cups of water and of milk and honey mingled before the chalice of the eucharist. Hippolytus tells us that the water represented the " living water " of the baptismal " fountain of life." (Has it a connection with John vii. 37?) That of milk and honey is " in fulfilment of the promise to the fathers wherein He said ' I will give you a land flowing with milk and honey '; which Christ indeed gave, even His Flesh, whereby the faithful are nourished like little children, making the bitterness of man's heart sweet by the sweetness of the Word." The threefold formula " In God the Father Almighty and in the Lord Jesus Christ and in the Holy Spirit in the Holy Church " forms a perfect climax to the rite, describing as it does the compenetration of God and the soul in communion which is the end of the spiritual life.

III. The Idea of The Church and the Eucharist

1. *The ' People of God '*

We have seen that certain notions about the Church emerge clearly from a consideration of the primitive eucharistic rite : 1. That in the Eucharist the Church is both priest and victim like her Master, offering *herself* as a " sacrifice to God for a savour of sweetness." 2. That in virtue of her indissoluble unity with Christ the Church is authorised to offer to God the Paschal sacrifice of Christ in its *anamnesis*, its ' re-calling,' which makes it here and now operative by its effects. 3. That in virtue of His unity with the Church, Christ offers the Church which is His mystical Body in union with His pleading of His own sacrifice at the heavenly altar. 4. That the Eucharist is emphatically a sacrifice offered by the Church in its corporate unity, and not a sacrifice offered by a celebrant on behalf of the Church, as in much later thought on this question.

It will be useful to consider for a moment how the Church conceived of herself in the abstract, and then to relate this to her eucharistic worship.

Deep in the mind of the primitive Church, and colouring every strand of her belief, is the strong consciousness of the unique privilege with God of the 'Holy Church.' She is the new 'Israel of the Spirit' which has replaced the old 'Israel according to the flesh' in the Divine love and in the Divine plan for the universe. The incurable Semitic tendency to conceive of " blood and soil " as the only basis of all human associations had led the Hebrews only too often to think and speak of the " Israel of God " as a purely racial or national corporation. But there had always been another side even to Hebrew tradition. The mockery of the Prophets for the boast of a mythical racial purity represented admitted historical fact. Such things as the necessity of Circumcision, even for born Israelites, as the 'seal of the covenant,' the phrasing of many prayers of the Synagogue liturgy, and above all the annual Passover rite—such things insistently recalled to the mind of the Jew that the privileges and destiny and even the existence of his race had a wholly different origin. 'The People' as such was a direct Divine *creation*. Just as the world came into being by a spontaneous fiat of God, so Israel owed its existence to a fresh spontaneous volition of God intervening in the history of the world He had created. " With His own right hand and with His holy arm," God Himself of His own motion had violently plucked the fathers from Egyptian bondage, fashioning " a people of what was not a people." With long and tender personal travail God had fused the " mixed multitude " of Egyptian refugees with the riff-raff of the desert and its border lands into " a kingdom of priests and a holy nation." He had set them in a land flowing with milk and honey, that there in ideal conditions they might be *His* people. And the purpose of it all was—*worship*. " Send forth the People that they may worship (λατρεύσῃ) Me." Israel was created in the midst of a world created long before, that God might therein be known and proclaimed as " the True God," and as such be truly worshipped.

Christians also habitually spoke of themselves as a " race," though with them the phrase was consciously a metaphor.[1]

---

[1] It is curious to find Hippolytus (*In Dan.*, iv. 9) denouncing the supra-racial unity of the Roman Empire as a diabolical parody of the supra-racial unity of the Catholic Church.

What was not a metaphor was that by baptism and confirmation a man became a 'laic,' one of 'The People' (λαός) in the strictest Old Testament sense. As with the old 'People' so with the new. Its very existence was the result of a Divine action. It was, again, a fresh *creation*, the result of a spontaneous intervention of God in His world—of that supreme intervention dimly foreseen by Jewish apocalypse as a vague but tremendous 'Messianic crisis,' ushering in the age to come. That crisis, in the Christian view, was the rejection of the Messiah by God's own chosen instrument in the world, the 'People of God,' followed by the sacrificial death, resurrection and ascension of Jesus, who constituted in Himself the transformed Israel which the Messianic crisis was to bring about. He " being by the right hand of God exalted hath shed forth " from the throne of heaven the " new Spirit " prophetically foretold as the mark of the " age to come " upon all who accept Him as " Lord and Messiah." By that acceptance they are members of the 'new Israel.' Baptized into His death and resurrection, in which and in the consequences of which they share sacramentally (*i.e.* really, but by grace not by racial descent), and being made partakers by Confirmation of His very 'Spirit' (*i.e.* of that which *constituted* Him Messiah), the new 'People' has passed with Him into the Messianic Kingdom. The Church is an *eschatological* fact. The darkness and terrors of Calvary were the new plagues of Egypt, the Resurrection and Ascension the new Exodus, the waters of the Paschal Baptism the new Red Sea, Confirmation the new Sinai (where the Law is given no more on tables of stone but written by the " new Spirit " in the " new heart "), the Paschal Mass with the draught of milk and honey the entrance into the new Canaan. And the Paschal Lamb, whose death brought liberty, whose Blood avails for a token against " the destroyer," of which no stranger and none without the 'seal of the covenant' in circumcision may eat, and whose flesh may not be borne outside the one household—this is " the Lamb of God that taketh away the sins of the world," whereof no heathen and none without the 'seal of the covenant' in the Spirit (Confirmation) may eat, whose

Flesh can never be distributed outside the one household of the Holy Church. All these identifications are made by Hippolytus in his recently-discovered Περὶ τοῦ Πάσχα.[1] The whole attitude they imply has to be borne in mind in considering the primitive liturgy.

2. *The Hierarchy in the Church*

Only when we have clearly grasped this conception of the Church as a whole as the corporate priest of a divinely ordained worship, can we rightly grasp the position of the primitive Christian hierarchy. For it is a true hierarchy, its members distinguished from the laity and from one another not only by office or function, but by differences of ' order,' *i.e.* of sacramental power. Yet the hierarchy is not *over* the Church, but *in* the Church. It is indeed the product of the Church, though not its creature. Bishop, presbyter, or deacon, every member of the hierarchy must be the nominee of a genuine *election* by the whole Church. This is as necessary for the lawful exercise of the sacramental power of orders as the imposition of episcopal hands. And the Pope himself cannot ordain the man of his own choice to the presbyterate without the election of the people; if they are unwilling he must plead and argue till they will consent.[2] It might indeed have been said by the Church as she presented the man of her choice for ordination, "Thine own of Thine own do we offer unto Thee," as the later liturgies say of the Eucharistic oblation of the Church. The only factor which does not seem to have been taken much into account was the man's own inner consciousness of vocation. The early Church thrust Holy Orders on many who were most sincerely reluctant to receive them, and refused many who were strongly conscious of their own call to the episcopate. It was the Church's oblation of the man for the bishop's prayer that mattered, and having offered him with her prayer she received him back as she received back the Eucharist, her own still but

[1] An edition is in preparation by P. Ch. Martin, S.J., to whose kindness I owe my own knowledge of it.
[2] Eusebius, *Eccl. Hist.*, vi. 43, 17.

now taken up into the High-priesthood of Christ, that by
his ministry she might receive afresh something of her own
character as the Body of Christ, and the gifts of unity and
the Spirit and ' the confirmation of faith in truth.'

It is hard for us whose clergy are largely the appointment
of irresponsible nominators—bishops by politicians, incumbents by patrons, assistant clergy by incumbents—to realise
how greatly this choice of the clergy by the whole Church,
taken in conjunction with the ' charismatic ' (in the true
sense) rather than ' official ' notion then held of the Sacrament of Holy Orders, intensified the idea of the ' spirit-
bearing ' Body of Christ as in itself *priestly*. It was not that
the clergy were viewed in an unsacerdotal way. There
was the clearest insistence on their exclusive sacramental
functions.[1] But they were members *of* the Church—doubtless its ' honourable members,' but members only like the
laity, in fact as well as in theory, set apart by the whole
Body to perform its ' liturgies ' and endowed by God at
the Church's prayer with the power to perform them in
the Body. They had their inalienable prerogatives in the
administration of the sacraments, not as a sacerdotal caste,
but as members of the Body. No layman could usurp
those prerogatives, simply because they were ultimately
the *Church's* prerogatives, and the layman had not been
empowered by the Church's choice and prayer to fulfil
them.[2]

3. The ' Clericalisation ' of the Eucharist

Formal theological teaching concerning the Eucharist is
not entirely a static thing in Christian history, though it
has probably changed less than most departments of
theology.[3] The Liturgy too undergoes considerable de-

[1] *E.g. Ap. Trad.*, xxvi. 12.
[2] It is to be noted that down to the fourth century the Church rejected
the very *possibility* of valid orders outside the Catholic Church, because
outside the Catholic Church the Holy Ghost does not operate. It is
when orders begin to be conceived of as something personal to the *man*,
and not as something pertaining to the Body of Christ, that difficulties
begin to multiply.
[3] I venture to say that *e.g.* St. Justin's theological teaching on the
Eucharist is a good deal nearer to that of St. Thomas than is his teaching
on the Trinity.

velopments, though they are for the most part true developments and not revolutions. Some of these changes of
teaching and rite have permanently enriched the Christian
understanding of the Eucharist, while others have expressed
only passing devotional fashions, and laid false emphasis on
unessentials to the obscuring of the real meaning of the
sacrament. But there is one change which, so far as I
know, has left little trace on dogmatic definitions, and
which in many cases has left liturgical formulæ verbally
unaffected for many centuries after their original meaning
had vanished, and which yet seems to me by far the most
momentous change in the whole history of the rite. I
mean what for want of a better word I have called the
'clericalisation' of the Eucharist, that steady tendency
which begins in the fourth century to take the eucharistic
action away from the Church as a whole and to concen-
trate it exclusively in the hands of the ministers, so that it
becomes in fact something done *by* the clergy *for* the laity,
instead of the action of the Body of Christ. However much
we may emphasise the verbal relics of the ancient conception still to be found in the great historic rites, that is how
the Eucharist is regarded in practice to-day all over Christendom by the plain layman and also by the plain parish priest.
The emergence of this wholly post-Nicene conception of
the Eucharist is nowhere marked by protests or incidents
of any kind. Indeed, it is nowhere discernible at all as
an event. Only by scrutiny of the sort of language current
about the offering of the sacrifice in one age and by comparison with that of another, we become aware that a vast
unconscious revolution has silently taken place, that both
clergy and laity have come to think quite differently of
their own and each other's function in the Eucharist. Far
more truly and deeply than any doctrinal definition does
the acceptance of this change from a 'collective' to a
'clerical' sacrifice mark off 'Mediæval' or 'Byzantine'
(as the case may be) from primitive eucharistic thought.

The history of this revolution has never yet been traced
and there is no space even to outline it here. In the East
it is easy to trace the change beginning in the fourth cen-

tury, and it is virtually completed by the end of the fifth.
And all the evidence points to that fruitful source of liturgical
innovations, Syria, as the region where the change was first
apparent, and most swiftly became an accomplished fact.
In the West the story is more complicated, but the evidence
seems clearly to indicate that the change reached Rome
last of all the Churches.   However it may be in the
matter of dominion, Rome was never particularly sacerdotalist
in the realm of liturgy; witness *e.g.* the prominence in the
eighth and ninth century Papal Mass ceremonial of unordained
laymen like the *primicerius* and *secundicerius*.   Rather we must
look at the countries of the Gallican rite.   The sort of
evidence I have in mind in saying this is perhaps worth
illustrating.   We have from the pen of St. Cæsarius of
Arles a collection of episcopal sermons as ' popular ' in tone
as anything in the whole patrology.   Here we find the
reiterated complaint that the laity behave as mere passive—
and somewhat uninterested—spectators of the liturgy performed by clergy, and do not seem to realise that they have
any share whatever in its performance.   For instance, when
the deacon's cry *Flectamus genua*, ' Let us bow the knee,'
rings out, " the most part of you " scolds the bishop,
" remain standing as stiff as columns." [1]   His sermons
abound in vigorous entreaties to the laity to come to communion.   Yet *c.* 18 of the Council of Agde (A.D. 506) in
which he took a prominent part, is forced to declare that
those who will not communicate at least on the three
great feasts *catholici non credantur*, ' shall not be accounted
catholics,' and later Gallican councils (*e.g.* Chalons-sur-
Saone, can. 47) were already content with the mediæval
rule of once a year.   Yet in the eighth century Bede tells
us that at Rome the greater part of the faithful still communicate every Sunday and on the feasts of the Apostles,
an example which he wishes the Anglo-Saxons would

---

[1] *Serm.* in app. *Spuria*, of St. Augustine, 285, P.L. 38, 2285.   In *Sermon*
307 (*ibid.* 2334) he practically admits that the real function of the laity
in religion is to support the clergy and monks by their alms while the
latter perform their devotion for them.   It is necessary to add that
Cæsarius' electors first sought the consent of an Arian monarch before
they would elect him to the episcopate.

K

imitate.[1] There are traces later still at Rome that general and frequent communion of the laity was still the custom after it had altogether vanished elsewhere in Western Europe.

Those who have the patience to explore those weary volumes of Migne—a few are quite beyond endurance—which collect the Merovingian and Carolingian authors of Gaul and the Rhineland, will find they have watched the gradual formulation of every single characteristic which distinguishes the religion of the Western Middle Ages from that which preceded them—in fact of what passes nowadays for distinctively 'Roman' Catholicism. Yet Rome in the geographical sense contributed singularly little to 'mediævalism' in the sphere of liturgy. (In the sphere of canon law things are very different.) The main purpose of the Carolingian reformers was avowedly the 'Romanisation' of the liturgy of the West, and in a sense they achieved their aim. But in a much deeper sense the real result of their work was the 'Westernisation' of Rome. All that remained in Gaul at the death of Charlemagne of the Gallican rite was some of its decorations—*and its spirit*, the spirit that by contrast with the old Roman 'collective' tradition of the Eucharist is so strikingly 'clerical.' It was in the Frankish monasteries that there was evolved the conception of Low Mass, as each priest's own individual offering of the sacrifice, with all that this implies.[2] The first known *Roman* directions for Low Mass are those of the *Ordo Missae* of John Burkhard (A.D. 1502).[3] Similarly, it was in the Frankish dominions that there was evolved the *Missale Plenarium*, the book of the sacrificing priest, by contrast with the Roman 'Sacramentary,' a book that was useless without the co-operation of other ministers each with his own book. The real end of the old 'collective'

---

[1] *Ep.*, ii. P.L. 94, 665 *sq.*

[2] I am not attacking the conception of Private Masses; I say one every day. But in the monasteries this was balanced by the continuance of the corporate conventual Mass. It was a different thing when a laudable practice of individual monastic piety became the normal presentation of the liturgy to the laity.

[3] Of course Low Masses were said at Rome throughout the Middle Ages, but it was not officially a Roman rite.

liturgy in Christendom comes in the eleventh century. A long series of imperially-nominated reforming Popes brought with them from beyond the Alps the new Romano-Gallican rite of the Carolingians with its accompanying ideas, and only relics of the old ' collective ' Roman rite lingered on till the days of the Avignon Captivity.

I think that when the history of this momentous change comes to be written in full there will be only one conclusion possible from the facts, namely, that the change in euchar-istic theory and practice from a collective to a wrongly sacerdotalist conception of sacrifice is itself the result of a certain fading in the Church's own consciousness of herself as the Body of Christ. There are indications everywhere in the history of a subtle and (to me) unexpected connection between three things which at first sight might be supposed independent questions. 1. The conception of the Church as a whole, and not the ' celebrant,' as the priest of the eucharistic offering. 2. The practice of frequent and general communion by the laity. 3. The extent to which the Church, regarding herself as a particular creation of God distinct from the world into which she was created, vindi-cates her own freedom in choosing her hierarchy in inde-pendence of the secular power. This last point may seem irrelevant, but I believe that upon consideration of the first part of this section the reader will discern for himself that the abandonment of the choice of the hierarchy by the ' Spirit-bearing ' Body of Christ does pre-suppose a very definite change from the idea of the church held by *e.g.* Hippolytus. And I think it will be found that wherever and whenever that right has been effectively lost to the secular ruler (it often survives *in theory*), there and then with a curious precision it will be found that the practice of frequent and general communion by the laity rapidly declines, and the ' collective ' character of the eucharistic sacrifice is soon lost sight of.

The Middle Ages in the West, for all their faith and devotion, are in truth an age of unexampled liturgical decay. The mediæval man brought to the liturgy all his natural love of pageantry and his admirable taste in the arts, so that it became a thing of conscious beauty as it had never been before. But he brought to it, too, all his profound ignorance of history, and its deepest meaning was largely hidden from him. Underneath all its unessential ornament the heart of the liturgy slowly withered. The people had no organic part in the offering of the sacrifice; all that was left to them was communion. And divorced from sacrifice, communion finds its fruition *apart from* the liturgy, between the soul and its Lord.[1]

4. *The Reformation in England*

This was the situation in England at the Reformation. The articles of the Devonshire rebels on behalf of the old religion in 1549 make instructive reading, particularly for those inclined to cherish a regret for fifteenth-century unreformed mediævalism. " We will have the Mass . . . celebrated by the Priest without any man or woman to communicate with him. We will have the Sacrament only at Easter delivered to the lay-people." The laity had lost their part in the offering of the Church's sacrifice centuries before. When they could sincerely believe that it was *wrong* for them even to communicate, the final end of the primitive conception of the Eucharist had arrived.

I have not to judge here of the doctrinal comparison of the two books of 1549 and 1552 with primitive eucharistic rites. " We are not worthy to offer unto thee any sacrifice." " Doing the *anamnesis* of His death and resurrection we offer to thee the bread and the cup making eucharist to thee because thou hast made us worthy to stand before thee and minister as priests to thee." Such statements measure the extent of the contradiction. But I think it is fair to say that bearing in mind the unreformed fifteenth-century religion such contradiction was only to be expected. After all, the eucharistic controversies of the sixteenth century are only by-products. The real dispute (as here) was on ' Justification.'

Nor does it seem necessary to compare the book of 1552,

---

[1] The primitive church was not on the wrong line in providing no corporate thanksgiving for communion.

the ancestor of our present rite, in detail with the primitive rites. Its defects from that point of view are well known. All that need be said is that of the swift clear eucharistic outline with its four scriptural acts there remain only fragments interspersed with mediævalisms. But it is un-generous to insist on this. The truth is that the primi-tive eucharistic rite *could* not be reconstituted in 1550 because the technical historical knowledge was not then available. The historical ignorance concerning Chris-tian origins which had brooded more and more darkly over the Middle Ages only began to be lifted at the end of the sixteenth century. These defects are only formal and have not the importance sometimes attributed to them. On the contrary, no criticism is fair which does not take full account of the fact that the rite of 1552 was an entirely honest attempt at a remedy within the limitations of con-temporary knowledge. So far as it went the diagnosis was excellent. It insisted on the one thing which seemed essential at the time, the Communion of the laity—even to the extent of forbidding any Eucharist at all without it, an heroic measure. Estimates as to the extent to which the remedy achieved its object have varied. On the whole it must be confessed that it never accomplished anything like the old weekly corporate communion of the whole Church of pre-Nicene times. It does not accomplish it to-day in any parish in England, as the figures for Easter communions show.

It may sound paradoxical to suggest that one pre-eminent cause of this is the inherent ' mediævalism ' of the Anglican rite, yet such appears to be the truth. We have been so obsessed with the technical questions of ' Catholic ' or ' Protestant,' that we have largely failed to see that on the one absolutely glaring point of distinction between the mediæval and the primitive eucharistic rites Cranmer stands foursquare with the mediæval against the primitive. It is the tragedy of English Church history that the Re-formation developed as a reaction and not as a positive movement. It meant that like all reactions it simply adhered to the last revolution but one. In offering the laity communion and urging it upon them, the English Church simply returned to the essential position of the developed 'clerical' rite at the beginning of the Middle Ages, which provided for the laity the opportunity of communion, *and nothing more*. The fact must be faced that the laity have no more organic function in the Anglican Communion Service than they had in the mediæval Mass; in fact rather less. It is still wholly a service done *by* the clergy *for* the laity; all that has changed is that instead of offering the sacrifice for the laity the function of the clergy is now to 'provide communion' for the laity. But the rite itself is still a purely clerical performance.[1] The primitive intercessions, for instance, were really the 'Prayers *of* the Faithful'; it was the people, the Church, that prayed. The celebrant served only to cohere the Church's prayer. In the rites of 1549 and 1552 the intercessions have become a long monologue by the celebrant. The prayer of the Church is now one word—'Amen.' Exactly how much of the rite of 1552 (which is normative in Anglican history) is assigned to the People? In the Eucharist proper—*two sentences*: "We lift them up unto the Lord" and "It is meet and right," and the Lord's Prayer, "the people repeating after him every petition." (1549 gives them four more sentences but only one petition of the Lord's Prayer.) For the rest the people are reduced to passive 'Amens.' They are there to be hectored with exhortations and comforted by the celebrant's recitation of texts; but the poor dumb beasts are not even allowed to confess their own sins.[2] The old rite had ordered that at each fresh movement of the liturgy the celebrant should turn and greet the Church with "The Lord be with you," to associate the Church with himself in what he did. All these eight separate ex-

---

[1] I speak, of course, of the rite as the Church of England gives it to us to use. The modern (unauthorised) attempts to get over the defect with hymns, etc., merely advertise the defect of the rite *as a rite*. They are usually an attempt to occupy the laity with something else while the clergy proceed with the liturgical action.

[2] "Then shall this general confession be made in the name of all those that are mynded to receiue the holy Communion, eyther by one of them or els by one of the ministers, or by the Priest himself, al kneling humbly upon theyr knees." 1662 adds "and saying."

pressions of the fact that the Eucharist is a corporate
action the book of 1552 swept away. (1549 retained three
of them and the people's response at the Pax.) The ancient
psalmody of the Mass, since Apostolic days the *Church's*
scriptural comment on and accompaniment to the minister's
lections and prayers, 1552 utterly removed. (1549 retained
the introit psalm.) For the old offertory psalm with its
antiphon by the choir, " The Curate shal . . . earnestly
exhort them . . . saying one or more of these Sentences."
For the rest—a succession of clerical addresses to God and
to the laity, punctuated with Amens—the *ne plus ultra* of the
essential mediæval spirit that had made the Eucharist a
clerical preserve.[1] It is an accident and an unimportant
one, but it is also symbolic that Cranmer ended by rejecting
the Mass Vestments, which were at least ancient and of
lay origin and a natural development, and retained the
only ecclesiastical vestures which were of deliberate clerical
invention and of mediæval date, the surplice and academic
hood and the rochet and chimere.

It will be obvious from what has been already said in
the first part of this essay, that in isolating the communion
of the people as their only effective share in the eucharistic
action the English rite is far from being a reversion to
primitive practice. Rather it is exceedingly typical of
sixteenth century post-mediæval religion. One may read
whole pages of eloquent (and on the whole fairly successful)
exhortations to the laity by St. Philip Neri and St. Charles
Borromeo to communicate often, with never a single suggestion that the layman's communion, like the priest's, is
the consummation of his offering of the sacrifice. Most
Jesuit spiritual writers taught that Sunday communion
should be the general rule for the laity, and they were very
successful in securing its observance by those who came
under their influence. Communion divorced from the idea
of sacrificial offering is no mere Anglicanism in the sixteenth
century. The Congregation of the Council was obliged to

---

[1] Morning and Evening Prayer give a much greater share to the laity,
which may account for their ' popularity ' compared with the Communion in many places to-day.

condemn several Spanish devotional writers who taught that it is *better* for the laity to communicate out of Mass. It is in the sixteenth century, too, that Communion quite apart from Mass and sacrifice, ' Communion from the Tabernacle' with the reserved sacrament, first becomes a common practice of the Roman Catholic laity. Looking at the matter broadly, from the standpoint of the history of eucharistic devotion rather than of technical eucharistic theology, it is not unjust to say that Cranmer's Communion Service would seem to be only one instance among many of that ' atomised' individualistic eucharistic piety which was common to the devotion of the Reformation and the Counter-Reformation alike in the sixteenth century. We can trace its roots back into the individualistic mystical piety of the unreformed sixteenth century. Its real stimulus was the mediæval breakdown of the whole idea of the ' liturgy' as the priestly service to God of His whole ' Holy People,' which included the laity just as fully as the clergy, in a single corporate action.

5. *The Church and the World*

If we seek the real explanation of this mediæval breakdown of the idea of the liturgy, we must, I think, again observe how closely it is connected with the breakdown of the primitive conception of the Church as " not of the world," as a separate creation from the world into which it was placed as the Body of Christ. In the magnificent but wrong-headed attempt to gain the whole world for God the Church came very near to losing her own soul. Outwardly the mediæval Church was dominant in the world; in fact the world and its princes dominated and constrained the action of the Church at every turn. Even in the fourth century the Church and the world were growing into one polity in the East. The process was quickly completed, to produce the Byzantine Empire, a Church-State neither secular nor religious. In the West it is the work of Charlemagne carried on by the Saxon and Suabian Emperors which achieves something of the same result—a Christian world in which the Church and the World are at one, but in which the Church loses much of that " separateness " which is the mark of the Body of Christ in a fallen world.   In the result, there never was a time when the Church had *less* freedom from political control of purely spiritual things by the secular power than in the Middle Ages.   The idea of the corporate action of the whole Body of Christ, either in the life of the Church or in the Eucharist almost disappears as an effective principle in the fourteenth and fifteenth centuries (witness *e.g.* the failure of the Conciliar Movement), though it subsists in ideals and phrases.

Here, too, Cranmer seems only to reduce what had been in fact the mediæval practice to theory, and to round off the whole mediæval development.   He has left us in his own hand and with his own signature his ideas on the nature of the " spirit-bearing " Body of Christ and its relations with the world.   " All Christian princes have committed unto them immediately of God the whole cure of all their subjects, as well concerning the administration of God's word for the cure of souls, as concerning the ministration of things political and civil governance.   And in both these ministrations they must have sundry ministers under them. . . . The civil ministers be those whom it shall please his highness for the time to put under him as *e.g.* the lord chancellor, the lord treasurer . . . sheriffs, etc.   The ministers of God's word under his majesty be the bishops, parsons, vicars and such other priests as shall be appointed by his highness to that ministration, as *e.g.* the bishop of Canterbury, the bishop of Durham . . . the parson of Winwick, etc.   In the admission of these officers be divers comely ceremonies and solemnities used, which be not of necessity, but only for a good order and seemly fashion; for if such offices and ministration were committed without such solemnity, they were nevertheless truly committed.   And there is no more promise of God that grace is given in the committing of the ecclesiastical office than it is in the committing of the civil office." [1]

[1] Cranmer (Parker Soc.), *Remains and Letters*, p. 116.

This was written in 1540. Fifteen years later he had not changed his mind. At his trial he insisted on defending the thesis that " Nero was the head of the Church, that is in worldly respect of the temporal bodies of men, of whom the Church consisteth. For so he beheaded Peter and the Apostles. And the Turk is head of the Church of Turkey." [1] Doubtless the civil ruler is a " minister of God "—but to be head of the Church it is at least necessary to be baptised and a member of it. And Nero—whom the Apostolic Church took for " the Beast " and Antichrist!

This is a doctrine which is ultimately irreconcilable with that of the Church as the mystical Body of Christ. It may be that one day the English Church will have to choose between them. But it is perhaps not surprising that rites compiled under the influence of such ideas fail adequately to express the primitive conception of the eucharist as the corporate act of the " spirit-bearing " Body of Christ.

The ' Liturgical Movement,' now rapidly growing in strength in the French and German Churches, has at least begun among the exiled Russians, and in the Greek *Zoe* movement, and in various ways among ourselves. It is no merely ecclesiological or archæological fad. It seeks to return behind the mediæval ' clerical ' distortion of the eucharist to the truer and deeper conception of the Church of the Martyrs, only because it has first recovered a more authentic notion of what is involved in the doctrine that the Church is the mystical Body of Christ, that the sovereign Spirit of the Risen Life of Jesus is the very breath of her life. It will be found that just in those quarters where the Liturgical Movement has obtained the strongest hold, there that new longing for the unity of all Christians, that new Catholic zeal for scientifically truthful historical studies, that new Catholic demand for social reforms, that new Catholic energy of Apostolate among those that have not the faith, both at home and abroad, have also found their most remarkable developments. This is not surprising. Where the Church is true to her calling as the Body of Christ, she must needs offer herself and all her members in

[1] Cranmer (Parker Soc.), *Remains and Letters*, p. 219.

sacrifice to God in union with the sacrifice of her Head. Like Him she can only find *thus* the consummation and fulfilment of her life in the world. And in Him this sacrifice of herself is perpetually accepted, perpetually fruitful " for the life of the world." But its price is a continual " dying to the world " that she may live, for she is " not of the world " as her Lord is " not of the world," and it must needs be that the world should hate that which is not its own, the " redemption " it perpetually needs.

These things are all in the Eucharist, rightly understood. St. Augustine said them long ago in words that have never been surpassed :

" The Congregation and Society of the Saints is offered in an universal sacrifice to God by the High Priest, who offered even Himself in the form of a servant for us in His passion, that we might be the Body of so great a Head. This form of a servant He offered, in this He was offered; for in this He is mediator and priest and sacrifice. And so the Apostle exhorted us that we should present our bodies a living sacrifice, holy, pleasing to God, our reasonable service, and that we be not conformed to this world but reformed in the newness of our mind, to prove what is the will of God, that which is good and well-pleasing and complete; which whole sacrifice we ourselves are. . . . This is the sacrifice of Christians: ' The many one Body in Christ.' Which also the Church celebrates in the sacrament of the altar, familiar to the faithful, wherein she is shown that in this that she offers, she herself is offered to God." [1]

[1] *de Civitate Dei*, ix. 6.

VI

LITURGY AND PERSONAL DEVOTION

By the Rev. C. PATRICK HANKEY
Vicar of St Mary's-the-less, Cambridge

LITURGY AND PERSONAL DEVOTION

1. Common Prayer and Private Prayer

Shortly after the war a young Englishman, who was working for the Y.M.C.A. in Salonika, took the opportunity provided by a short furlough to visit Mt. Athos and its monasteries. He had arranged, when his visit was at an end, to return to Salonika on foot through the hills, and as it chanced that an old monk of Athos had also to make that journey, it was agreed that they should travel together. All day they tramped over the hills, and at nightfall, having supped at a country inn, they shared a small bedroom. The young man knelt by his bedside and said his prayers before sleeping; when he rose from his knees he was startled to find that his companion was already in bed. Could he have gone to bed prayerless? In the morning the same thing happened; while the young Englishman was shaving, the monk rose, performed his hurried ablutions and undoubtedly left the room without prayer.

At the end of three days of one another's company, the Englishman, who had said his prayers night and morning without fail, was quite certain that the old ' religious ' had not once prayed. This omission was to him as incongruous as it was shocking. Before they parted at their journey's end he plucked up courage to ask the old man for an explanation of this omission of so obvious a duty. The monk was clearly surprised by the question, but quite ready to answer it. He pointed out that he was a member of a community—a worshipping body; every day and always the community offered its common prayer in liturgy and office. When he was there the monk took part in that prayer; when he was not there he could not take part in it, but the prayer went

147

on just the same. Was there anything else his young friend would like to know? He was very ready to instruct him.

The incident may serve as an introduction to the study of the subject of this essay, inasmuch as it shows how wide the cleavage can become, and has become, between the Liturgy and personal devotion. Common prayer and personal devotion, each so necessary to the other, are here seen almost completely separated—and yet sharing the same bedroom. It is only because they are sharing the same bedroom that the contrast becomes startling; the cleavage has been in existence for centuries and underlies the problem of our divisions and misunderstandings. Christians are continually puzzling one another and shocking one another in much the same way and for much the same reasons that the monk was puzzled by the representative of the Y.M.C.A. and the Y.M.C.A. man was shocked by the monk. We can agree that both were wrong, but may still be divided on the question ' which of them was farthest from the truth '?

The vast majority of our own people would affirm without hesitation that their countryman was nearest to the truth —indeed, it is doubtful whether they would admit that he was in the wrong at all. Private prayer was, until fairly recently, about the only religious exercise which church-people in this land regarded as being of obligation. (Not that we now recognise other religious exercises as having this nature; it is doubtful whether any religious act is now regarded as obligatory.) Daily private prayer was considered to be an obligation by the English churchman in the same sense as the Sunday Mass is an obligation for the Roman Catholic. His sense of the value of corporate prayer was weak, but he was touchingly regular about those he said in private.

These daily private prayers are still generally recognised as a Christian's duty, and a man will go on saying his prayers when every other religious practice has become infrequent or been abandoned. He feels that he can understand what they are for; they fit into his picture of reality; they are part of a man's individual religion, and religion is primarily the relation between the individual soul and God. These private prayers provide the means by which he holds communion with his Maker; they are the acknowledgment of the call of Jesus to each of us to a moral and spiritual reformation of life. The basis of all true religion is the soul saying to God 'My Father, which art in heaven.' [1]

Having given their vote emphatically in favour of the young Englishman and his private prayer, the same judges would go on to criticise the attitude of the monk towards corporate prayer. It seems so clear to them that the object of 'services' is to stimulate personal devotion—that if a service does not do that, if it does not fit into a man's life of personal devotion and help him to grow in holiness, it has no object, and can safely be neglected. There is even something insincere in taking part in a service unless it is the expression at that moment of the worshipper's religious feelings. The monk knew nothing apparently of this personal aspect; he only seemed to know about corporate prayer, to which he attached extraordinary importance; indeed, he seemed to believe that his liturgy and offices had, as it were, a life of their own and that he could rest on the knowledge that they were being offered to God in his absence. It was certain that he would assert the supremacy of corporate prayer over private prayer; it was probable that he would assert that there was no such thing as private prayer.

We are not bound to answer the question 'which was

[1] In view of this, it is curious to observe how small a contribution to the knowledge of the subject has been made by the English Church since the Reformation—or indeed before it. In spite of the importance attached to it, it does not appear that her members have ever received much instruction on the subject of how they should offer those private prayers or have been led to believe that there was anything much to be learnt. They receive the impression that praying is something which any Christian should be able to do without instruction. A child, of course, must be taught some prayers to say; an adult can easily find out for himself. There is nothing to be learnt from the experience of others in the present or the past. The result in many cases is known to have been that men and women have continued to say childish prayers, with a few additional petitions, until old age. And it is beyond question that many people in our day abandon even the practice of private prayer as having no value for them, before they have learnt how to pray or have taken any steps at all to discover elementary facts about its nature—as though one laid aside the violin as a 'rotten instrument' after some desultory attempts to teach oneself to play it.

L

farthest from the truth?' Common prayer and personal devotion are not rivals. But we recognise that the monk has right on his side to this extent, inasmuch as common prayer is prior to personal private devotion. The person who gives his unhesitating judgment in favour of private prayer would also unhesitatingly say that the primary business of religion is to help the individual to lead a good life. If this is indeed so, the Church has changed her mind as to the nature of her being and the purpose of her existence, for her belief *was* that she was a worshipping body, not a body of worshippers, and that her worshipping prayer—the common prayer she offered as the Church—was her great task.

No one would be so foolhardy as to depreciate the importance of the religious experience of the soul. As Dr. Wotherspoon wrote, " The truth that Christianity and its exercise necessarily demand social faith and social life may be overstated: Robinson Crusoe might be a sound Christian before the arrival of Man Friday, and St. Simeon on his pillar was surely a Christian of some sort. The spiritual life is always lonely because it is personal and in much cannot be shared, and the salvation of one's own soul is not so contemptible a quest as some hold it to be. Personal religion is all important." [1] But we must recognise, as the monk of Mt. Athos recognised, that we exist primarily as members of a worshipping body. Those prayers by the bedside, so infinitely important, cannot be regarded as the norm of Christian prayer if he who offers them thinks of them as being his private business.

We belong, we are told, to a praying Church, but that might imply no more than a belief that we belong to a body of people which regards prayer as one of its various duties. The truth is more important and exciting than that. The Church does indeed say to us, ' Remember, my children, to say your prayers '; but she says first and says more emphatically, ' Remember, my children, that you belong to a body which is a praying body, in the sense that it is itself,

[1] *Religious Values in the Sacraments.* Croall Lectures, 1926–27 (p. 290).

so to speak, a prayer.' The prayer of the Church is there
already: that is where the monk was so right. What we
have to learn to do—or to remember to do—is to join in it,
to put *our* prayer, such as it is, into that living stream: that
is where the monk was surely remiss. The Church's prayer
is for the Christian *the* prayer, and there is no other Christian
prayer beside or in addition to the prayer of the Church:
our private prayers have no existence of their own: they
live only as part of the prayer of the Church.

2. THE CHURCH'S PRAYER

"Mutual prayer," wrote Khomiakoff, "is the blood of
the Church." We do not describe the circulation of the
blood as a duty of man, but as part of his physical existence.
So prayer is not a duty of the Church, which is the Lord's
Body, but a part of her being. The Church has no life of
her own; she has only the Lord's life—His livingness: the
Church's aliveness is the Lord's aliveness; and the Lord
Himself is the Christian prayer.

> And having with us Him that pleads above,
> We here present, we here spread forth to Thee
> That only offering perfect in Thine eyes,
> The one, true, pure, immortal sacrifice.

That is not the gushing fervour of a 'dévot,' but the
sober statement of a theologian. The Body of the Lord
which He presents to the Father as a sacrifice pure and
immortal, bearing still the marks of our usage of Him, is
the Christian prayer. And the Church is the Lord's Body;
not in the sense that she is a body of people who have
declared their allegiance to the Lord, but in the sense that
she is primarily Christ Himself in His own being. He is
the living whole: we are only part of that whole. Prayer,
then, is not one of the duties which the Church undertakes,
as once she undertook the duty of providing the means of
education. It is part of her being, because it is part of the
Lord's being. To be a member of the Church is to be part
of that prayer which is the Lord's prayer. When, therefore,
we make our most private and urgent prayers in some

private and urgent need of our own or of someone we love, we *can* only pray as *church people*, and so must join our poor little private prayer to the corporate prayer which is always going up to God out of the Church's being, which is Christ Himself. It is of this truth that we are reminded when we end each prayer " through Jesus Christ our Lord."

It is in the Liturgy that this fact receives its most complete earthly expression. It was in the breaking of the bread that the Church first learned what Christian prayer is, and Christians of to-day must still learn this lesson there. The standard type of Christian prayer is common prayer: that is what the Lord taught us not only in the Liturgy, but also in the ' Our Father.' We are to learn how to pray by ourselves by having learned first how to take part in corporate prayer, for it is in that act that we discover how to pray as members of the Body of Christ. If we try to reverse this process —thinking of prayer as being primarily our private communion with God—we shall hardly keep from thinking of common prayer as the gathering of a number of people to say their private prayers together, a thing very difficult to achieve and of doubtful utility.

The objections to corporate prayer which are commonly met with to-day are due in large measure to a reversal of this process. It is indeed difficult to offer private prayers in public. The presence of other people, the necessity for making the concerted movements of the service—these and many other necessaries of common worship distract the individual in his private devotion. One reason for the popularity of Low Mass in Western Europe is the opportunity it provides for undisturbed private prayer.[1] The solemn Eucharist, in which as many as possible, both clergy and laity, have a specific part to perform in the service, and everything is used for worship which can be used for that

---

[1] This is not an adverse criticism of the quiet and the silences of that service. These are as valuable as the corporate silences of Quaker worship. It is a criticism of the person who prefers the low celebration of the Holy Communion because there is there the least interference with the soul's private communion with God. One cannot help suspecting that some Christians would prefer that the Church should not be thronged with worshippers at that service.

purpose, is often appreciated as an act of congregational worship to be preferred to sung Mattins as the leisurely and not too exacting devotion of the later hours of Sunday morning. But although this whole, corporate, dramatic act is the least inadequate form of worship, not so much because of its dignity as because it is most clearly the act of the whole Christian people, yet many devout church-people express a preference for making their communion at a Low Mass, in spite of its inadequacies and sacerdotalisms. In effect they are saying 'Since corporate prayer is at times unavoidable, let it be as little distracting as possible; that is what matters most.' This suggests that the task of living in communion and fellowship with one's fellow-men is not particularly difficult or important, and that the final vision of God is to be like a private view of an exhibition of pictures.

It is precisely these difficulties and distractions of common prayer which make it so valuable, and which help to keep Christians within the stream of the catholic and apostolic life. The stuff of religion is not the refined desires and delicate movements of the soul reaching out after spiritual experience as though it were disembodied, but the common things of life—its 'bread and wineness,' and the bodies which the Apostle besought his brethren to offer as a living sacrifice, and our human environment which is largely a physical environment. It is out of this stuff that our prayer is made.

We are to learn, then, how to make prayer in private by having learnt first how to join in common prayer: we do not learn how to take our part in common prayer by learning first how to pray as individuals. Common prayer provides the visible setting of the earthly Church and its earthliness, which we have to make ourselves remember when we are praying by ourselves. That is why the church-man finds corporate prayer so great a means of grace; but when we use prayer as a means of self-perfection—praying, in order to make ourselves better—we find common prayer tiresome. We have forgotten then that 'being made better' is a by-product of prayer, not its purpose.

3. The Training of the Laity in Prayer

For their training in this life of personal devotion—a devotion of which the Lord explained the nature in the breaking of bread and the Our Father—the Church made ample provision for both the clergy and laity of her first generations. The clergy are still adequately provided for: whether they use the means or not, their part in the Liturgy and their duties in the matter of the daily offices afford them ample opportunity for this training. We shall deal with this subject at a later stage. What concerns us at the moment is the fact that, for many centuries, the training of the laity in personal devotion after the Scripture model has been laborious and difficult owing to their virtual exclusion from the action of the Liturgy. The service has come more and more to have the appearance of an offering made by the priest in the presence of the people. This is due in part to the substitution of Low Mass for High Mass as the normal communion service; in part also it is due to alteration in the manner of celebrating High Mass; in the process of simplification some of the acts which used to remind the people of their share in the mystery have disappeared.

In our own country this training in personal devotion through participation in common prayer has a history of its own. On the one hand we have had certain advantages denied to other church-people. The use of the vernacular in the Liturgy has made it possible for the laity to take part in the prayer of the Church and prevented them from feeling that they are quite unnecessary. Of equal importance has been their admission to the offices. In this matter the Church in these provinces set herself the task of making a morning and an evening office which could be used by clergy and people: they were built out of the old materials which had been used for the prayer of God's people for centuries: they fitted on to the Liturgy and derived their life from it in the way the offices should. This was potentially a great aid to the people's personal devotion. They could grow accustomed to the Church's prayer and learn how to make their own prayers in union with her prayer

—learn to say ' Our Father ' instead of ' My Father.' But the fate of the Liturgy prevented this reform from having its full effect. The admirable desire that every Mass should have its consummation in a general communion led to the Liturgy being celebrated infrequently: the offices became separate services—services one attended instead of the Liturgy. The people no longer learnt how to take their part in them by having first learnt how to take their part in the Eucharist. Divorced from the Eucharist, the meaning of Mattins and Evensong was not apparent, and they could not be the guide to personal devotion which they should have been. Moreover, when people did attend the Liturgy, it was celebrated without any active assistance from them beyond the collection of the alms by a clerk or churchwarden. In view of these grave deficiencies in his training, it would hardly be surprising if the layman believed that he was most Christian when he was alone; if he thought that his religious feelings and experiences were the all-important thing in religion; if he failed to realise that the sustaining element alike in common worship and private prayer is the pleading of Christ's Name, and that his personal devotion can only be grounded on that act of faith which is without ceasing.

Further, when it is remembered that for several centuries there has been no effective reminder in any liturgical service of the communion of saints, no petition direct or indirect for their prayers; that during that same period there has also been no public memorial of the departed such as formerly occurred in almost every office: that the people of God have been taught that it was useless to ask the saints for their intercession and wrong to go on making those prayers for departed souls which they offered for them when they lived—it would again be hardly surprising if the present generation of Christians tried to pray alone instead of with the Church on earth and in communion with the faithful departed and the blessed company of heaven.

In point of fact this has not happened as generally as, and to the extent that, one might have expected, though such grave deficiencies have necessarily had grave conse-

quences. That it has not happened to a greater extent
among church-people is due, in large measure, to the
observance among us of the liturgical year. There have
been periods when even this became feeble, but at the
present time it is steadily becoming more widespread and
more thorough. Even among Free Churchmen the
observance is gaining ground.

The Church's observance of the liturgical year is a
practice which has immense value and a deep effect on the
personal devotion of her members. Especially is it valuable
as a means of preserving and increasing the sense of fellowship in prayer. By directing the attention of everyone to
one particular mystery of God and His Christ, so that all
worship God at the same time for the same blessing of His
manifested love, the Church keeps us together and draws
into the stream of her prayer the most private worship of
her individual members. By setting forth her Lord's
incarnate life in its glorious order, she leads her children,
almost without their knowing it, to realise that He Himself is
their one prayer and to think of themselves as members of
that Body. By her commemoration of the saints—their
birth, their conversion or their death—she does something
to keep before her children the destiny which God has for
them as members of the Christian family, and the nature
of that heavenly life for which they must prepare themselves
here—that life as part of the beloved community whose
animating spirit is God. Finally, by her appointed seasons
for general fasting and penitence she sets them all thinking
and praying together about the actual estate of life in
which they live here, and joining corporately in the penance
and discipline which the facts of that estate make necessary.
They learn then that sin itself is corporate in its nature—that
" men make an implicit compact not with Death and Hell
alone but with one another, to hold down the truth in
unrighteousness, to connive at an outraged social order, to
tolerate the inertia of selfishness, to prostitute the divine
standard of purity to the debased usage of the world." And
because sin is corporate, the penance, the discipline, and the
sorrow must be corporate too.[1]

[1] Dr. Kirk on the Atonement, in *Essays Catholic and Critical*, p. 269.

Such is in brief outline the provision made by the Church in this land for the training of her children for the vision of God. Her directions are sufficiently clear, and the means she has provided for following those directions are adequate. That her children have not always followed her directions as carefully as they should, and that some of the means she provided fell almost into disuse for a considerable period of time, are due to causes which it is not the business of the present essay to discuss. What is of great interest to observe is—that when men began to take her formularies seriously once again and to study her directions, as the Tractarians did, the result was not only a renewed sense of the Church and her fellowship, but also a great deepening of the desire for personal devotion. The history of the last hundred years provides strong proof that common worship, when it is really worship, is the parent of that private devotion which is its counterpart. Such great changes as the startling revival of the Religious Life for men and women, the renewed study of prayer and its orderly practice, the growth of the habit of making a retreat, and the use of confession as a normal means of grace, are immensely significant. Although each of these can be regarded as the result of an individual desire for personal growth in holiness, yet each of them has arisen out of the movement which the Tractarians originated, each has been born of a new sense of the fellowship of the Church, and each depends for its fruitfulness upon a lively awareness of membership of the Church.

We do not propose to deal here with the revival of the Religious Life; but something further should be said about those three means of graces for ordinary church-people to which we have just referred—prayer, retreats and confession.

(a) *Prayer*. In these last decades we have witnessed a great change in the practice of private prayer. Among church-people and also among the ' religious-minded ' it is increasingly realised that there is much to learn about it. Many new books have been written on the subject and old books have been reprinted; most of these have a considerable sale. As evidence of interest in the study of prayer this is very encouraging, but in some ways it is not without its danger. In the first place, while it is true that the Christian ought to know about prayer as a subject of study, in outline at least, such knowledge by itself will not enable him to pray. It would be possible to be an expert in the literature of the subject without knowing anything of prayer itself. Secondly, it is confusing to read many books on such a theme. It is much more profitable to know one or two books thoroughly and to read them often at intervals in one's life. Thirdly, the great books about prayer have been written by men who have assumed that their readers had around them a strong Church life. Their description of prayer and their advice about its practice can be gravely misleading to those who are living outside the Church's fellowship and without her sacraments.

These writers assume, in fact, that their readers think of themselves as members of a worshipping body, that they know that man cannot " present himself before God in and from the midst of his natural desires and necessities," [1] that " mere man cannot pray at all." When eucharistic worship is a normal activity of our life, we naturally think of our private prayer as having that nature—or rather we do not think of it, for we do not know of any other way to pray. " The Eucharist is our co-operation with Christ in his heavenly ministry " (what else is prayer?), " or equally it is His co-operation with us in our approach to God " (again, like prayer). " Christ cannot be alone: there is nothing in which He says to us ' I have no need of you; ' in His glory as in Gethsemane He calls us to be with Him. And apart from Christ we can do nothing—least of all ' do this.' " [2]

Without that background of eucharistic worship, it is so easy to conclude that it is a good thing to pray because prayer provides the best means of dealing with our reactions to the difficult and tiresome elements in our lives, or because it comforts us to do so. We do not pray in order to make our lives, even our interior lives, easier. We do not even

[1] A. L. Lilley, *Prayer in Christian Thought*, quoted by Dr. Kirk, *Vision of God*, p. 438.
[2] Wotherspoon, *ibid.*, p. 242.

pray in order to make ourselves better. Either or both of these may be the result of prayer, but neither is its purpose. That purpose is to see God in the face of Jesus Christ and, having seen, to adore: it is to engage ourselves in that human activity by which we express an unselfish love of God: of that love so expressed there is bred the desire that God's will may be done by us and all men, in order that His love of us may have fruit.

The nourishment of the Christian's prayer is the Christian's Communion. In the Communion there is immediate contact with the actual Divine: there is also the vital unity of all believers inhering together in Christ. He prays as a communicant, aware of God-given communion with God and man; he is wise if he brings his private prayer into as close a contact with his Communion as he can contrive, either by offering it before or after that act, if there is opportunity, or by deliberately recollecting the gift he has received before he begins to pray, or by making his prayer in a place where the Sacrament is reserved.

Another practice which is most profitable for lay people is the reading of the psalms and lessons appointed for the day, or of some part of them. For a busy Christian this may be impossible, or at least inadvisable, owing to the danger of his reading through the passage in a hurry as a task to be accomplished; but there is a large number of people who can make sufficient time for this, and should be able to exercise the discipline necessary for its profitable performance. There are many who already use this means of grace; but it is doubtful whether their number is increasing, as it should be.

As a school of personal devotion the psalms and lessons are invaluable. They speak the same language as the Mass; " for both in the Old and New Testament everlasting life is offered to Mankind by Christ, who is the only Mediator between God and Man, being both God and Man " (Article VII). The psalms teach us to worship God through Jesus Christ: in them we hear Christ speak on His own and on our behalf as the Lord's Anointed and as our Mediator. The very fact that their sentences so often make nonsense if we try to think of them as our prayer rather than His, teaches us what prayer is and how it is to be made, almost without our being aware of it. As for the lessons from the other Scriptures, they provide the food which is essential for our meditation. From them we derive the knowledge of God and of His ways with man which is the substance of prayer; to read them with thought and slowly is to obey His injunction to us 'learn of Me.' Here God reveals to us what we are like and what the world needs by showing us Himself: here also He teaches us how these selves of ours may be changed, and what we are to do for other people.[1] The private prayers of church-people would be immeasurably healthier if the Church's office or some part of it was more generally used as their basis.

(b) *Retreats.* The increase in the number of lay people who go into retreat from time to time is a most important change —especially as this habit begins to extend to the busy and the 'not particularly religious.' Parish priests have plenty of experience of the spiritual growth which generally results from the use of this means of grace. They can also bear witness to the fact that the desire to make a retreat normally arises in a soul when a sense of membership of the Church has been quickened, and is not the result of a desire to find its own way to God. Even a few members of a parish who make an annual retreat have the effect of strengthening the sense of membership of Christ's Body in the rest of the Family in that place. Certainly the fruitfulness of a retreat depends, as we have said, in large measure on a lively awareness of that membership in the retreatant.

For this reason it is not to be regretted that the laity generally take part in a retreat which is given for a number

---

[1] On the subject of the use of the Gospel as a source of our meditation Fr. W. Knox writes: " Our use of these subjects will have the further advantage of our counteracting the tendency, which is quite noticeably common in modern Christianity, to regard the person of our Lord as if He was merely the hero of a 'mystery religion,' who has saved us by His death and resurrection, and has handed down to us certain means of salvation, but of whom nothing else is known. We must always remember that He is not merely a divine Redeemer, but also a human example; the modern decline of Bible reading makes us liable to forget this." *Meditation and Mental Prayer*, p. 36.

of people, instead of doing so in solitude. The presence of others, even though they are strangers, checks individualism; but it is a pity that parochial retreats are so difficult to arrange, for they could be most profitable. When individuals, by choice or of necessity, make a retreat by themselves, they may well be advised to do so at a religious house. The community life, its common prayer and common table, provide a background which may counteract the effects of their solitariness as retreatants.

(c) *Confession.* Another change which has occurred in these last decades is the increased use of sacramental confession as an ordinary means of grace. Here again the parish priest can testify that the use of this sacrament not only marks very often the abandonment of a superficial religiousness, but is the result of a deepening of the desire to share the mind of the Church towards sin, and to be united with her in her penitence, as completely as possible.

It may indeed happen that at the beginning the adoption of this practice is due to a sense of the soul's individual uncleanness and the desire to have for oneself that pardon, peace and quiet mind which everyone naturally desires to have. Nor does it ever cease to be something that happens between the soul and God, a movement of the soul in penitence towards Him, a movement of God in forgiveness towards the soul. But as it becomes a normal part of the Christian's practice, the Church both in heaven and on earth and all his fellow-creatures are more and more present to the mind of the penitent. Not only does he learn to think of himself as joining as fully and as radically as he can in the Church's penance, but he realises also ever more vividly the extent of his indebtedness both to the elect people of God and to all mankind, because he is what he is and has done what he has done. He knows more clearly than he ever knew before the need of submitting his acts and omissions to their judgment, and the need of receiving their forgiveness for the injury he has done them by his secret sins as well as those that are known, since all alike have altered for the worse that person they had a right to have as their fellow-creature and fellow-member of the Church.

Sacramental confession, like those other practices, depends for its fruitfulness very much upon the strength of our awareness of being a member of God's family.

4. THE PRAYER-LIFE OF THE PRIEST

We have dealt, very briefly, with the personal devotion of the laity before considering that of the clergy, because much that has been said about the former applies equally to the latter. There is, for instance, nothing special to be noted about the use of sacramental confession or a retreat by a priest. But it may be well, in conclusion, to give special attention to the priest's duties in the matter of the Liturgy and the offices, and observe what it is that he learns from them about the life of prayer.

First, he cannot very well make any mistake about the Liturgy as the common prayer of the Church. When he is himself the officiant at the service he has no opportunity and therefore no temptation to turn it into a private prayer: nor will he then regard his official duties in the conduct of the service as a distraction from true devotion, since everything he is ordered to do, every gesture he has to make, as well as every word he is ordered to say, is part of the prayer. His particular function in the Church teaches him how to make himself part of the Church's prayer, and he does not forget this lesson even when he takes part in the Eucharist without being the celebrant.

What he has learnt in the Liturgy he applies to his private prayers. He will do this the more readily if he is able to offer some portion of them before or after the Mass. Part at least of his pastoral intercession should be offered after the thanksgiving, while the Lord as our only Mediator and Advocate is still vividly present to his mind. Many priests find great profit in making their meditation immediately before or after they celebrate, since this helps them to avoid thinking of that difficult prayer as merely an individual exercise. This is not always possible; but it can anyway be made at an hour sufficiently early for them to be perceiving still the fruits of Christ's Redemption very clearly.

Both the Liturgy and the daily office will be in any case the source of his meditation, and indeed of his whole personal devotion.

Secondly, the divine office: the priest will bear in mind that, whether it is said in public or in private, it is always common prayer, and must never be treated as part of his private devotions. How much more possible it is for us to avoid this pitfall than it is for the Roman Catholic priest, whose office is of such length and so unsuitable for public recitation as a complete whole, that it has become in effect a part of the private prayer of the clergy—sometimes it almost seems as though the Mass itself was suffering this fate also. Whenever it is possible, the office should be said with others to take part in it. The priest must also exercise an interior discipline to prevent this prayer, which is part of the external discipline to which he is subject, from becoming merely the performance of a compulsory task. Only exceptional claims on his time can excuse him if he hurries into church to say the office and hurries out of it immediately afterwards. The recitation of the office is a more solemn undertaking than his private devotions. He may very profitably make a large part of his own evening prayers, such as his thanksgivings, self-examination and daily intercessions, before or after the Church's evening prayer, in the same way that he makes the Church's morning prayer the basis of his meditation.

Finally, to say that a priest's devotions are subsidiary to his public prayer is not of course to say that they are not of great importance. To neglect them in the least degree is to run the risk of becoming formal in the discharge of his primary duties. Indeed, the dependence of the priest upon his private devotions is far greater than that of the layman. There is, for instance, the preparation and thanksgiving for his communion—communions which he is bound to make as often as the Liturgy is to be celebrated, and not as often as he privately thinks best for him. Preparation and thanksgiving for communion received in such circumstances, with such frequency, must have the support of much meditation and prayer if they too are not to become formal. Furthermore, his dependence upon private devotion is greater than the layman's, for the very reason that his business is the doing of good works and the leadership in the people's common prayer. He may so easily suppose, unless his own prayer is deep and strong, that his public labours and prayers are a sufficient offering—forgetting that they are his job, like any other Christian's job. It is in his private devotions that he forms and expresses his intention to mean what the Church means and to will what the Church wills when he offers the Church's prayer.

VII

IDEALS FOR THE PARISH

By the Rev. J. F. LOVEL SOUTHAM
Canon of Chester

M

IDEALS FOR THE PARISH

I. IDEALS

1. *Churchmanship*

EVERY parish priest, if he is to do constructive work for the Kingdom of God, must have an ideal for his parish. At his institution he is solemnly handed the ' cure of souls ' from the Bishop; none can divest him of this, and nothing must stay his constant endeavour to be true to his trust. He is responsible for trying to discover what God would do with him and his people, and through them for the Church. The parish, though a unit, can never be regarded in separation from the whole Body, with which the Bishop who gave him his cure is the link. He must set himself constantly to seek to know the will of God, and he will find that will revealed to him not only in direct contact with God, but through consideration of God's call to the Church generally and the direction in which the Holy Spirit is guiding it at the particular time in which he is called upon to exercise the responsibility of leadership. It is urgent both for priest and people that they should be quick and alive to the fact that they are under obedience to God; the one thing that matters is that they should know the will of God and have courage to fulfil it. There can therefore be no place for self-will.

This involves a great plunge of faith in a present, living Lord. To hear the voice of the living God is to have the thrilling call and the glorious opportunity to enter into Life. Life, however, in the Chrisian sense, is always Resurrection; it therefore involves death. The Cross means the crossing out of self, personal and parochial. The conflict means conflict with the old Adam, with the mind of the flesh which always turns in on self, and is therefore deadly. It may mean

167

conflict with a wrong loyalty to the past which is a real treachery to the future. It will most surely mean conflict with principalities and powers which muster their unseen array whenever and wherever the Kingdom comes and the power of the Spirit is manifest. Christ promised ' not peace but a sword '; the sword comes and the sword divides. There must be a conflict of loyalties and a responsibility of choice, wherever religion is alive and issues are laid bare. The peace of Christ is a thing that has to be fought for, that we have to prove ourselves worthy of; it is never, even when possessed, an end in itself, but to be prized as the condition of effective work to the glory of God.

" It takes the ideal to blow an inch inside the dust of the actual "; this is true in parochial life, as many a parish priest knows to his cost. His first problem lies with the number of people to whom peace means stagnation, who do not want to think, and do not want to change themselves, the Church or the world. Yet the God with whom we have to do has made mankind and His creation new at the price of the Cross; and He calls on His Church to fulfil His work. This is impossible without a renewal of those to whom ' religion ' is a convention, and ' Christian ' a name, and ' faith ' a peradventure, with a query and a note of caution.

If this be so in a parish—there are few of which it is not in some measure true—it is clear that fresh starts will have to be made and new developments be called for. The parish priest therefore whose care is for the Kingdom of God must be oppressed with a sense of urgency: he will only be saved from that sense of urgency passing into one of impotence, by being beaten to his knees, and his people with him. It becomes clear that, under present conditions of Church life, ' the people ' will not be represented by the whole congregation. Not all the congregation will be prepared to count the cost or pay the price that a revolution of love involves. It is precisely such a revolution that the Church is waiting for—and the world—but the Church must undergo it first. Revolutions are things of blood, and the revolution of love involves the blood of sacrifice. That is the pith of the New Testament message.

There must be a process of testing, of sifting—a ' calling out ' of those who are ready to be ' the soul of the Church.' These people will set out with their parish priest to learn to know the will of God, and to witness to that will at any cost to themselves, by translating it into action. For this there are no short cuts, no easy ways. It is not a mere question of new methods or fresh organisation; people matter more than methods, and the living Body of Christ more than any organisation. The Body of Christ is created, not made; its life is dependent upon the God who gave it. Pentecost follows Calvary and Resurrection; we must know this not as a fact only, but as a living present practical experience. The Spirit descends to-day where He can find a group of people prepared to receive and transmit Him.

So Christ worked through comparatively few on whom He spent Himself; His purpose for them was fulfilled only when He got them—with how much labour—past Calvary to Resurrection and to Pentecost. Dead, they could become— the Church: not simply ' a fortuitous concourse of (spiritual) atoms,' but the mystical Body in being, built up in sacramental worship and fellowship, learning together what Christian love and service really mean.

It is evident that such a corporate life must make demands upon the individual. " I, the prisoner in the Lord, beseech you to walk worthily of the calling wherewith ye were called, with all lowliness and meekness, with long suffering, forbearing one another in love; giving diligence to keep the unity of the Spirit in the bond of peace. There is one Body and one Spirit, even as also ye were called in one hope of your calling; one Lord, one faith, one baptism, one God and Father of all." Humility will be the hall-mark of such Christians. There can be no turning in on self, for each will be coming to realise that the purpose of their existence in that Body is that of an apostolate. " Many parishes have not begun to understand what healthy corporate living is. Therefore right adjustment in fellowship must come through the formation of a central group which is training itself in the understanding of corporate life."

There must, however, be no direct and overt attempt to

form a group.   The call will be given to the whole congregation, to come and make something of the Church.   The
Church itself is the only Christian ' guild,' and that fact must
be recognised by all who respond to this invitation.   Priest
and people must grow together and act and react on each
other.   The people make the priest, as well as the priest the
people, through the Spirit.

Those who are setting themselves to ' live in the Spirit '
will inevitably begin to ' walk in the Spirit,' *i.e.* to find the
Christian way of life.   In this way they will grow in a living
theology, born of the experience that can only be won by the
experiment of faith.   No one who has shared this can ever
doubt the reality of what is to him the deepest and most
compelling experience in life.   Membership of a Communion
that embraces earth and heaven, that stretches beyond
humanity and time to the Eternal Father ' of whom and unto
whom are all things,' provides something worth living for.
It is because so much is involved in this, which is almost
completely unrecognised by a large majority of those who
compose our congregations, that it seems clear that the only
way to bring it home is through those, be they few or many,
who will set themselves to live out Churchmanship in the
New Testament sense.

We pass on to consider how they are to grow in the knowledge of that which a living Church exists ultimately to impart.
We must possess before we can transmit.   Speaking broadly,
we may say that their life will grow in a ' virtuous circle '
of prayer, fellowship and service.   In this, they will follow
in spirit in the steps of the Scriptural Church.   They will
express their life in action, and by that action find both their
faith and their life increasingly deepened and renewed.   We
seem so often in the world to be in the grip of vicious circles,
that it is all the more inspiring to try to trace a virtuous one.

2. *Development through Teaching*

Christ was first a Teacher: His theme was God and His
Kingdom, and the meaning of human life in relation to Him.
The law and the prophets had been until John: from that
time onwards the Kingdom of God was being preached.

He pointed forward to a new dispensation in which the Holy
Spirit should be the Teacher, leading into all Truth. In
the upper room before the Passion His great desire was to
prepare them to pass on in thought, from a Christ whom they
had 'beheld' and 'known' after the flesh, to one whom they
should 'see' with the eye of faith, and therefore know in a
fuller way, after the Spirit. In the great forty days there
came the teaching on 'the things pertaining to the Kingdom
of God,' the sacramental Kingdom. They should find it to
be the special sphere of grace and truth, through the Spirit.
This Kingdom is created, not made, at Pentecost. Into it
the Christian is born, not merely co-opted, by a Baptism of
the Spirit into one Body. This, because it has to do with
birth, is fundamental and primary. The doctrine of
Baptism is a 'first principle' of the Catholic Church.

This is one of the first things the group would have to set
themselves to think out. Holy Baptism, the Sacrament
of Initiation, has been allowed to fall far too much into the
background in thought and practice. A new recognition of
the true place of the Font can be created in the parish, by
Holy Baptism being ministered within the Divine Office,
as the Prayer-book directs. The Sermon, which is not
ordered at Evensong, can be omitted, or be briefly directed
towards this particular point—the meaning of Holy Baptism
in Church life. There are here many significant things to
be learned. All must be born again, all must alike pass
through this door. Here is the beginning of that unity
which is the priceless possession and characteristic of the
Catholic Church: a spiritual unity that on the level of grace
transcends all the natural things that divide and which
are too strong for human nature to conquer. "Rational
ethics cannot form a community; irrational instincts are
too strong." Holy Baptism points to the one transcendent
source of fellowship which the Church in every parish needs
to realise, to a brotherhood that is as wide as the Fatherhood
of God.

Baptism into a common Faith is the root of the obligation
of Sponsorship in the widest sense—that mutual care for
the highest good of one another which should be the glory of

the Church. It is because of our common Baptism that we should help one another to live out our Christian profession. Indeed, the seed-germ of the mystical Body lies in the Font: it is here, therefore, that a revived Churchmanship must begin, it is here that we learn our first lessons in the meaning of Catholicity. It is here too, alas, that nominal Christians have been manufactured by the thousand: no one could imagine indiscriminate Baptism being practised by the scriptural Church, nor is it possible to square it with the teaching of our Prayer-Book. The Acts and the Epistles gain fresh interest when we go to them to discover how the Apostles and those associated with them taught and practised the fundamentals of Church life. The rank and file of the Church need to study Apostolic first principles. Faith and Life must go together; the only way to know is to " do the doctrine." " If we live by the Spirit, by the Spirit let us also walk." We now pass on to consider how this life which has its centre in God is to find its true expression.

3. *The Expression of Life in Worship*

There is perhaps no direction in which we have more widely gone astray from reality than in our thought and practice of Worship. We have only to reflect upon what the phrase ' a place of worship ' denotes in the popular mind. So far from reaching out and up towards high heaven, it is concerned primarily with self: a place where one goes to get something, and the highest thing that is expected is the personal achievement of spiritual uplift. It is doubtful what a self-centred soul can conceive this to be, or for what particular end it is sought. One thing is certain: that it is an entirely different thing from that complete losing of self in God which true worship involves; it begins at the wrong end.

From much of the teaching that is given about worship it would be hard to gather that ours is a religion that has its centre in the being and in the claim of God, and not in the needs of men. Here the word ' cater ' has much to answer for, and its implications are far-reaching. Great is the responsibility of those whose duty it is to lead and to teach God's people in this vital matter.

Christian Worship ascends to the Father through Christ, humanity's High Priest, " who through the eternal Spirit offered himself without spot to God " : in the worship of the Apocalypse the Lamb is on the Throne. In other words, it is sacrificial worship, a response to God which is essentially a dying to live. It is God Himself, not spiritual uplift, that the assembled hosts are seeking there, and it is because God is the object of their search that they, losing themselves, are caught up to highest heaven.

All life finds its true purpose in surrendering to and serving the order of being that is higher than itself. Life rises upwards only through sacrifice. Life in man finds its goal in a willed and purposeful surrender to the divine eternal Order, and by that surrender is capable of the transforming touch of grace.

Clearly it is in the Holy Eucharist that we are at the centre of Worship and of Grace. Here we offer Nature's offerings of corn and grape transformed by men's hands into bread and wine, a sacrament of labour offered for use in the eternal Order, to be transfigured into the sacramental Body and Blood of Christ, a sacrament of grace. The reception of that transforming gift from above welds us anew into the mystical Body, while ' strengthening and refreshing ' our personal lives. It is by that self-oblation which is Worship that the Church perpetually offers itself; it is through that sacrificial activity that we are made capable of grace.

It is significant that ' the Name of God ' constantly recurs in the eucharistic Liturgy. In the fixed parts of the Prayer Book rite it comes eight times, and each of these contexts is worthy of study : and the recitation of the Creed is a great proclaiming of the Name. The Name of God denotes His being, His character, and His relationship to men; and round the Name the thread of devotion is woven. We see this very clearly in the Psalms, which will always remain the classics of Christian devotion. It is on this principle that the Lord's Prayer is built; and it must guide all prayer that is to be in line with that and with the Liturgy. The basis of our approach to God in both Scripture and Prayer Book is what we believe about God—the Creed—not our own needs and desires.

Such prayer will save us from the self-centred attitude which has penetrated so deeply both into our thought about God and into our religious practice, corporate and personal. Here lies the root of many difficulties about prayer, both speculative and practical.

It is indeed a matter of fundamental importance for us all, clergy and people, whether our worship is really ' in spirit and in truth,' as God would wish to see it. ' Lift up your hearts ' is the trumpet-call which summons to such worship; the living heart of the Church in a parish consists of those who are setting themselves in spirit and in truth to answer ' We lift them up unto the Lord.'

Here is the centre; but this liturgical attitude and spirit must be carried out into all prayer-life. It is not too much to say that in many parishes and many lives this must involve a revolution. It will demand a steadfast seeking to find and to respond to God in prayer; it means that all prayer will be linked on to Eucharist—a sacrificial activity, an activity that depends on the realisation of the promised Presence: " Where two or three are gathered together in my name, there am I in the midst of them." " Thy Father seeth in secret."

A living Church will set itself not only to make the altar the centre of worship, but also to learn more fully to know the meaning of this; to develop corporate prayer in other ways and to grow in the personal prayer-life of its members. All this must accompany and lie behind the development of worship at the altar, if it is to be an offering of life such as conducts us to the threshold of heaven. It is God, and God alone, that such worship seeks. It is significant that the words of dismissal at the close of the Liturgy are these: " The Peace of God which passeth all understanding keep your hearts and minds in the knowledge and love of God." Our worship must correspond with the nature and character of the God we worship, and it is our worship that makes *us*, for it sets God free to touch our inmost hearts with His transforming grace.

4. *The Expression of Life in Fellowship*

" Worship and Charity are the twin glories of our destiny."
Worship is primary, but it has to be translated into terms of
Charity. " God is love." " Love is of God, and everyone
that loveth is born of God and knoweth God." " We know
that we have passed from death unto life because we love the
brethren." It is self-centred worship which is the root
cause of the low level of our spiritual fellowship in the Family
of God.

Not only has the Sacrament of Fellowship been made a
storm-centre of discussion and dispute among Christians
generally, but an individualistic outlook has penetrated into
the attitude of many of our regular communicants: they
live by the Body, and they are not of it. The individual goes
' to make his Communion ' oblivious of the fact, and the
implications of the fact, that it is *in* and *through* the Body
that he receives it. Such private souls can kneel week by
week at the same altar with the same people without ever
bothering to know who their neighbour is.

It was said in the Archbishops' Report on the Evangelistic
Work of the Church (1918): " Nothing appears more dis-
tinctly in the evidence than that the lack of fellowship within
the Church is at once a cause of stumbling to those without
and a source of weakness to those within. Men ask to see a
greater spirit of justice, brotherliness and kindness among
Christian people. The idea of the Church as a Fellowship
is almost non-existent. Men do not see in the Church a
brotherhood where those who worship together regard
themselves as belonging to one family in Christ." We look
at the Scriptural Church, and we see a unity that trans-
cended all differences on the human level and held in spite
of attacks from without, of divergences in outlook and policy,
of disagreements as to methods and differences in tempera-
ment within; through everything unity was never broken—
' in all things charity.' We look at the spiritual realities
represented in the Apocalypse, and we see a fellowship of
love surrounding the Throne in the midst of which is the
Lamb. It is a fellowship that is of like nature with the God

worshipped—a fellowship of the redeemed, of hearts in which pride is broken and where the writ of God's Love runs.

Charity is the hall-mark of the Church, Charity that begets humility in the soul and fellowship in the Body. " Where the Spirit is, there is the Church." It is Charity in its grand true sense that the world wants of the Church; it is going spiritually bankrupt for lack of it. Failure therefore in Charity is the failure that really matters.

It is a hard saying if we have to confess that we are not always conspicious for Charity in parish life, that often our fellowship is a spurious one spiritually, derived from hot air rather than the Holy Spirit. It is not Charity to reduce the demands that love and truth must make: at the heart of Christian truth and fellowship is the Cross of the Redeemer. It is not Charity to fail to bear witness to the truth, because the truth hurts: Charity often has to hurt, and hurt badly, and be hurt too in order to save: ' speaking truth in love.' It is not Charity to treat sin lightly; for its consequences are not light to the sinner or to the Church.

Failure in humility, in fellowship, in truth, in penitence, is first failure in worship. If people are learning to worship right, all things will follow—there is a wonderful inevitable-ness about the working of the Spirit of God in surrendered hearts. It is, indeed, only in realising how sin destroys corporate life that some souls come to penitence—" I have sinned against heaven and before thee." The ravages of self-will on the Body of Christ are open wounds, the effects of which all can see.

Often as we sadly watch people drifting away from the Church, we incline to attribute it to any other cause than that which is the true cause more often than we dare to think—poverty of spiritual life within the Body. Love has grown cold, that distinctively Christian thing for which a special word had to be coined: ' Agape.' Hence there has been nothing strong enough to hold in face of the insistent attacks from outside and a treacherous divided allegiance within. A renewing must come to the Church of such Charity as will make its fellowship a strong and compelling reality. This is especially so in the case of young people, whose human family is too often not a fellowship alive with Christian love; this makes it all the more important that the divine Family of the Church should be so.

Love begets life. Where the Body of Christ is alive it will grow, where it is not alive it is better by far that it should not attempt to extend. We have no right, in the Name of Christ, to bring people into something that cannot save them from themselves unto God. " That ye may have fellowship with us, and truly (as you shall find) our fellowship is with the Father and with his Son, Jesus Christ " —we must be able to say that or we can say nothing. The parish that is striving to represent the fellowship of the Catholic Church needs to ponder these things: and it will be a heart-searching business.

Here is an ideal of Catholic love that humanity on its own level is incapable of reaching. Men in their hearts know that nothing less than the universal will do, that anything less is counterfeit fellowship, a brotherhood without sonship, and therefore contrary to Nature, not above it. To ask for it is, indeed, to ask for a miracle in the old bad sense of something unnatural. Grace can accomplish what sinful men on the natural level, with their unruly wills and affections have no hope of achieving. The one enduring source of such fellowship is the altar. He who knows what is in man gave us that sacramental means of sacrificial fellowship—' one Bread, one Body.' We must make our Communion together the centre of our fellowship, in spirit and in truth, in our regular Church life. We need to enter more deeply into its meaning; and of the ways and means thereto the greatest is the ' sacrament of silence.'

This can be entered into by groups meeting together in church or private houses, but best of all by a group of people going away together into a *parochial* Retreat. It is the existing bond of fellowship which enables the Holy Spirit to weld them more deeply into one, and to bring home the great truth that there is no unity so strong as that which comes through the sharing of God together. When this exists it is wonderful what mighty works can be accomplished

in the souls of individuals even in one week-end, what entering into prayer and penitence, what hopes enkindled, what
resolves offered, what opportunities for service realised.
The greatest works of God are done in silence. The group
will descend from the ' mountain ' into the ' valley ' capable
of mighty works, with a new trust in God and confidence in
one another. Those who know that they belong to God
know that they belong to one another. It was out of the
heart of such a fellowship that the Apostles went out ' to
turn the world upside down,' to teach, to heal, to save with
a power which they knew was not theirs and belonged to
none of them individually, but the power of God possessed
in fellowship. Neither the Church nor individual Christians
can approach to being what God means them to be, save by
prayer. Prayer is the fundamental activity of the People
of God.

5. *The Manifestation of Life in Service*

Christian service is the fruit of worship and fellowship.
It has the glory of God for its motive, the Kingdom of God
as its goal, at its heart lies Charity: it is there ' disinfected
of egoism ': alive unto God, it is therefore life-giving. It
will be recognised that all such service must be inspired by
prayer—indeed, that intercession is itself the highest act of
service, the most real act of Charity. There will be groups
gathering for prayer, with the Parish Eucharist as the centre.
Thus will appear the working of the Spirit in the bestowal
of spiritual gifts—teaching, helps, healings, interpretations.
Some will find the children, others the sick, others their own
circle of friends the special sphere of their ministry. There
are many who need educated and spiritually developed
lay-people to help them—people who can give a reason for
the faith that is in them and speak wisdom amongst them
that are perfect. Certain it is that opportunities to witness
will come, and the power.

At the Parish Eucharist will be found the centre of spiritual
giving. It is significant that almsgiving, as opposed to pay-
ment, is contemplated in the Prayer Book only at this Service,
where the Church makes sacrificial response to the ' God
who so loved the world that He gave . . .' Systems of

giving are important, but more important is the inspiration of the spirit of giving, the development of givers. If giving is to be as St. Paul contemplated in ideal " a matter of bounty not of extortion," the givers must first give themselves to the Lord and to the Church. The secret of that spiritual thing, Christian Finance, is to be found at the altar: it is the motive that makes an alms. Under ' alms ' must be also included all acts of social service undertaken by Church-people for the love of God. These must not be merely haphazard, but directed, organised and technically effective. Charity needs to be crystallised: it has been too often allowed to evaporate. A living congregation will recognise that the work of the Church, including its extension at home and abroad, is their business because it is God's. There is no need to tug at the purse-strings of converted people; indeed, it is an outrage to do so. Equally outrageous is it to give or expect thanks for any act of service or offering that is done in the name of the Lord. It is a very dangerous thing to fail to foster the sense of privilege in all that has to do with Christian worship and life.

Here at the altar is the source of evangelistic zeal: true worship, real fellowship, sanctified service, have converting power. If there come into such a congregation " one unbelieving or unlearned, he is reproved by all, he is judged by all; the secrets of his heart are made manifest; and so he will fall down on his face and worship God, declaring that God is among you indeed " (I Cor. xiv. 24, 25). When life is ascending in the rhythm of worship other lives will be caught up, and " borne along unto perfection." When this is present, evangelisation is inevitable; without it, no true evangelisation is possible.

Bishop Westcott wrote, in *The Historic Faith*: " Constant habit deadens our sense of the grandeur of our communion of faith. If only a single congregation could enter into full possession of all that lies in the acknowledgment of the Divine allegiance which we agree to profess: if we could each feel, and then all act together as feeling, that faith in God as He has revealed Himself is the foundation, the rule, the life of our lives: there would be a force present to move the world."

6. *The Sunday Service*

The ideal here set forth is that of a ' corporate communion ' of the Church every Sunday, individuals coming because they love our Lord and are endeavouring to live in right relationship with Him and with the Family of God.

It must be recognised that this is an altogether different thing from an occasional ' corporate Communion ' of any organisation within the Church. In such there lies a grave danger of a cross loyalty and obligation cutting across that of the Church itself, and of a ' Test Act' attitude being fostered. Not only this, but the individual is often encouraged to come to such a corporate Communion from motives other than the love of God—this is a subtle and insidious danger which often seems to be quite unregarded. To make such a Parish Eucharist the central act of the week means in many a parish a reorientation, if not a revolution in eucharistic thought and practice.

From a practical point of view one obvious matter for serious thought is the hour. Time must be our servant, not our master. One important consideration is that it should not be so late as to make fasting Communion practically impossible. Some parishes might think it best to develop the 8 a.m. service into the Parish Eucharist. This has its difficulties. There will probably be some to whom the tradition of a quiet said service is of great and life-long value, and these must have provision made for them, though perhaps not every Sunday. It is also early for a great deal of singing or for a fairly lengthy service. There are usually difficulties also in getting school children at an earlier hour than they and their homes are accustomed to during the week. 10.30 or 11.0 is late for fasting Communion, late too for Sunday-School Teachers if there is a morning session. Those who want to get away after service will wish for an earlier hour, and it is wisdom to take this into consideration. If the service held at this hour is Morning Prayer, it is hopeless to attempt to build a Parish Communion, with all that is implied, upon that congregation.

We seem therefore almost compelled to try a fresh hour,

and if we are to begin with such a group as has been considered as a nucleus, it is far the best thing to do.   Such a
change as is contemplated should not be made without
at least a year of preparation and teaching about the
Sacrament and the Mystical Body of Christ which has its
life built up thereby; otherwise the attempt will be still-
born—just another idea that has not worked.   That way, the
last state is likely to be worse than the first.

Details are discussed elsewhere in this book.   But a word
must be said here about an important subsidiary point:
the Parish Breakfast.   This is, of course, a separate matter
from the Parish Communion; it is obviously not essential,
but there are advantages of a positive kind which argue for
its where it may be had.

1. A social meal in connection with ' the Breaking of
Bread ' was held in New Testament times—the ' Agape ' or
Feast of Charity.   It is more likely than not that there will be
something of spiritual value in a practice of the Scriptural
Church.   The fact that anything has been abused or misused
never contradicts the reality for which it stands.

2. Such a meal is of value in expressing the true idea and
place of social life within the Church.   It provides an
expression on the ordinary social level of that fellowship of
grace which has been found first at the Altar: the higher
comes first and transcends the lower but manifests itself
through it.   This is the right order; it produces social life that
is Christian: the other order does not work.   The Parish
Breakfast ought to set the tone of the social life of the
parish.

3. Here the fellowship of the Christian Family is deepened,
and in ideal it will include and embrace the natural human
families.   It is a delightful thing when a whole family is
able to be there together: the greater includes the less.
It is true that where this is not possible one or two members
of a family will not be at Sunday breakfast at home; but
often that is the least formal and social meal of the day,
whilst the advantage of the strengthening of the ties that
bind to the spiritual Family is great.

4. Unless such opportunity is given, it may mean in the
N

case of some, especially young people, that breakfast after communion is impossible. This is especially so with Sunday-school teachers where there is a morning session; and nothing could be better in ideal than that they should be able to go on to give their lesson straight from the heart of the Christian Fellowship.

II. The Final Goal

" Our citizenship is in heaven." However little we may know of the heavenly state, at least we know this—that it is a corporate life lived in the Presence of God, a fellowship of the redeemed. We want to be in line with the glimpse given to us in the Apocalypse of the spiritual realities that are true for earth and heaven. A worship, which is the adoration of the Lamb: a fellowship, redeemed, reconciled, and reconciling, which is the great Catholic Communion that no man can number: service, which is the selfless joy of the Saints, itself an act of praise: " His servants shall serve Him, and they shall see His face."

It is as if this is the end of the whole matter: there is no more to be said. This is indeed the *summum bonum* for which we are being prepared; it is in relation to this that our parish life must be tried and weighed. " Let us be borne along unto perfection." Here is an ideal which will save us from ever thinking that we have attained, that will keep us on the march to the City of God, our final goal. " Till we all come . . ."

VIII

THE HALLOWING OF DAILY LIFE AND WORK

By the Rev. E. DENIS TYNDALL
Vicar of St. Jude's, Birmingham

THE HALLOWING OF DAILY LIFE AND WORK

THE prayer, " that we may ever perceive within ourselves the fruits of Thy redemption," perfectly expresses the meaning of the corporate life lived in, and through, and by, the Eucharist. It is not a prayer that we as individuals may inspect ourselves and see the wonders which the practice of going to Holy Communion has wrought in us; it is a petition that by this blessed means of grace the daily life and work of every communicant, and so of the Church corporate, may be hallowed. That this ideal may be realised is the true aim and object of every parish priest and his people.

There is a certain parish church (typical, no doubt, of many others), where one of the activities which is most prized, and by which much store is set, is the annual parish camp. This is generally held at the sea-side, but it always starts at the altar of the church, where all the campers assemble before they set off for the train. At the camp itself, each day starts with the Eucharist and ends with the chanting of Compline. There is no kind of obligation to attend either of these services, but it is clearly understood, without its ever being put into so many words, that everyone shall take part in the two corporate Communions which are held on the Sunday and on the last morning of the camp. To this particular camp a number of people go, of widely differing ages, outlook, and education. The communicant life is the basis of the whole undertaking, but in practice it is very little talked about, for it is the natural, normal life for all the party. The work of the camp is divided up on lines of strict equality, a list of ' duties ' being posted up. At various times organised games of diverse kinds are arranged, in which all can join or not, exactly as they wish, for the campers are free to spend such time as is free from the duty they give to the community as their fancy takes them.

There is nothing in the least remarkable about all this; indeed, that is the point. It is a very normal and ordinary way for a sensible body of Christians to spend a cheap and wholly enjoyable holiday. And it is just because it is so very ordinary that it provides at any rate a rough picture of the ideal ordinary life of a parish in the heart of which stands the parish church. The difficulty is, that this is so often the very opposite of what the life of a parish church actually is.

It is a truism to say that all life is social, and that we depend at all points upon each other for the supply of all our needs. But it is a truism which needs consistently stressing, since in practice it is so often entirely forgotten. And if it is forgotten in ordinary every-day life, it is to be feared that it is far more often forgotten in religion. Yet every Christian virtue is essentially corporate, for love, joy, peace, long-suffering and the rest mean absolutely nothing apart from the brotherhood. This all needs tremendous emphasis to-day; and it is probably true to say that it is a truth which has not so much been forgotten by the majority of people, as never grasped. The result is, that religion as such has become very largely separated and cut off from life, with quite disastrous results to the life of Church and people.

It is not the purpose of this essay to try to show how the Eucharist is the life and very heart of all parish life and activities. That is being done elsewhere. Nevertheless, it is necessary, in order to deal with the subject of the carrying of the Eucharist into life, to be sure that that is the standpoint from which a start is made. In the Eucharist all Christians join together to offer sacrifice, to plead the one Sacrifice once offered, and to give—to give themselves, their souls and bodies—to give all that they have, all that they are, and all that they do. They come and do this as individuals, but never as mere individuals, for they come as members of a family. As members of the family they leave the altar, and each goes out into the world to live his or her private life. They carry with them something which is intensely precious, but which is not given to them to be precious only to themselves. It is the very life of the incarnate, risen and ascended Jesus, which they have received through participation in the sacred mysteries of His Body and Blood. Endowed with this power, they have become evangelists, for Christianity in practice does not consist in doing things, but in being something. It is only thus that the great gulf which, as we have said, exists in the lives of so many Church-people, separating their religion from their secular lives, can be bridged over and effective contact established between the two spheres. But what does all this mean practically? How can this ideal become a reality?

It must start with the personal consecration of the individual, to whom the fact that he has been " accepted in the Beloved " must be the over-ruling fact of his whole life. To one who has grasped in any way the significance of the Church, this will involve a consecration which is both individual and also social; for at Baptism a man is brought into the family of God, that in the fellowship of that family he may continue to live. By his Baptism he was, in fact, accepted also 'in the beloved,' in the family. Only as he maintains his membership by partaking of the fulness of the family life, is he carrying out all that that consecration means. As the very heart of the family life is found at the Eucharist, the personal consecration of each individual continually issues into the world from that. Thus the κοινωνία can never be something which stops at the altar. In the lives of the faithful it must go into every corner of the world. The important thing to realise is that, since the life of the Crucified is to be found and received in the Sacrament of His love, so only from that source can the fulness of Christian life permeate the world. The Eucharist is the ordinance which Christ has bequeathed to His Church. No private way of evangelism nor of life can ever take its place. It follows that every Christian must continually strive to live his life as one who ever recollects the altar, and thinks and speaks and acts in its strength. For a Christian—it will bear saying again—is one who is something, not one who does something. The hallowing of life must start with a body of what may perhaps be described as ' κοινωνία-bearers.'

Eighteen hundred years ago Aristides wrote these words in his famous letter about the Christians to the Emperor Hadrian: "And because they acknowledge the goodness of God towards them, lo, on account of them there flows forth the beauty that is in the world." With shame it must be admitted that to-day this is by no means always true of those who profess to be Christians. It is not to be wondered at that there are multitudes who, although they make no Christian profession, yet in fact live a Christian life, for the Spirit of God is like the wind which " bloweth where it listeth." The tragedy is—and it must be faced by the Church as a reality—that full often the lives of non-believers put those of Christians to shame. Not only are they more attractive; they are also frequently more full of love and breathe more of the spirit and teaching of our Master. This ought to be impossible, not because the lives of non-believers cannot be in practice Christian, but because those who live by the life of the Saviour should show forth that life in their own lives. Christianity transcends all the artificial divisions into which the world has divided itself, and still continues to divide itself. There can be no such thing as a ' class distinction ' which makes one man superior to his neighbour. In Christ there is neither Jew nor Greek, bond nor free. If the Eucharist means anything, it means that those who partake of it live in that higher atmosphere which is above and beyond any such natural or artificial divisions. This is the only true solution of all the international and social problems which to-day beset a distracted and puzzled world. Put in the simplest possible way, it means that life can only be hallowed by the followers of Jesus who have in them the mind of Christ.

But further, what a communicant is must issue in the most natural way possible into what he does. How the world of this rushing age in which we live needs kindness and unselfishness in the common ways of daily life! The Christian must seek out ways of being kind and unselfish. Because he is a Christian who partakes of the life-giving food, he must see to it that he 'feeds others' in all manner of ways. How often do Christians succeed in being the most unpleasant of neighbours when, if they only remembered and realised the precious gift of Christ, nothing could prevent them from being the most charming people one could possibly find with whom to share one's garden hedge. Daily life can only be hallowed by the putting into practice of the 'every-day' Christian virtues, of which kindness, gentleness, patience and long-suffering will serve as examples.

It is in the home, for some obscure reason, that it is hardest of all to practise the Christian virtues. But unless a Christian can make some beginning at any rate of carrying his faith into practice there, it is useless for him to imagine that he will be able to do so in a wider sphere. But home-life can, and will, be hallowed by the grace of eucharistic worship, if the faithful communicant will only determine that it shall be. All Christian life is a perfect unity, and the Christian law of marriage is part and parcel of the Christian home, which is founded and maintained by the Christian Eucharist.

In eucharistic life, again, there cannot be a separation between business and religion. Difficult though it undoubtedly is in the midst of a world often definitely unchristian, the spirit and laws of Jesus must be fearlessly and resolutely applied in the work-a-day business world. To many this will seem an impossibility, and it will remain a seeming impossibility until it is tried. Yet the amazing truth is that it can be done, as it is being done in countless places, and has been done through all the Christian ages. Unless, indeed, the religion of Sunday is carried into every nook and corner of Monday, it is a worthless and useless thing. For the worthy reception of the Holy Communion is not only to be *followed by* the faithful witness in factory, office or workshop; that faithful witness is in very truth part of, and one with, the Eucharist itself.

The same may be said, too, of all works of love and

mercy of whatever kind. Philanthropy is not a virtue which naturally some possess, while others do not. If a man lives by the law of Christ he must be a philanthropist, and what he is must just as naturally show itself in what he does. One cannot be a Christian and fail to care about the plight of the unemployed. The miserable conditions under which tens of thousands of men and women have to live to-day owing to housing evils, the toil of the multitudes who still have to work in jobs in which they are overworked and underpaid—no one can be living the eucharistic life who does not care about these things, for Christianity has to be carried into the whole of life.

These truths are so self-evident that in a Christian community there should be no need to state them. Happily there is much to show that at the present time the urgent necessity for linking up worship with daily life is being more and more realised; but it is nevertheless true that unless the Church in this land puts forth every possible endeavour to teach her children to do so, she will more and more lose her hold upon the life of the people, while her own spiritual power will evaporate.

Of late years an interesting experiment has been made, at first in one or two isolated places, but recently in a considerable number. This is the establishment of a Parish Breakfast, which is held in some place near to the church after the Parish Eucharist on Sunday morning. This is not the place for a full consideration of the Parish Breakfast, since that is being undertaken elsewhere in this book, but one aspect of it is very much germane to the particular subject with which this essay deals. That is, that the Breakfast must not be considered merely as a convenient way in which a number of people who have come together for Holy Communion may be fed. If it is really to be understood, it must be seen that it is the social counterpart of the solemn spiritual meal in which the family has partaken. As such it is definitely a social obligation, for it is an organised social event for the purpose of carrying out into social spheres that which has been offered by the family at the altar. In it there must be an atmosphere which breathes the very spirit of the Communion. It is indeed an Agape, a love-feast of those who together have feasted on Christ.

This breakfast has been found of the greatest possible value in the hallowing of the common life in many parishes, so much so that there are priests to be found who will almost claim that it is not merely of the *bene esse* but of the *esse* of parish life. It must be remembered, however, that there are certain practical difficulties which have to be squarely faced. With these it is proposed to deal at a subsequent point in this essay. For the moment it will suffice to stress the fact that its value is to be found in the practical way in which, if it is what it ought to be, it can be a hallowing of the social life of the church and congregation, before that hallowed life is carried out into the wider world of home and office, factory, field and shop.

In the same way all parish activities will find their inspiration where their treasure is, at the altar. It cannot meet the case merely to make a rule of monthly Communion for the men's club, the football team, the Scouts, the Guides and the Mothers' Union. Good and helpful as that or a similar rule may be, it is never enough by itself. It is in the strength of the κοινωνία that the Club or Guild must find its common life; it is in this spirit that all its activities must be carried out. This does not mean that there are not often circumstances when a Guild or Club will not be found useful as a means of evangelisation; but it does mean that no parish Society will ever be carrying out its life in all its fulness unless its work is based consistently upon the communicant life of all its members. This can be a very different thing from ' coming to the early service once a month.' It is with this latter kind of obligation that the Church is so often tempted to be content.

The late Canon Scott Holland in one of his sermons points out that the motive of all that our Blessed Lord was and did on earth was that of compassion. " I have compassion on the multitude " was His continuing motive. That same compassion is ever the motive of His Church; and if daily life and work is to be hallowed by the common feeding upon and worshipping of Him, it must be constantly shown forth in the lives of individual members. Compassion still flows forth unceasingly from the broken Body and streaming Blood of the Saviour, but He wills that it flows forth through those whom He has strengthened with His life in the sacred Mysteries. Christians must then go forth into the world possessed of that infinite sympathy and understanding which can only be learnt from communion with our Lord Himself.

There is far too much loose thinking about what passes by the name of ' broad-mindedness ' in the world to-day. ' It does not matter,' people often say, ' what you believe, so long as you do the right thing '; or, put in a different way, ' I am not one who goes very often to church. My religion, you see, is to do all the good I can in the world.' That kind of attitude is not broad-mindedness at all. It is merely an attempt to live one's life without any kind of satisfactory basis. True broad-mindedness is in no way incompatible with the holding of very definite dogmas. The man who is really broad-minded can perhaps best be described as the man who has an infinite capacity for understanding another person's point of view; this in no way involves subscription to it as a right one. Now surely Christians must be men and women who go about the world with this capacity, and who consequently reflect something at any rate of the compassion of Him who died for us all. There is no place in the life of one whose life is being lived with Christ for any kind of self-complacency, and still less for any fancied superiority. Too often is it possible to say of Christians that they are narrow, bigoted, and self-satisfied, or that they despise those whom they ignorantly think to be less righteous than themselves. These things ought not to be.

Then there is the great difficulty of any attempt to present to the world which knows Him not the beauty and the power of the Saviour. This difficulty presents itself in countless ways, but there are two definite aspects of it which may be considered here. First, there is the fact that the majority of people in this country to-day simply have no conception of what the Church stands for, of what are its ideals, and indeed, of what it is. It is quite an ordinary thing to find those who look upon it as a Relieving Office where not quite so many unpleasant questions will be asked as in other official places. It is almost generally thought that the Church exists only to give. This is true also of very many who would scorn to ask for anything material, but who feel that the primary object of their church-going is to acquire for themselves comfort, strength, help and forgiveness. It need hardly be said here that the only real secret of love and penitence (as, indeed, of everything else which is worth having) is that it must always be a giving before it is a getting. But most sad of all is the fact that to the mass of our fellow-countrymen the Church is a society of the elect and not the home of poor sinners. ' If I was good enough, I should like to be a Christian.' To a certain point, of course, this is an admirable sentiment, for it means that there is a clear vision of the demands which Christ makes. As it often works out in practice, however, it is deplorable, for it goes on adding fuel to the evil fire which burns so brightly and extensively—the fire of the separation of those who ' go to Church ' from the multitude on whom the divine Saviour ever has compassion. Only, under God, the hallowed lives of those who have learnt something of that compassion from Him, can quench that fire.

Secondly, there is the increasing secularisation of modern life. Life which feels no need for God, life lived apart from God, is more and more being put before people as the normal life. Formerly, the ideals of Christian ethics were always in the background, and held up as desirable. The books which were read fifty or sixty years ago, however much to-day we may revolt from the sentimentality of some of them, generally speaking held up at least a Christian standard as an aim. To-day the novels which are commonly read and the pictures which for the most part are seen are not so much bad in themselves (though of course many of them undoubtedly are), as a continual presentation of an imagined normal life into which the idea of God simply does not enter. To the minds of those who have had little or no teaching about the things of God, it naturally appears that the normal life which is generally being lived is a life in which there is no need for God at all. Side by side with this, there is the ever-increasing use of Sunday, not as a day primarily for God and secondarily for man's rest and re-creation, but simply as a day of rest and pleasure. More and more the whole of civilisation is becoming ordered upon a humanitarian basis; and the tragic result is, that while, although all too slowly, the amenities of life are gradually being secured for the mass of the people, God is being forgotten in the so-called improved ordering of society. It cannot cause a thoughtful person any surprise if there is a serious amount of juvenile crime everywhere, since education is becoming increasingly conceived of as something which can be complete in itself apart from God; whereas the truth is that no education can be in any sense complete unless it is given and received against the background of God, and unless it has its basis in the worship which it is man's duty to give to God.

There is much else, too, which might be said in a similar connection of the ruthless demands of modern industry. Man is more and more treated as a machine, and consequently comes to be considered as less than man, so that the sanctity of the individual has become a doctrine which is in danger of being cast out as obsolete. Naturally, again, all this has its bearings upon the family, the true unit of the nation's life. The secularising tendencies of our age are steadily undermining the Christian ideal of family life in practice. What wonder is it, then, that the majority of mankind have little use for the Church and her ways, since there is so general an ignorance of what the Church is and for what she stands?

The moral of all this is very simple and straightforward. The ideal of the Church must be shown by Christians as something which is both real and ' livable ' in practice. It is in this way, and in this way alone, that the parish church, with its faithful sons and daughters, can in its own day and generation carry on the Church's age-long task of the hallowing of daily life and work.

Thus the Parish Eucharist, as the heart of all parish life, must enable the Christian life to be lived. Any conception of the reception of the Holy Communion which is merely individual is utterly inadequate to equip the Christian for his main task of life, that of evangelisation by means of personal consecration; for this alone can lead to the process of hallowing in the world at large. It follows naturally that whatever the particular arrangements for the Eucharist in any parish may be, the spirit of " the fellowship of the Gospel " must permeate them. It cannot be denied, as indeed is clearly set forth elsewhere in this book, that the ideal is the one Eucharist celebrated at that hour which is most convenient for all, and at which all can communicate together. From the very nature of things this must be an ideal which is very seldom capable of *complete* fulfilment; but the biggest possible step towards that goal will be taken when in any parish it is possible to have a Eucharist which is the chief service of the day and at which the great majority of the faithful are able to communicate. That this should be followed by a social meal is, as has been said, most highly desirable. It is, however, no use shutting one's eyes to the fact that in practice it is far from being merely a question of getting the good-will and co-operation of the congregation and starting these things. There are certain pitfalls both as regards the hour of the Eucharist and as regards the breakfast into which it is only too possible to fall, and there are certain difficulties which in many a parish make the ideal at present impossible of attainment. Some of them may be briefly sketched as follows:

(1) It will generally be found that the most fitting hour for the Parish Eucharist is one between 8.45 and 9.30. Where this is adopted it will involve, if not the discontinuance, at any rate the very considerable curtailment in numbers and in importance of the usual 8.0 service. At present this service is the chief source of life in countless parishes, and the fact that it is so may be said to be the chief fruit of the Catholic Revival of the last hundred

years. It has an immense value, moreover, in the fact that it is held at a time which makes it easy for the parish priest to inculcate through it the obligation of receiving the Holy Communion fasting. It will be more difficult for him to carry out his duty in this respect if the normal hour for receiving Communion becomes changed to, say, 9.0. There will in that case be a considerably greater danger of young people growing up in the habit of receiving not fasting. There is, furthermore, a value which cannot be over-estimated in the growth of the habit of self-denial which is engendered by early rising. It may be a thousand pities if Sunday becomes in the mind of the average man the one day in the week on which he comes to Holy Communion, and at the same time the one day in which he has to make the least effort to rise from the comfort of his bed. Is it not right that Holy Communion should be associated in the mind of a Christian with at any rate some measure of self-denial such as the necessity of early rising so well provides? There is much which may easily be sacrificed in the establishment of a Parish Eucharist at a later hour than that of 8.0, and all too possibly regretted when it is too late.

(2) It is surely possible that the value of a Parish Breakfast may be unduly stressed. It is courting trouble to imagine that it is of anything like so great an importance as the Eucharist itself. As an adjunct where it is possible, it is difficult to over-estimate its value; but it is a pity to treat it as if it were always and everywhere a *sine qua non* of the proper ordering of parish life. For in practice it will be found that there are certain quite considerable dangers. Is it not possible that the Parish Breakfast may sometimes effect something of a great social value at too great a cost? Present-day social conditions must be borne in mind, even though they are all too often far from ideal. Nevertheless Sunday is the chief home day in the majority of families to-day. Social family life needs strengthening and not weakening. If Sunday by Sunday all the members of the family attend the Parish Breakfast, well and good; but if instead only certain members go, something in the

family life is in danger of being broken up. Again, although we deplore, and rightly, anything in the nature of class-distinction, it is undeniable that different sections of the community live in different ways. Even if it is felt that this should not be so, it is undoubtedly a fact that it is. As such it has to be faced, and in the present ordering of English life, good as the Parish Breakfast may be from time to time, it will be found that in many parishes it is utterly unsuitable *as a regular thing*. There are, of course, many parishes where this objection will have no force at all, but that does not affect the fact that there are certainly many where it will.

There is another danger, too, which it will be well care-fully to watch, and that is the danger that the Parish Break-fast will be a source of temptation to selfishness for the young people. It would be far from the ideal which has been envisaged that this should be so, yet very often the hallowing of the Eucharist is to be carried out first at the sink in the kitchen at home. If Sunday by Sunday the devout youth of the family attend the breakfast, while mother and the undevout members of the same family do the washing up and get the dinner, has the desired result been achieved? It is certainly doubtful.

It is probable that many who read this essay will think that these dangers are either purely the result of imagina-tion or greatly exaggerated. This may be so, but they are certainly in the mind of many who are giving the whole question most searching consideration, and since this is so, it is good that they should find expression and be con-sidered. The solution of them as difficulties lies, of course, at the very heart of things, in the spirit in which the Eucharist itself is offered. If that is right, then that of itself will make other things right; but a right spirit cannot be achieved by forgetting obligations and refusing to face facts. The subject may be summed up by saying that the Parish Breakfast must not become a fetish: its true meaning is seen in its relation to the Sacrament which precedes it.

It is all too easy to forget that Christianity is a way of life. Ideally, in practice, it is life properly interpreted and

o

rightly lived. It is more than believing something, though that something is the very being of one's life. It is more than devotion to Someone, though that Someone is Very God of Very God. It is this belief, this devotion, so made a part of a man's life, that he *is* it, and it is his true life, as he lives his life and passes through the world. All this has to be found and learnt at the altar of God. Thus, and only thus, will lives and homes and work and actions be hallowed, because they are permeated with the very Life of Him who died. For from the altar there flow forth into the world the very rivers of life, as in the vision of the prophet Ezekiel when he said, " And it shall come to pass, that every thing that liveth, which moveth, whithersoever the rivers shall come, shall live."

IX

THE PRIEST HIMSELF

BY THE REV. J. F. BRISCOE
Rector of Bagborough

THE PRIEST HIMSELF

Vita clericorum liber laicorum. The quality and effectiveness of the ministry of a priest in his parish depend not so much on what on specific occasions he says or does, as on what he is. When he has left his parish, when he is dead, what will be found to have had most influence will be his character. A holy priest leaves behind him a fragrant memory which is still able to stir the heart and spur the will. A holy priest unconsciously creates around him an atmosphere of holiness: he is himself a radiating centre of spiritual power and light.

This is not to say that a priest is free to neglect the technique of parish worship and parish work. A good priest will find absorbing interest in the arrangement of the worship and the administration of his parish. But the most careful attention to the technique of worship and the most up-to-date and business-like methods of administration will be almost entirely without spiritual value unless both alike are inspired by the devotion of the priest to the service of God.

It is difficult to exaggerate the importance of a right technique of worship. I do not think the average country congregation is much affected by the details of the decoration of the church or of the ceremonial of the services. The dullest peasant will nevertheless be discouraged and disgusted if the look of the church is shabby and slovenly, if the preaching is lifeless and perfunctory, if it is evident that no pains have been taken to make the music as good as possible. It counts for a great deal that the altar is solemn and beautiful, the walls of the church white and clean, and all the necessary apparatus of worship worthy and decent. Though the ordinary countryman may be oblivious to detail, he is alert and responsive to a general atmosphere of reverence and smartness and order.

Under the direction of the bishop, the parish priest is responsible for the arrangement of the Sunday services. He has for his guidance the Catholic rules which require attendance at the Eucharist on all Sundays, and communion at least once a year from all adult Christians. He does not forget the rule that under normal circumstances the holy sacrament should be received by communicants who are fasting. If he reads this book, he will learn with interest and sympathy that here and there are parishes where it has become the practice to sing the service of the Eucharist at such an hour on Sundays as makes it possible for most of the congregation to receive communion fasting, and he will recognise that only with such revival of the custom of the primitive Church will the full glory of the eucharistic rite be restored.

My experience, however, during thirty years would lead me to insist that in such a parish as mine the least satisfactory hour for the central service of Sunday is nine.[1] A village priest has normally to deal with three classes of people among his parishioners: the squire and his family, the farmers, and the workers on the land. He has to consider not only what is ideally the best, but also what is actually feasible. He will be very reluctant to ask the squire or the farmers or the working-people to upset the *régime* of their households without absolute necessity. At nine o'clock the squire is busy with his breakfast, and on the farms and in the cottages there is necessary work to be done. By eleven nearly everyone can be ready if he will, and all the parishioners who desire to serve God can be gathered in church for the offering of the holy sacrifice. The children

---

[1] Note by the Editor: " I have received other testimonies to the effect that, in many country places, nine o'clock is an impossible hour; nor, it would seem, is eight o'clock any better, at least for those who work on the land. On the other hand, we have in this book Fr. Fairbairn's testimony that he has found 8.45 the ideal hour (see pp. 261, 266–7). Another testimony from a country church is that 9 a.m. suits three-quarters of the people very well: but that it is found to be almost impossible to get the children of non-churchgoing parents to church at that hour, even on Easter Day. For the problem presented by such children in a town parish, see p. 274."

of the Sunday School should be there, and should sit, if possible, with their parents. The service should be done by twelve, so that the family dinner may be ready at home at the usual time. This plan secures leisure for the central Sunday service, and involves no undue strain on the congregation. They have had their breakfast; a good part of the work of the day is done; they are ready to join in the simple singing, and listen gladly to the admirable scriptures read from the altar,[1] and patiently to the sermon provided by the rector. The present writer is sure that the best time for the reception of communion is early in the morning, and that this service for communion should be as brief as may be, with a good deal of silence, to give the rare and precious opportunity for prayer in an atmosphere of stillness.

Sheep must not be over-driven; and there is a real danger of exacting from simple people a higher standard of frequent communion than they can happily attain. The priest will indeed be very far from content till his people are receiving Holy Communion much more frequently than the minimum which the Church demands. Nevertheless he will remember a letter by the Venerable Bede to Egbert the Bishop of York, in which the writer complains of the grievous lack of frequent communion among the English, as compared with the Christians of other nations.[2] I expect it is certain that the vast majority of the practising members of the Church of England have never at any time received communion more often than three or four times a year, and generally they have received it more seldom still. Attendance at Mass every Sunday, and careful and respectful communion at the great feasts, represent a standard of conformity to Catholic rule which may and does sustain a deep and true religious life.

It is hard to exaggerate the importance of a right technique of worship. The priest must provide opportunities for frequent and fasting communion for all his parishioners, and he must try to gather all the Christian people of the

---

[1] The long lessons of Morning Prayer are surely very ill-adjusted to the needs of an ordinary congregation.

[2] *Historia Eccles. Bædæ*, ed. Moberly, p. 403.

place for a common act of eucharistic worship every Sunday morning. He has now the necessary apparatus for the practice of the Catholic religion.

But—and here we return to the point that was emphasised at the start—it will largely depend on the priest himself whether the system lives or not. It is not sufficient that he should have good intentions and be trying to do his best: there is need that he should be living a life of spiritual discipline, a life lived in a regular rhythm of sacrament and prayer. His exhortations to his parishioners will inevitably be illustrated by his own devotional habits. He must be seen to use as the articulation of his own religion the apparatus he commends to his people.

It is quite futile to decorate the church and arrange a careful service once a week unless it is plain to all that the priest uses the church for his own devotions. Almost alone of men, the priest has no ' office-hours '; it is not with him as with the doctor and policeman and farmer, who can continually be seen busy about their work. The priest is free. It is therefore absolutely essential that the priest shall be seen early every morning on his way to church for the blessing of the day, and every evening for the blessing of the night.

Mr. Belloc has written admirably in *The Path to Rome* [1] of " the pleasing sensation of order and accomplishment which attaches to a day one has opened by Mass." If it means so much to a layman, how much more it ought to mean for a priest. There at the altar he stands between earth and heaven, between the living and the dead ; in his hands is the Divine Victim once offered for the sins of the world. There at the altar he gives highest praise to God, for the sacrifice he brings is worthy even of the Divine Majesty. There he bears all human needs in his heart, and intercedes most prevailingly in the Name of Jesus Christ. His regular visiting throughout the parish has made him familiar with the special necessities of the individuals committed to his care : now is the moment when he brings them before God.

The rule of the Church of England that the Divine Office

[1] Pp. 51-3.

shall be said in church should be obeyed so far as possible. The priest will find that the duty of being punctually in church twice every day will be an excellent discipline.

Discipline is needed by no one more than by a priest living by himself in a country village. But mere precision of external observance is not enough. Because so much depends on him, there is urgent need for the priest to keep alive the spirit of his vocation and consecration to God.

There are three aids for this.

Every year the priest should make a retreat of not less than three days. The retreat is an opportunity for prayer, for self-examination, for consideration, for resolution. Here the priest will adjust his sense of values; he will weigh time against eternity. He will scrutinise his habitual motives and his standards of priestly conduct. He will review his life as it were from outside, asking himself why so many opportunities of grace have produced so little result. He will leave his retreat with a new simplicity of aim, a quiet conscience, and a cheerful determination by the help of God to do better in the future than in the past.

The Church requires a very high degreee of fitness from those who approach the Holy Communion. Only those who are ' holy and clean ' may receive that holy Sacrament in which Almighty God gives His Son ' to be our spiritual food and sustenance.' What is required from his parishioners the priest must very rigorously exact from himself. If he keeps a rule of going to confession at certain definite times, he will carry on his work in the peace and freedom of a good conscience, he will be helped to be on the alert against the insidious growth of bad habits, he will be saved from acquiescence in venial sins.

Massillon, the Bishop of Clermont, spoke as follows to his Synod in 1732 : " La prière est comme l'âme du sacerdoce ; elle seule fait toute la force et tout le succès de notre ministère ; c'est cette eau sainte qui arrose la semence que nous jettons dans les cœurs, et qui lui donne l'accroissement. Un Pasteur, un Prêtre qui ne prie pas, est un canal aride et une nuée sans eau." [1] The priest must have a rule of personal

---

[1] *Conferences et discours synodaux*, Tome II, p. 262.

and individual prayer apart from his official prayer at the altar and in the choir. A priest may sometimes say that he finds it ' impossible to keep a rule of meditation.' This may be because he imagines that meditation means an intricate process of intellectual consideration of which he thinks himself incapable. In fact, Meditation is a convenient word to cover any personal and deliberate waiting on God. There was no methodising of such intimate personal prayer before the thirteenth century, and little before the sixteenth.[1] Every priest should have a rule about the time he will give every day and every week to quiet communion with God apart from the fulfilment of any obligation with respect to vocal prayers, and if he is faithful to his rule there is no need for him to burden himself with any of the technical regulations on the subject. There is no need: any lifting up of the heart to God is true prayer: a regular time secured for this every day is a loyal keeping of a rule of meditation. There is no need. Nevertheless those who have faithfully used one or other of the various methods of meditation are those who say that they have found this method an excellent and fruitful discipline at least for the first stages of training in the life of prayer. The temptation to shirk what is exacting and difficult is never far away.

Vita clericorum liber laicorum. The priest will effect much more in his parish by his example than by his exhortations: he will effect much more by the continuous influence of a consecrated character than by any specific words or deeds. Charles de Foucauld used no methods of missionary propaganda: only he set himself to live in the midst of the wild tribes of the Sahara the life of a Christian priest. We may not imitate his complete independence of the ordinary methods of pastoral work, but we shall make no mistake if we believe that the most powerful contribution we can make to the spiritual welfare of our parish is to try to live among our people the life of a holy priest.

[1] *Spiritual Letters of Dom John Chapman*, p. 104.

X

THE LITURGICAL SERMON

By the Rev. M. R. NEWBOLT
Canon of Chester

THE LITURGICAL SERMON

1. PREACHING

MANY a single-handed priest has moods when he feels that the production of two discourses a week is a weary burden. " My people," he complains, " must get tired of the sound of my voice; it is so hard to find anything fresh to say to them." On the other hand, it is a commonplace that our laity are ill-instructed; we are sometimes startled by the ignorance even of regular church-goers about matters which concern their life in Christ. If we deplore this lack of knowledge, let us remember that it is our duty to cure it, and that we are almost the only teachers to whom the laity can look. Two periods of twenty minutes each per week is not excessive for such a thing as the Word of God. There ought to be something to show for one hundred and four sermons a year. If indeed a year's preaching represents a succession of unrelated discourses on topics chosen at random, then the complaint that the clergy have to preach too often may be justified, and much devoted labour may run to waste. But if the priest's object is to educate, the situation is transformed; he may find himself lamenting, as a keen teacher in such a movement as the Workers' Educational Association might lament, that he had to compress so much into so short a time.

Is it not true that some of us need to make a new start in this matter? Many priests are not clear about the objective of their teaching, and this may be a reason why they do not make a strong impression on their people.

This is a plea for the Liturgical Sermon, based upon the ideal of Liturgical Prayer. It is not claimed that all sermons ought to be 'liturgical,' any more than that all prayer can be. Liturgical Prayer cannot do everything; that kind of prayer is limited to what is of universal application—equally appropriate to the West End of London and the West Coast of Africa—and must be supplemented by popular devotions which minister to individual piety, and by private prayer. Likewise there are other kinds of sermon which are essential to the preacher's task.   But the Liturgical Sermon ought to be the normal type of sermon for the parish pulpit. There may rightly be occasions where a Savonarola is billed to preach at Mass, and the people come to hear Savonarola; but this should be exceptional. The ordinary Sunday sermon should not be a purple patch, however splendid, inserted into the formal background of the Liturgy. The pulpit should serve the altar, not obscure it like the old ' three-decker ' in a Georgian church. The congregation should not normally be invited to turn their attention from what they have been doing in the service in order to stop and listen for twenty minutes to the Vicar talking about something else.[1]

We should all agree that the preacher is not there to air his own pet ideas, nor ' to say a few words ' because something has to be said; his is the humble obedience of the man who accept the duty to speak to God's people in His name. And this is a great responsibility. " Any priest," said Bossuet, " who should give from the altar common bread instead of the Holy Sacrament, would be guilty of sacrilege. So also any priest, who from the pulpit gives to the faithful, not the word of God, but his own speculations, is guilty of nothing less than sacrilege."   A greater than Bossuet lays an anathema on any man " or an angel from heaven " who preaches any " other gospel."

The priest cannot go far wrong if he aims at making the sermon at the Eucharist an integral part of the whole act of worship, linking on to it, growing out of it and illustrating it,

---

[1] As in preaching, so also in the conduct of the service, the priest who values the Liturgy will never obtrude his own personality; he will not preach the prayers to the people, nor declaim them as if their effect depended on his own beautiful and impressive rendering. He speaks, as the mouthpiece of the Body, words which belong to the Body. His is the responsibility of a steward, not the dominant position of the Lord of the inheritance.

remaining, as it were, within the framework of the Liturgical action. His teaching thus becomes the spear-head of the service and drives home some lesson associated with the Sunday or the feast, so that the sermon interprets the Liturgy and the Liturgy reinforces the message of the sermon.

2. THE LITURGICAL IDEA

Before we can approach our subject, it is essential to appreciate what the Liturgy itself should mean to us, to grasp its spiritual opportunity, to understand its dignity and the part it plays in making men, women and children into living members of Christ in His mystical Body, the Church. We clergy have first to learn this for ourselves, and then to teach our people. It is not indeed altogether unfamiliar to them, for the Church of England is rich in the spirit of liturgy; they have a better tradition of it than their Roman brethren; they like to hear and understand the service, and Evensong, which they know and love, demands a good deal of capacity for liturgical worship. The spirit is there, but it has sadly deteriorated in recent years. We must face the fact that ground has been lost; " a generation is growing up," it has been said, " which knows neither the A.V. nor the P.B.," and our people are forgetting the tradition of church-going. Perhaps our ill-starred efforts at Prayer Book reform have had the result of arousing a critical spirit; whatever the reason, we know how widespread is the disposition to carp at almost any form of liturgical prayer.

The effect of the Liturgy on the mind is cumulative; we grow into the spirit of it by slow process of use. Through it God has taught you and me from our youth up until now; we " feel it in our bones." But only a minority of English people now know the secret of its associations; they come to it almost as strangers, if not with prejudice, yet without enthusiasm.

It is otherwise with mystical or individual prayer. The last thirty-five years, since the publication of Dr. Inge's Bampton lectures on *Christian Mysticism* in 1899 and William James's *Varieties of Religious Experience* in 1902, have seen a remarkable output of literature on this subject and a considerable growth of devotion among individuals. Miss Evelyn Underhill's work alone has had an amazing influence. We thank God for it, but this represents one side only of the spiritual life.

During the same period—the period of Prayer Book revision—Common Prayer has suffered a setback; we have been experimenting with it, criticising our formulas (not always wisely), and trying, not very successfully, to 'brighten' our services, yet all the while our congregations have been diminishing. There has grown up a habit, even among spiritually minded people, of decrying 'institutional religion,' with the implication that the genuine Christian is he who keeps his spiritual life to himself. It is quite certain that unless we can bring our people back to the true spirit of corporate worship in the Body of Christ, no development of mystical religion, in which the faithful Christian draws near to God *solus cum solo*, is going to convert the nation. We must teach people to pray in unison in Church, not as unrelated units each seeking God in quiet and in silence. The request 'Teach us to pray' comes not only from the individual, but from the congregation conceived of as a unit.

The nature of man is twofold: he is at once an individual and a social being. As an individual he must be converted and must grow in personal devotion. At the same time, as a being who can only realise his true nature in a society, he must be built up into the Body of Christ.

For these two things are different; they are two sides of the shield. Both sides of the spiritual life are essential, and it would be supremely disastrous to lose an atom of what we have gained in the kind of prayer that is exercised in meditation, contemplation and personal intercession. But real mystics will always be few; liturgical prayer is the prayer of the many; it belongs to us and to the people of God in common, not only to a few devout persons, but to all of us because we are baptised Christians. The first kind of prayer may be compared to singing a solo, a solo moreover which must be improvised. The second is like joining in a chorus where the singer has to follow a score with attention and is set a piece of classical music to interpret. It keeps before us a great pattern of prayer, training the spirit in a school of worship which is based upon the word of God. It may be ' above our people's heads '; but so is heaven.

Liturgical worship is not so simple as that superficial devotion which finds its expression in singing *Abide with Me*. It is never sentimental; also its discipline corrects the over-complicated tendencies of the mystic and is a sovereign remedy for the self-centredness of the *dévot*.

Public worship is a public witness, and there is a special sanctity in the very act of ' going to church,' in the situation which the people find when they enter the sacred building. This is something much more than an association of ideas, or an effect of psychological suggestion. It has been well said by Friedrich Heiler that the purest and most primitive ideal of Christian worship may be summed up in the familiar words of the Fourth Gospel. "On the first day of the week, when the doors were shut where the disciples were gathered together . . . came Jesus and stood in the midst and said, Peace be unto you." Every Sunday morning these conditions are in very truth repeated. We have to help our people to realise this fact.

The bells have summoned the faithful to a tryst; this is the reason why they are assembled; their demeanour, their whole action and procedure, imply that God has made a rendezvous with them. They have said implicitly "We will go into the House of the Lord "; our Lord has promised explicitly " Where two or three are gathered together in My Name, there am I in the midst of them." This is a promise made to the assembly as such, and not conditioned by its size. Liturgical prayer is the prayer of the Holy Church throughout all the world (of which the particular congregation is a part), acknowledging God in union with goodly fellowships, noble armies and glorious companies of saints in heaven, whither with Cherubin and Seraphim, Angels and Archangels we lift up our hearts, in Christ, to Him.

Only in the assembly of the faithful can we achieve this high enterprise of worship; it transcends space, for it is

P

simultaneous, world-wide, and heaven-wide; it transcends time, for it is offered in unison with eternity and uses forms inherited from the Church's past. Yet obviously it cannot be achieved without intelligence and will; a merely formal and external worship is a mockery. The group mind of the Church must be educated up to the ideal " that ye should be of one mind with one another according to Christ Jesus; that with one accord ye may with one mouth glorify the God and Father of our Lord Jesus Christ." The priest's duty as a preacher is to make worship intelligent and to stir up the will to worship.

Moreover the congregation represents, not merely an assembly of people, but the Family of God and the Body of Christ; the Liturgical Sermon is addressed to the faithful in the same spirit in which " Paul called to be an apostle of Jesus Christ," addressed " the Church of God which is at Corinth, them that are sanctified in Christ Jesus, called to be saints " (*i.e.* " to be Christians "). " Now ye," he says, " are the Body of Christ "—*Vos autem estis corpus Christi.* These words point to a deep mystery. Christ is in those people in the pews, " except they be reprobate." However sparse and humble the congregation, even if it only consists of a few little old women, some children, and the priest, it is the Body of Christ in that parish. Their prayer mounts into the heavenly places ' in the Name of Christ '; it is Christ speaking from the parish church; their utterance in psalms and prayers is the voice of the Body of Christ made audible. If the Body of Christ be there, the preacher must speak with love and reverence; indeed, unless he loves his people, or rather, the Lord Christ in His people, unless he " discerns the Lord's Body " in them, it is hard to see how he can speak effectively to them at all. We who preach cannot remind ourselves too often that we speak in the bosom of a sacred family. We are not like John the Baptist, confronting a generation of vipers.

People inevitably divide the world into " them " and " us." To the poor, who form the majority, everyone in a position of authority, from parliament to railway companies, including magistrates and parsons, are " they "; and

" they " are looked upon as in another camp from " us."
So do the ruling classes look upon the ruled. So does the
Englishman look on the foreigner, or the Bolshevik on the
" class enemy." But in the Body of Christ there is neither
the national division of Greek or Jew, nor the social cleavage
between bond or free. " Christ is all and in all "; high and
low, rich and poor, one with another, young men and
maidens, old men and children, praise the Lord in the parish
church, their common meeting place and home. A
Children's service or a Men's service, being popular devotions
intended to appeal to an artificially selected class, can never
be truly liturgical; [1] invaluable as such services are for
arousing personal devotion. Liturgical prayer is the prayer
of the redeemed race—the people of God. God, we say, hath
visited His people and hath raised up a mighty salvation
for *us*, and *we* being delivered out of the hand of *our* enemies
may serve Him without fear. God has visited *us*, guides
our feet into the way of peace—*we*, the Body of Christ, claim
one forefather Abraham. If one must draw a line of cleavage
between " them " and " us," " we " are the people of God;
the World, or society organised apart from God, is " they."

In public worship this sense of corporate, affectionate
family life which is " the fellowship of the Holy Ghost," is
fostered; the Body of Christ finds self-expression on Sunday
just as the regiment, itself one unit of an army, " finds itself "
and comes alive on parade. Without common worship the
Church must languish and would eventually cease to
function as a living spiritual body. No small part of the
preacher's task is to make men, women and children know
that in the church they are at home. He speaks in the
family language to members of a family which feels its
continuity with a glorious past, enjoys the privileges of a
blessed present, and looks with calm assurance to a glorious
future.

[1] The School Chapel, with services specially designed for the young,
for this very reason often creates a distaste for the parish church service.
The School is ' we '—the congregation in the holidays (and after) are
' they.'

3. THE LITURGICAL ACTION

St. Paul tells us that the apostolic Ministry is ordained for three great ends. *For the perfecting of the saints*; that is, the personal sanctification of individual Christians. *For the work of the Ministry*:—that is *diaconia*, the cure of souls; and *for the edifying of the Body of Christ*. We are alive to the duty of converting and sanctifying individuals; we work hard at visiting and pastoral activities of various kinds; are we at the same time edifying, or building up, a strong and living Church? The proper place to do it is *in* church, and one of the chief means we can use is the sermon; the centre from which we start is the congregation who are there. It is not enough merely to 'introduce the sung Eucharist,' and expect people to like it. They need to be taught, with patient allowance for their loyal conservatism and with an equal loyalty to the tradition of the Holy Catholic Church. Something is wrong if they accept the sung Eucharist as a personal fancy of a priest whom they respect; but if the preacher can get them to see for themselves the meaning of the things which the Church service sets before them, they are wonderfully happy and delighted.

First he must make them feel the significance of the common action in which they are engaged, how the Holy Mysteries are themselves a dramatic expression of the Gospel, passing through the stages of penitence, in the *Kyrie Eleison*, of the proclamation of the Word of God, in the Collect, Epistle and Gospel together with the sermon which applies their teaching; he must show how our own contribution to and union with Christ's action is signified in the Offertory (it is *our* bread and wine which is placed upon the altar); how we join with Angels and Archangels and all the company of heaven in adoration of the all-holy God; and how all this leads up to the culmination, the showing forth of the Lord's death in the Broken Body and the Blood, whereby we plead that great act of God which includes Christ's death, resurrection and glorious ascension. All this is brought home to ourselves in the act of communion, whereby we are united to Him in His victory and triumph through the Cross, and to one another, in His mystical Body the Church. Such points as these may be explained from time to time till they become a part of the people's general awareness of the meaning of the eucharistic action, and once they are grasped, the Liturgy, or rather the Holy Ghost, who is in their hearts, and who teaches them through the Liturgy, deepens and expands the meaning of their customary worship. Each step of the service may convey some definite idea and be filled with meaning. *Kyrie Eleison* may be connected with the opening words of the fifty-first Psalm, " Have mercy upon me, O God," from which this liturgical ejaculation is taken; or it may be illustrated by reference to the words of the Publican in the Temple: " Lord be merciful to me, a sinner "; the gesture which he used is that of the priest as he says the Preparation at the foot of the altar (*percutit sibi pectus*). It is appropriate to us who " stand afar off " at the beginning of the holy mysteries, acknowledging our sins before we dare " draw near."

Our people should understand how the Gospel is read as being the Word of Christ. When the service is performed with three ministers (which is more primitive than the low mass in which the priest celebrates alone), at the time when the deacon, surrounded by attendants, proclaims the Gospel, he is the centre of the action—the celebrant being left in the background at the altar—in order to emphasise the dignity of the Word of Christ. Jesus Himself speaks in the Gospel.

The placing of the bread and wine on the altar at the Offertory may be linked to the offerings of corn and wine in the Old Testament; the Harvest Thanksgiving familiarises us with this idea, and it may be made more significant by describing how, in the first Christian centuries, the congregation brought white cakes of bread made of their home-grown wheat, and wine from their vineyards, and offered their gifts, part of which were taken for sacramental use, at this dramatic moment of the service.

By their contributions, the congregation testify to their share in the Christian sacrifice; they are connected up with all that happens at the altar. It is " *our* sacrifice of praise and thanksgiving."

The *Sursum Corda* may be illustrated by the word " Come up hither " which John heard in the isle of Patmos when the door was opened in Heaven and he, entering, saw the worship of Him that sits upon the Throne and of the Lamb. This serves to remind them that the whole eucharistic action is directed to the Eternal Father, through Jesus Christ as the Eternal Victim, the Lamb standing as it had been slain.

The Consecration and the Fraction, as they know well, are associated with the Last Supper and with Cavalry ; but it is good to make them see how our commemoration of the death of Christ is one of joy and triumph, not a mournful but a glad memorial, since we are mindful not only of His Cross and Passion, but of His Resurrection and glorious Ascension.

In the act of communion is all the teaching of the sixth chapter of St. John. We have brought our poor share—" it shall suffice if it be the best and purest wheaten bread that can be gotten "—and offer it to God. He takes it and gives it back to us as Jesus Himself the " Bread of Life," to preserve our body and soul unto everlasting life. For though the act of worship is corporate, a communal and social act in which the individual is blended in the Body, yet the gift is given to each separate one of us. " The Body of our Lord Jesus Christ which was given for *thee* " ; " the Blood of our Lord Jesus Christ which was shed for *thee*." When we receive the Chalice, the Atonement, at that moment, actually makes contact with ourselves. It helps to make worship intelligent if we tell them the meaning of familiar things. Such ancient words as *Amen* and *Alleluia* remind us that our worship has roots in the Old Testament. For *Amen* in the Old Testament we can refer to Deut. xxvii. 15, etc., in the New to Rev. i. 5, 6, and xxii. 21, to I Tim. vi. 21, Phil. iv. 23.

To respond *Amen* means " We agree with you and join your prayer." " The Lord be with you " of Mattins and Evensong is also a most ancient Jewish salutation. Boaz says, " The Lord be with you " to his reapers at Bethlehem (Ruth ii. 4). It is a common exchange of greetings between

priest and people. The answer " And with thy spirit " is
the people's blessing to the man who is to speak for them to
God. Such points can be woven into our teaching from
time to time till they become familiar.

4. LITURGICAL PREACHING

Ordinarily, the preacher's subject is that of the service for
that morning. " This," he says, " is what the Church has
to say to us to-day."

In the Proper, the ' manifold ' or ' many-coloured '
wisdom of God is unfolded in the set course of the liturgical
year. Every Sunday and Holy Day the Church speaks its
appropriate message in Collect, Epistle and Gospel and in
those ancient minor elements of the office—the Introit, the
Gradual, the Offertory and the Communion. They have
dropped from our Prayer Book, but are in the hands of any
congregation which uses the *English Hymnal*, and even if
they are not sung, we may find in them many fruitful
suggestions for the interpretation of the message of the
Liturgy.

Thus on the Second Sunday after Easter the *Introit* sets the
key-note of Easter gladness: " The loving kindness of the
Lord filleth the whole world, alleluya ; by the word of the Lord
were the heavens made, alleluya, alleluya. Rejoice in the
Lord, O ye righteous, for it becometh well the just to be
thankful." For the *Gradual* is sung " Alleluya. I am the
Good Shepherd : and know my sheep and am known of
mine. Alleluya. The Good Shepherd hath risen : he
hath given his life for the sheep." The *Offertory* : " O God,
thou art my God : early will I seek thee, and lift up my
hands in thy Name, alleluya." The *Communion*, " I am the
Good Shepherd, alleluya, and know my sheep and am known
of mine. Alleluya, alleluya," gives us a word which we can
take with us to our communion. That is why it was
originally chosen.

The preacher who has read these words and meditated
on them can hardly fail to make his people hear the voice of
the Good Shepherd whose flock they are, in whose pasture it
is their lot to feed. The Alleluyas remind us that the Good

Shepherd is the Risen Lord present with His people.
(" Then came Jesus, where the disciples were assembled,
and said, Peace be with you.") The whole Psalm of the
Good Shepherd speaks of passing through the valley of the
shadow of death, and assures us that since the Good Shepherd
has passed through that valley, we, His flock, need fear
no evil, for He is with us. He prepares a table before us
against them that trouble us, and feeds us with the Bread
of Life and immortality.

Or if we turn to Quinquagesima Sunday, instead of the
Paschal chant stammering with Alleluyas, the *Introit*,
voicing the petition of one who is in direct need: " Be thou
my God and defender and a place of refuge that thou mayest
save me," fits harmoniously with the Gospel story of Bar-
timæus. We ourselves are the blind man sitting by the
dusty roadside where Jesus passeth by,[1] going up to Jerusalem
to the Cross of Good Friday and to the triumph of Easter.
The matchless Collect and Epistle, telling us of the supreme
virtue of Charity, whereby alone we can follow Jesus in the
way, make in themselves a theme for Quinquagesima
Sunday.

A concordance helps us to gather together texts bearing on
one point, and it is a great help to our people if they can have
such texts printed on their minds, even if they forget most of
our words; for the liturgical spirit is the scriptural spirit,
and the place where the Holy Scriptures are most at home
and framed in their proper setting is the Liturgy.

The preacher is "like unto a man that is an householder
which bringeth out of his treasures things new and old."
The treasures of Holy Scripture are heirlooms; the preacher
must know their history—treat them, that is, as the
Church has treated them in their liturgical use; and he
must love them well himself. For family treasures should
be explained to the family by one learned in their associations. The old sword hanging in the passage means infinitely more to the children when they are told how their
ancestor bore it at Culloden; the " miniature of a gentle-

[1] Similarly in all the many healings of the sick occurring in the Sunday
Gospels we listen to stories about our own position with regard to Christ.
I am the deaf man. I am the paralytic. My need is there depicted.

man " is treasured because it reminds us that we have a poet among our forebears; the piece of Crown Derby acquires an interest beyond its function as a teapot when we are told the price a collector offered for it. Liturgical worship is an art, and it is the business of the preacher to know its canons; he must cultivate a sensitive feeling for it, as a musician cultivates an educated taste. The priest must not allow the church service to suffer from that formal monotony which its critics are so apt to profess to find in it. The wisdom of God is " many-coloured," not a drab uniformity, nor yet a jumble of unharmonious colours. The place of ' Introits and other Anthems ' is, with us, usually taken by hymns—which are popular devotions, inserted in order to sweeten and enliven the service. We must exercise liturgical tact in choosing them, not singing " Ye Watchers and Ye Holy Ones " in Lent, for instance.[1] The first essential is to make the hymns appropriate to the Sunday— and most hymn-books print a guide in the shape of Hymns arranged for Sunday and Holy Days.

Each season, even each holy day, has its own ' tonality.' That of Lent is the sense of preparation, with the dominant notes of humility, prayer, penitence and discipline, and this is the best observed of all liturgical seasons. Eastertide, which also lasts for forty days, is far less carefully treated. It is as if when Easter Day is done, we were too exhausted by our preparation to enjoy that for which we have been prepared.

The tone of Easter is triumphant; in every Sunday of the Paschal season the service should resound with the proclamation of victory and joy. The preacher can more clearly bring to light the special spirit in which the Body of Christ is intended to worship God when every component

---

[1] Let there be some limit to our charitable desire to ' give the people what they like.' " Jerusalem " is what they like at present, probably for the sake of one fine sentiment and a magnificent tune, but what meaning can we attach to a rhetorical question whether Christ did in ancient times walk on the hills of Somerset? The answer is in the negative. Mere vague melodious aspirations for a " bow of burning gold and chariot of fire " build up nothing very solid. " Give the public what they like " is the motto of Hollywood. The policy of the B.B.C. is better.

No teacher of a serious subject gives people what they like, but something much better which they will learn to like.

element in the service harmonises with the lesson of the season.

In the great primitive age, when the ancient liturgies were taking shape and crystallising from improvised prayer on a set theme into marvellous and stately forms, the Bishop chose then and there lections appropriate to the day, telling the minister who read the Gospel to begin at a certain place in one of the Four Evangelists and when to stop. He would then expound, either himself or by deputy, its message to the faithful. Many of the sermons of the Fathers which have been preserved to us were delivered in this way.

This is the liturgical sermon. It is more than an ethical exhortation saying in many words " Be Good." It is not a chance discourse on any topic. Its preparation does not involve fluttering the leaves of the Bible at random in the search for a text, but requires careful study. It must be more than a few hasty and jejune comments on the Gospel or Epistle, which may only increase our people's distaste for all liturgical worship.

Let us repeat that this is not the only sort of sermon: it would be a grave mistake to preach no other. Being a sermon addressed to the Family of God, to the Body of Christ, it is inappropriate and almost meaningless to the pagan or semi-pagan world; but it is obvious that we cannot be doing our duty unless we also preach to " them that are without." There is a place for exhortation to social righteousness, for teaching about holy marriage, about the Christian's attitude to war, for general apologetics and kindred subjects which may be treated apart from any reference to the service for the day.

Quite obviously, the liturgical sermon itself admits of a vast variety of subjects and of treatment; it may be an ethical instruction, based on the Parable of the Good Samaritan on the 15th Sunday after Trinity, it may be doctrinal on Whit Sunday, on the 3rd Sunday after Trinity it may be a lesson on God's love for sinners or on Preventive and Rescue Work. It is not ecclesiastical in the narrow sense of the word, but a message given as the teaching of the Church and addressed to the Church.

This conception of the sermon does not mean that we are content to give hot-house spiritual consolation to the devout and to forget the world outside. Such an idea would never have occurred to St. Paul as he wrote to his Corinthians. If we follow this ideal of the sermon faithfully, we may find ourselves compelled to deal with aspects of the Gospel which, left to our private choice, we should have omitted or glossed over hastily.

The Word of God as interpreted in the Liturgy is bracing and strenuous; personal devotions, wrongly used, are more likely to produce the ' hot-house ' type of pietist. He is the kind of person who prefers " to pray at the mass " rather than to " pray the mass," who uses the most holy mysteries as a stimulant to sensible devotion in his private prayers and desires ' to be quiet in church,' dissociated from the corporate action and undisturbed by the sound of the voice of the priest—to be alone with his own thoughts. " You in your small corner and I in mine." The world will never be saved by individual piety alone. It can only be converted by a strong, well-knit, corporate body living the life of Christ in the midst of it. Mankind needs not only " the spirit of Christ "; it needs also the Body of Christ—not merely a set of disembodied principles, but the united overt witness of " the blessed company of all faithful people." Worship is the native air of that Body; in worship it lives and breathes and grows up to its stature in the Perfect Man.

5. THE WORD OF GOD

We have diverged into matters that seem to have little to do with preaching, such, for instance, as the choice of hymns. But it is partly the lack of co-ordination between pulpit, choir and altar which is responsible for much failure in the Church's witness. The Liturgy itself is " preaching " of a most essential kind; it embodies that kind of " preaching " looked upon as foolishness, by which St. Paul tells us that it " pleased God to save them that believe."

The word here used is, in the Greek, *Kerygma*, and Dr. Dodd, in his suggestive book, *The Apostolic Preaching and its Developments*, points out that in Gospels, Acts, Epistles and

Apocalypse alike a clear distinction is drawn between *Kerygma* and *Didache*. *Didache*, or " teaching," he says, in a large majority of cases, means in the New Testament ethical instruction; sometimes it means the reasoned commendation of Christianity to persons interested but not yet convinced; sometimes, in the Johannine writings, it includes theological doctrine. But " preaching " or *Kerygma* means proclaiming, " like a town crier, an auctioneer, a herald."

When we say " I believe in God . . . and in one Lord Jesus Christ, and I believe in the Holy Ghost, and the life everlasting " we publicly proclaim our faith. So when the words are said " The Lord Jesus Christ, in the same night that he was betrayed took Bread," we proclaim the Lord's death. Such sentences as " Glory be to God on high, and on earth peace, good will towards men " herald forth the Gospel. They are *Kerygma* or " preaching " in the Apostolic sense. We need not feel that Dr. Dodd disparages our sermons when he expresses a doubt whether much of our preaching in the Church at the present day would have been recognised by the early Christians as such. We do not as a rule proclaim these truths from the pulpit; indeed, it would be hard to do so effectively—at least for most of us. The Body of Christ itself proclaims them in the Liturgy.

What the Apostles did when they " preached Christ," " preached the Gospel," " preached the Kingdom of Heaven," the confident, brief, triumphant heralding of the essential elements of the Faith, is contained in the service itself. It is pre-supposed in all our teaching; it is the foundation of which the sermon is the super-structure. St. Paul's Epistles themselves are not *Kerygma* but *Didache*; but all his " teaching " is built upon the foundation of " Jesus Christ," on what he calls " The Gospel."

To illustrate this point by a concrete instance. On a spring evening, as I passed through the Abbey Gate at Chester, a street evangelist was declaiming his gospel in stentorian tones. " God so loved the world," he cried, " that He gave us His Son; His only Son. This is what I have to say to you people of Chester. I do not know what you are going to do about it. God gave His Son! " As I got further off I still heard in the distance, " His Son! His only

Son! Eternal Life! "—words hammered by the speaker into his audience with rhythmic, persistent repetition. "Why," I thought, "can we not get this kind of simple gospel appeal inside the Cathedral? Must this message be only given in the street, with an implied challenge to the official Church, outside the House of God, under its very walls?"

Two days afterwards, while we were singing the solemn Eucharist in the choir on Whit Monday, the nave of the Cathedral was packed with tourists, casual sight-seers, taking the Cathedral as part of their day's outing. It happened that I remembered the street preacher; his words were still running in my head, but I had forgotten the opening of the Gospel for the day. It came with a shock of surprise when the Deacon from the chancel steps intoned "God so loved the world that He gave His only begotten Son." Those very words, surrounded by what may have seemed the unusual pageantry [1] of lights and coloured vestments, may well have rung in the ears of some excursionist from the Potteries on that Bank Holiday, as the street missioner's had done in mine.

The tone in which Gospel is declaimed is that of assertion: Amen, Amen, I say to you. The Church is not the lecture room; there are other places for the scientific analysis of the Word of God; our liturgical sermon need not smell of the synoptic problem. The Bible Class is the place to argue and discuss, but there is also a place to listen to the Word of God with a simple, obedient and receptive mind. "He that hath an ear, let him hear what the Spirit saith unto the Churches."

The *Kerygma* of the Church is committed to the whole Body which "with one mind and one mouth glorifies God." The *Didache* is entrusted to the preacher. The good news of the Gospel is the foundation; the sermon is the superstructure; it may be of gold, silver, precious stones, wood, hay or stubble, but the foundation must always be the same; "Other foundation can no man lay than that is laid, which is Jesus Christ."

[1] The Church surely ought to make its witness solemn and arresting. Pageantry is not inappropriate to the herald. The town crier has his bell and his cocked hat, the auctioneer his hammer, the herald has his tabard and his trumpeters.

A LIST OF TITLES FOR SUNDAYS AND HOLY-DAYS

According to the Book of Common Prayer

Based on the title-headings in the *Evangeliebok* of the Church of Sweden.[1]

	General Heading.	Heading to Epistle.	Heading to Gospel.
Advent Sunday.	The Lord's coming to His Church.	The new day demands a new way of life.	The entry of Jesus into Jerusalem.
Advent II.	Waiting for the Day of the Lord.	Patience sustains hope.	Signs of the Lord's coming.
Advent III.	The Lord's forerunner.	The faithful servant appeals to the Lord's judgment.	The message of John to Jesus.
Advent IV.	The Lord is at hand.	The nearness of the Lord's coming awakens joy.	The witness of John.
Christmas Day.	The birth of Jesus.	*The glory of the Son.	*The Word made flesh.
St. Stephen.	The martyrs.	The first martyr bears witness to Christ.	The fate of God's messengers.
*St. John Evangelist.	*The apostolic testimony to the Light.	*The Word manifested in the flesh.	*God works with life-times.
*Holy Innocents.	*God glorified in the children.	*Blessed are the pure in heart.	*The children's deaths.
Sunday after Christmas.	The lowliness of Jesus' childhood.	Christ bestows son-ship to God.	*The birth of Jesus.
Circumcision.	The new year.	*The circumcision of the Spirit.	The name Jesus.
Epiphany.	The arising of the Light.	*The Gospel for all nations.	The wise men from the east.
Epiphany I.	Jesus learning and teaching.	A Christian offers spiritual temple-worship.	Jesus in the temple at 12 years of age.
Epiphany II.	The presence of Jesus sanctifies the home.	Common life demands faithfulness and love.	The marriage at Cana.
Epiphany III.	The power of Jesus to create faith on earth.	Evil overcome by good.	Jesus heals the centurion's servant.
Epiphany IV.	The power of Jesus to help in danger and perplexity.	*The Christian under the civil power.	Jesus stills the storm.
Epiphany V.	The power of Jesus to gather and to keep His own.	Love creates unity.	The wheat and the tares.

[1] In this list, the Swedish title is translated in every case where the Swedish usage corresponds to ours : all that is not derived from the Swedish book is marked with an asterisk *. The translations have been made and additional titles compiled by the Rev. A. G. Hebert, S.S.M.

	General Heading.	Heading to Epistle.	Heading to Gospel.
Epiphany VI.	*The hope of the second advent.	*The Lord to whom all hearts are open.	*The coming of the Lord to gather His elect.
Septuagesima.	All is of grace.	An incorruptible prize to be won.	The labourers in the vineyard.
Sexagesima.	The word of God.	Toil and danger must not frighten the ministers of the word.	Four kinds of soil.
Quinquagesima.	The way of the passion.	Greatest of all is charity.	Jesus goes up to Jerusalem.
*Ash Wednesday.	*Fasting according to the spirit.	*Humiliation for sin.	*Treasure in heaven.
Lent I.	Temptation.	God gives His servants patience.	Jesus tempted in the wilderness.
Lent II.	Faith under conflict.	God calls us to holiness.	The Canaanite woman.
Lent III.	Assault and defence.	The children of light are to walk in the light.	Teaching of Jesus about the power of evil.
Lent IV.	Bread for the hungry.	The covenant of freedom is better than that of bondage.	Jesus feeds 5000 men.
Lent V.	Increasing hatred.	The sacrifice of Christ cleanses the conscience.	The bitterness of the Jews against Jesus.
Palm Sunday.	The going away.	The humiliation of Christ.	*The Passion according to St. Matthew.
*Monday in Holy week.	*The conflict with evil.	*The Divine Warrior.	*The Passion according to St. Mark.
*Tuesday in Holy Week.	*The suffering of Love.	*The Servant of the Lord in patient endurance.	*The Passion according to St. Mark.
*Wednesday in Holy Week.	*Redemption through suffering.	*The One Sacrifice.	*The Passion according to St. Luke.
*Maundy Thursday.	*Looking forward through the Passion to the Feast in the heavenly kingdom.	*The sacrament of the Sacrifice.	*The Passion according to St. Luke.
Good Friday.	The crucifixion of Jesus.	*The obedience of the Divine Victim.	*The Passion according to St. John.
*Easter Eve.	*Buried with Christ in his death.	*Put to death in the flesh.	*Waiting in the grave.
Easter Day.	The resurrection of Christ.	*Risen with Christ.	*The first day of the week.
Easter Monday.	The witnesses of the resurrection.	The risen Lord is proclaimed to the heathen.	The disciples at Emmaus.
*Easter Tuesday.	*The Gospel of the resurrection.	*The mighty works of God.	*Jesus stood in the midst.
Easter I.	The Lord liveth.	The new life of faith overcomes the world.	*Peace be unto you.
Easter II.	The Shepherd and the sheep.	The example of Christ calls us to follow.	The Good Shepherd.

	General Heading.	Heading to Epistle.	Heading to Gospel.
Easter III.	The longing for home.	The Christian is a stranger and a pilgrim.	Jesus teaches the short duration of affliction.
Easter IV.	The benefits of Jesus' 'going away.'	Heavenly gifts involve responsibility.	Jesus teaches of growth in the Truth.
Rogation Sunday.	Prayer.	The hearers of the word must also be doers.	Jesus teaches prayer in His Name.
Ascension Day.	From humiliation to exaltation.	Jesus promises to establish the Kingdom of God.	Jesus sends forth the Apostles and ascends into heaven.
Sunday after Ascension.	Waiting for the Spirit.	The time of waiting is filled with work.	Jesus promises the Spirit.
Whitsunday.	The outpouring of the Spirit.	The Spirit poured out on the Apostles.	Jesus teaches of the guidance of the Spirit.
Whitmonday.	The way of the Spirit through the world.	The Spirit is poured out also upon the heathen.	God gave His only-begotten Son.
*Whittuesday.	*Ordination.	*The gift of the Spirit by the laying on of hands.	*True and false shepherds.
Trinity Sunday.	The new life of the Spirit.	*The heavenly worship.	Jesus and Nicodemus.
Trinity I.	Irreplaceable goods.	Perfect love casteth out fear.	The rich man and Lazarus.
Trinity II.	The call to God's kingdom.	He that loveth hath passed from death unto life.	The great banquet.
Trinity III.	God's prevenient grace.	God both calls and makes perfect.	The lost sheep and the lost coin.
Trinity IV.	Man's judgment and God's.	The creation longs for its liberty.	The mote and the beam.
Trinity V.	Discipleship.	The Christian is called to inherit a blessing.	The great catch of fish.
Trinity VI.	The law of God.	The old man is crucified with Christ.	Jesus teaches of his higher righteousness.
Trinity VII.	*Growth in grace.	*Bondage and freedom.	*The bread of life.
Trinity VIII.	Error.	The Spirit testifies that we are children of God.	False prophets.
Trinity IX.	Stewardship with responsibility.	Disorderly living leads to ruin.	The unjust steward.
Trinity X.	Lost opportunities.	The Spirit's gifts are manifold.	Jesus weeps over Jerusalem.
Trinity XI.	True and false righteousness.	Grace gives humility and strength.	The Pharisee and the Publican.
Trinity XII.	The use of the tongue.	The letter killeth and the Spirit giveth life.	Jesus heals the deaf and dumb man.
Trinity XIII.	Compassion.	The Promise is more ancient than the Law.	The Good Samaritan.

	General Heading.	Heading to Epistle.	Heading to Gospel.
Trinity XIV.	Thankfulness.	The Spirit suffereth not the works of the flesh.	The Ten Lepers.
Trinity XV.	Daily bread.	Christians are to bear one anothers' burdens.	The most important thing to take thought for.
Trinity XVI.	The shadow of death.	The Spirit gives strength in the inward man.	The widow's son at Nain.
Trinity XVII.	The freedom of a Christian man.	The unity of the Spirit must be kept.	Jesus at the Pharisee's dinner.
Trinity XVIII.	The way of perfection.	Christ bestows patience to the end.	The great commandment of the Law.
Trinity XIX.	Faith in time of tribulation.	The old man resists the new man.	The paralytic.
Trinity XX.	Spiritual neglect.	Time must be used well and wisely.	The man without the wedding garment.
Trinity XXI.	The true support of faith.	The Christian must wear the Divine armour.	The nobleman's son.
Trinity XXII.	Forgiving one another.	Abounding love gives spiritual wisdom.	The unmerciful servant.
Trinity XXIII.	Citizenship.	A Christian has citizenship in heaven.	Tribute to Cæsar.
Trinity XXIV.	The life that never dies.	The saints have inheritance in light.	Jairus' daughter.
Sunday before Advent.	*Perseverance.	*Hope in the living God.	*The Bread of Life.
*St. Andrew.	*Missionary vocation.	*The Gospel for all nations.	*Fishers of men.
*St. Thomas.	*From doubt to faith.	*God's spiritual temple.	*Faith perfected in self-abasement.
*St. Paul.	*The Apostle of the Gentiles.	*A chosen vessel.	*The reward unmerited.
Candlemas.	Revelation.	The Promised One comes.	Symeon's hymn.
*St. Matthias.	*False and true apostles.	*Rejection and election.	*Knowledge of God.
Annunciation.	The Annunciation.	The promise of Immanuel.	The Angels' tidings to Mary.
*St. Mark.	*The Resurrection and the Gospel.	*The Body of Christ.	*The Vine and the Branches.
*St. Philip and St. James.	*The Way of eternal life.	*Endurance of temptation.	*Christ the Way.
*St. Barnabas.	*Manifold gifts.	*Pastoral work at Antioch.	*Fruit that remains.
St. John Baptist.	Earth and heaven.	The Forerunner's message of consolation.	Birth of the Baptist.
*St. Peter.	*The apostolic office.	*Peter delivered from prison.	*The rock of Peter's faith.
*St. James.	*Obedience to vocation.	*James the martyr.	*The cup and the baptism.

Q

	General Heading.	Heading to Epistle.	Heading to Gospel.
*St. Bartholomew.	*The word preached and received.	*The word with power.	*Servants of the servants of God.
*St. Matthew.	*Consecration of wealth.	*The Gospel in sincerity and truth.	*Renunciation for the Gospel's sake.
St. Michael and all angels.	Greatness and lowliness.	Michael's conflict with the dragon.	The greatest in the Kingdom of Heaven.
*St. Luke.	*The Gospel for the healing of the nations.	*Labour and patience.	*The missionaries.
*St. Simon and St. Jude.	*The Church's foundation.	*Warning against false teaching.	*The Spirit of the Truth.
All Saints.	The Saints.	The great multitude before the throne.	The Beatitudes.

The following three Meditations [1] are submitted as a sample of the way in which these Titles may be used, as for instance at a Preparation for Communion after Saturday Evensong, or as providing the scheme of a Liturgical Sermon.

THIRD SUNDAY IN ADVENT

The Lord's forerunner

The church service for to-day suggests a striking picture: in the foreground one coming, bearing a message; and in the background, behind him, there comes Another, a vast figure, the Lord Himself. So the *Collect* speaks of the clergy as sent in the Lord's Name, sent not on their own errands but on His, to prepare His way.

In the *Epistle* one of the messengers explains what he is: only a minister (servant) of Christ, only a steward. As such, he must be faithful; but it is not for his people, nor even for himself, to pronounce judgment of approval or condemnation on his words and actions: it is the Lord, the Coming One, who is the final Judge.

In the *Gospel* we see another messenger, in direct contrast with the Lord Himself. The messenger is commended for his faithfulness: he is " a prophet, and more than a prophet." But behind him comes the Lord Himself, and

---

[1] A complete set of these Meditations is in preparation. Some of them are appearing in the *Chichester Diocesan Gazette*, beginning with Nov. 1936.

His mighty works show who He is: men are healed and saved in body and soul, and the poor have the Gospel preached to them.

Consider therefore what the Clergy are: ministers of Christ, stewards of God's mysteries, sent to prepare the Lord's way, as shepherds of His flock. Pray for them and for those who are being ordained this Embertide.

Second Sunday after Trinity
The Call to God's Kingdom

The Kingdom of Heaven is like a Banquet: compare St. Matthew's version of the same parable (see Gospel for Trinity XX), where it is said explicitly that the King (God) has made a marriage for His Son (Christ, the heavenly Bridegroom). To that Feast we are invited, here at the Lord's Supper, to be guests at His Table.

Some refuse the invitation through worldliness (*i.e.* loving other things more than God): one has just got a new garden, another a motor-car, another has just married; and they make these into excuses. But we are not told this in order that we may reflect how much better we are than those who do not come to church, but rather that we may take warning for ourselves, lest through loving other things more than God, we who come to the Sacrament should not give ourselves wholly to Him; lest, while *outwardly* accepting the invitation, we should *inwardly* be refusing or half-refusing it.

This is explained in the *Epistle*, which speaks to us of love: love means self-forgetting and self-giving. He who does not love is not coming in spirit to be a guest at the Lord's Table. To refuse the call of love is to refuse life and choose death; but he who loves has passed from death to life, and the gift of God in the Sacrament is life eternal.

Make us then to have a perpetual fear and love of Thy holy Name.

EIGHTEENTH SUNDAY AFTER TRINITY
The way of perfection

Apply the words of the *Epistle* to the congregation of which you are a member: thank God, with St. Paul, for His "favour and goodness towards you," and for the spiritual gifts which He has given to you all in different ways. Pray for all those who worship with you, that God will accept your common prayer and praise, and make you to abound more and more, and give you patience unto the end—for the growth of God's people in grace looks towards a final perfection—" that ye may be blameless in the Day of our Lord Jesus Christ." And not only for those here present, but for the Church of God throughout the world, with which and in which you pray: " let us pray for the whole state of Christ's Church."

The *Gospel* shows us the two bases of the Church's life: faith—Jesus our Lord is true Man and true God; Son of David, and Son of God seated at God's right hand—and " the great commandment of the law," the complete and whole-hearted love of God, and the love of man.

Pray therefore in the words of the *Collect* for all Christians and for yourself, that we may not through sin fall short of God's high calling.

A. G. H.

XI

INSTRUCTION IN WORSHIP

By the Rev. HENRY DE CANDOLE
Chaplain of Chichester Theological College

INSTRUCTION IN WORSHIP

IT is widely recognised that the best method of teaching is by actual practice, or 'expression work.' To be a Christian is to live in the Church. To learn Christianity the best means is to join in the Church's life, where it is to be caught, and supremely in the Church's worship, which expresses the essence of the Church's life. A grain of practice—of positive experience—is worth a heap of theory. The claim of these essays is that the Church's purpose is expressed most fully in the Church's eucharistic worship, and that the meaning of worship (and therefore of the purpose of the Christian society) is to be learned best by sharing in worship.

But there is an important point to be made first. Worship is the expression of the Church's life. It springs out of that life, not as something incidental or external, but as the blossom on the tree, an essential, integral, flowering of the plant. A Parish Eucharist, as the expression of the corporate family life of a Christian community, must be rooted in a real family life. Unless that background is present, a Parish Eucharist will be but the new patch on an essentially old, individualist, garment. Other essays in this book will have elaborated this theme. But it must be taken as the foundation of much that follows. Unless the parish priest has in his own mind the vision of his work as the building up of a genuine family life, a fellowship to be by its corporate witness the instrument of Christ, the suggestions of this essay will be largely irrelevant. That family life will have its centre in worship, and the worship will itself be a means of instruction in the corporate spirit.

1. Occasional and Daily Offices

'Liturgy,' in its sense of the ordered arrangements of the various acts of public worship, has its own message. It is indeed the best point at which to start instruction, for it is practice and not theory. But Liturgy needs to be interpreted. It is clothed in words. It is focussed in actions. It is expressed by ceremonial. It has a form and shape not always immediately recognisable. It is the product of history, woven from many strands of Christian experience. These need to be explained, partly by words, partly by proper ' presentation ' (and the dramatic term is consonant with Liturgy). This does not require specialist knowledge, but should be as much part of the parish priest's equipment as the parallel study of Theology which is the basis of his teaching in school or pulpit. Liturgy *is* Theology in another form, a form continually at hand, to use or fail to use.[1]

It is with the Sacrament of Initiation that we must start. There is perhaps no point at which reform is more needed or might be more fruitful for instruction, than in our practice here. Fr. Benson of Cowley was surely right when he claimed that if equal attention had been paid in the Church Revival of the last century to Holy Baptism as to the other great Sacrament of the Gospel, Churchmanship would be far better understood. For Baptism is the Sacrament of Churchmanship. Its benefits to the individual come to him through, and because of, his incorporation

[1] Reference should be made in any treatment of this subject to the very interesting ' Instructions on Worship ' known as the *Lectures on the Mysteries* of St. Cyril of Jerusalem, about 350 A.D. They were delivered to the newly-baptized on the days of Easter week succeeding their Baptism, Anointing, and First Communion, in order that they might " be taught the reasons of everything which has been done " (Lect. xviii. 33). He interprets in turn the Renunciation, Baptism, Anointing, the Body and Blood of Christ, and the Liturgy from the Lavabo to the end.

They are printed in St. Cyril's Catechetical Lectures, Nos. xix.– xxiii. (Wace and Schaff's *Nicene and Post-Nicene Fathers*, Vol. VII); an English translation by Dr. R. M. Woolley has been published by the Faith Press (1s.), entitled *Instructions on the Mysteries by St. Cyril of Jerusalem*.

into Christ and His Body the Church. The whole setting of the Baptismal Office is clearly assumed to be a public service, an act of admission to the Christian family—of course it is this, however few be present; but the fact should be given actual outward expression. The catechumen, infant or adult, is brought into a family, surrounding him at the font, and welcoming him by their presence and manifest interest in this great family occasion. Therefore Baptism is ordered by the Prayer Book to be normally on a Sunday or holy day, " when the most number of people come together," and as an integral part of one of the public Offices of the day. There is a congregation, who take their part in the framework of the service, thus performing a real and actual share in the liturgical action. There is also a smaller group with a more particular and personal part to play, the sponsors: themselves (as the whole tenor of their function and answers proclaim) practising Christians, pledging themselves on behalf of the child for whose Christian training they undertake responsibility. There is the priest with his attendants, performing the ceremony itself—the Baptism and naming, followed by the solemn Reception into the Church with the signing of the Cross. Here is a picture of Churchmanship: of the entry into a new relation with God, by membership in His covenanted people, with its privileges and responsibilities and opportunities. The Prayer Book service is indeed shorn of many of the old symbolic ceremonies—the white robes of forgiveness and purity; the oil (or rather chrism) of God's anointing, or sealing; [1] the draught of milk and honey proclaiming admission to the Promised Land of God's holy people. The immersion beneath the waters remains still the technical rule, with ' dipping ' as the alternative now practically universal. But the symbolism, even of the ' dipping,' brings back all the suggestions of the Christian's mystical share in Christ's death, burial, and resurrection, as worked out by St. Paul in Romans vi. Nothing can bring home more clearly the specific thoughts and teaching of Easter Even

---

[1] These are New Testament terms: II Cor. i. 22; Ephes. i. 13, 14; I John ii. 20, 27.

than a Solemn Baptism at Evensong, or as part of the ancient Easter Eve ceremonies—following as it does the precedent of all Christian antiquity. So too the use of the other ancient baptismal day, Whitsun Even, brings into prominence its close connection with Pentecost, with the birth of the Church Catholic, and membership in the Body of Christ. At least occasionally also Baptism should be administered publicly during Mattins or Evensong on a Sunday. Such an occasion is itself a 'visible sermon' on Christian discipleship and Church membership. After the Second Lesson, the choir, headed by cross, lights (and incense), will proceed, singing such a hymn as " In token that thou shalt not fear " (E.H. 337), to the font, followed by priest in cope and his servers to meet the parents and godparents with the children or adult catechumens at the font. After the saying of the introductory prayers, the Gospel (with its responses before and after) will be sung, and the homily said in the natural voice. The Questions will be put, in a lower but audible voice, to the group of godparents. The Blessing of the Water will be sung (at least if the 1928 Order is used) to the tone of a Preface. The naming, baptism and reception into the Church will follow with due dignity. The concluding section of Thanksgiving is an act of the whole congregation, who will join in the Lord's Prayer. The final exhortation, rightly headed in 1928 " The duties of the Godfathers and Godmothers," will be addressed to them, and the procession will re-form and be led back to the choir during the singing of the Nunc Dimittis.

Even at weekday Baptisms, such dignity and public character as are available will be given by public announcement, the provision if possible of a congregation, and the use of cope and servers with cross, or at least, lights. No Baptism but should give the impression of the Church's sense of the importance of the Sacrament. Notice should always be required at least two or three days beforehand; a form filled up, including names of Godparents; the home visited if possible before the Baptism, and of course afterwards; the child's name entered on a baptismal roll, kept perhaps by the Kindergarten or Sunday-School superintendents, who will invite it to join the appropriate school as soon as it is of age. An annual birthday card on the anniversary of baptism may provide a means of contact during the intervening years. When children have been privately baptized, the opportunity will always be taken of their public reception into the Church.

So the child (where, as with us, infant baptism is normal) begins his Christian life. From early days a great part of his instruction in Christianity will come from his sharing in the worship of the family; not at a separate Children's Eucharist, but at the Parish Communion, where he will see the older members making their Communion, and be aware that at present his participation is incomplete; where also he will form a habit of attendance which will last him beyond childhood, all his life. From the Eucharist he will catch the meaning of the Christian fellowship, and something of its fundamental beliefs—the reality of God, self-offering through Christ, the way made open into the heavenlies. Theology will be clothed in action; the great days marked by Processions; Christmas by the Crib, Lent or Passiontide by the veiling of pictures and statues, Palm Sunday by the palms, Eastertide by the Paschal Candle, while the varying colours of altar and vestment impress on his eye the changing course of the Christian Year.[1]

In due course he comes to be confirmed. Like Baptism, the service of Confirmation should carry its own message. It is a public service. The congregation is present to witness the profession of obedience made by the candidates, and to surround them with their prayers and fellowship. Some, as Confirmation godparents (according to the rubric [2]),

---

[1] *The Way of Churchmanship* (S.P.C.K., 4d.) and *Worshipping Together* ('Children and Life' series, no. 5—S.P.C.K., 4d.) have some valuable suggestions for the religious training of little children. *A Little Princess*, an allegory on the Eucharist for children (A. M. Tennant, Mowbray, 3s. 6d.), is an admirable introduction to the service for quite young children. Of Sunday School lessons for older ones, the best is probably A. H. Walker's *Lessons on the Eucharist* (the National Society). The National Society has recently published two courses of lessons on the Prayer Book which deserve mention: *Short Lessons on the Book of Common Prayer* (ages 8–11) by Hetty Lee: and *The Church's Book of Days* (ages over 11) by Sybil Longman (3s. each).

[2] Rubric after the Catechism (1662): before the Order of Confirmation (1928).

will be more particularly interested in individuals. At the centre is the Bishop as father of the whole family. After the Preface and the Question, he joins the candidates with him in the Versicles and Responses. The ancient prayer for the Holy Spirit precedes the sacramental laying on of hands, which should be unmistakably the central feature of the service. On its completion, the congregation take up their part again in the Family Prayer, and after two prayers and the Blessing, all is over. The service, intentionally short, is admirable in itself. It is a beginning, the door into full membership of the Church. Might we respectfully ask that it should more often be left to express its own meaning, and not overshadowed by long addresses? Most suitably of all, it may be administered before the Sunday Eucharist, in the presence of the family gathered for their weekly worship, the Bishop giving Communion to the newly confirmed with their brothers and sisters in Christ.

On other of the ' occasional Offices ' we can only touch, but all need to be explained. In the Marriage Service we have, despite all criticisms, a clear expression of the principles of Christian marriage. To go through it beforehand with the engaged couple would show the spirit in which the Church regards the marriage vows, and prevent many misconceptions. But the best expression of the meaning of marriage is the true Christian wedding—the joining in Holy Matrimony of two faithful members of the family, surrounded and supported by their brothers and sisters in Christ, and completed with the Communion of the bride and bridegroom as their first act of married life. To many, accustomed only to the Church service as part of a social ceremony, such a wedding gives a fresh vision of the Church's thought and teaching about marriage.

The same may be said also of the Church's rites of burial. The service for the Burial of the Dead is itself jejune, a meditation on death for the survivors rather than the expression of the natural and Christian instincts of mourners for a loved one. But its completion in the offering of the Eucharist—most of all, with the accompaniments of the music and ceremonial of a Solemn Requiem—bring home those mingled thoughts of penitence and hope, with which the Christian Church teaches us to regard the death of one of the faithful. Human frailty, even in the best; but Christ's perfect offering. Separation in visible presence; but continual and continuous unity in the fellowship of Christ's people. The sacred rites of the Church proclaim these truths more touchingly and with greater restraint than any sermon.

Mattins and Evensong, the daily Offices of our Prayer Book, would deserve longer treatment than we can give. Much criticism is levelled against them, not a little of it due to a misconception of their object. They are not meant for beginners in the way of worship. They were never constructed as a substitute for the Eucharist. They are the subsidiary services for the faithful communicant, satellites round the sun. To appreciate them demands considerable spiritual experience, and they lack the dramatic action of sacraments. Their essence lies in the regularity of Psalm and Lesson, their place in the continuous stream of worship offered by the Church to God on behalf of the forgetful world. The individual comes to put himself into that stream of the Church's prayer, not to be catered for as an individual. It may well be that for the little-instructed who may ' drop in ' to church on Sunday nights we need something quite different. To use or adapt the Offices for that purpose may be to misuse them. The Psalms and the Old Testament do not at once explain their meaning. They need knowledge, not of the critical sort, but of the ' Christian culture ' which has used them for generations, which has (maybe) read into them its own meaning, interpreted, applied, overlaid them. Israel and Jerusalem are God's people, His agelong Church, not Jewish now, but Catholic. Edom and Ammon are not national foes, but the eternal enemies of God and His Church, the hosts of spiritual wickedness. David, the anointed King, is His greater Son, the Christ. The cursing of an individual foe becomes the Church's detestation of the devil and all his works. The history of the Jewish people is typical of the Christian

Church; God's providence and God's judgments on the one, typical of the other.

Now, all this is the entry into a great world of traditional Christian devotion, which itself requires instruction; and this instruction we must provide. Some account will be given, first of the *rationale* of the services; the preparatory (and detachable) section of penitence; the Psalms, the backbone of the whole, the Church's expression of her varying moods, desires, aspirations Godward, into which the individual enters as he is able, and learns to grow thereby in knowledge and approach to God; the Lessons reflecting the vision of God in His Providence and His redemptive acts; the Canticles expressing the Church's answer to His revelation. Then all that has been caught afresh of God's glory is poured into the recitation of the Creed, and transmuted into prayer. We join in the Lord's Prayer now with fuller understanding and deeper meaning, and its accents are carried over into the remainder of the Office, the Collect for the week forging the link with the Eucharist of the morning or of the previous Sunday.[1]

On the principle of 'expression work,' such outline instruction may best be given *before* the recitation of the Office (in place of a sermon following). At another time, the Christian interpretation of the Psalms must be explained and illustrated. Bishop Walpole's *People's Psalter* [2] may well prove useful for the lines of such exposition. An experiment, which has proved valuable in Holy Week, is that of explaining before the service the application of the Psalms and Lessons, using the admirable revised selections. The Office then used becomes an intelligent spiritual participation in the liturgical keeping of the season. Such a method is also possible and valuable at Retreats or Quiet Days.

---

[1] Two small S.P.C.K. pamphlets (2*d.* each) may be mentioned as useful: *Evensong Explained*, by Dr. Lowther Clarke, and *How to Make Mattins and Evensong Real*, by the Rev. C. A. M. Stewart, though the latter misses the full corporate interpretation of the Psalms.

[2] Elliott Stock, 3*s.* 6*d.*

2. THE HOLY EUCHARIST

It is time to turn to the need of instruction on the Holy
Eucharist itself. We do not need to emphasise again the
truth that liturgical worship is essentially a corporate act.
Our aim then is the active and instructed worship of the
whole congregation, worship from which in turn they gain
further grasp of the meaning of their Christianity.

Part of such instruction is addressed deliberately to, or
through, the mind. In the Ante-Communion, instruction
of this kind plays the principal part. Each Sunday has its
own Collect and Scripture passages.[1] The Collect directs
the Church's intention for her members' common prayer
that day—Gospel and Epistle direct our minds towards
particular incidents in the Christian revelation, or particular
virtues of practical Christian life. They are meant to
colour the service of each Sunday, to provide not only
variety but an ordered round of teaching to stimulate worship,
and they will normally form the basis of the brief eucharistic
Sermon. Wherever possible, this may suitably be linked
with later moments in the service—the Gospels of Lent IV,
Trinity VII and XXV with the Offertory, Fraction or Communion; Lent II with the Prayer of Humble Access;
Michaelmas with the *Sanctus*; All Saints with the Prayer
of Thanksgiving; Advent I or Palm Sunday with the
Benedictus; Trinity XI with the Confession; Epiphany III
with the approach to Communion; Trinity XXII with the
" Ye that do truly "; and so on. Or with particular
sections of the Prayer for the Church, the Lord's Prayer or
the Post-Communion prayers, all of which should at some
time (probably not during the Eucharist) be analysed. At

[1] Until the Reformation (as still in the Roman Mass) also its psalmody
—Introit, Gradual, Offertory and Communion passages, the ' proper '
for the day. These passages have traditional connection with the
Sundays, and carry on the primitive custom of using the Psalms at the
Liturgy. They are printed at the end of the *English Hymnal* and are not
beyond the capacity of an ordinary choir. They can be followed by
congregational hymns at *e.g.* the Offertory and the Communion.
The Introit might well be restored, as already in some churches, by
the use of the complete Psalm of which the opening verse only survives,
e.g. as printed in the *English Hymnal*.

some convenient time, possibly as a Lenten course, or in recurring series of instructions, the scheme and structure of the whole service should similarly be explained: [1] its two main divisions, the Ante-Communion or Preparation, and the Eucharist itself or Liturgy proper; the course of the latter—Offertory, penitential preparation of communicants, Canon or Consecration, Communion, Thanksgiving. This articulation of the structure of the Liturgy, as a dramatic action with a definite form, each part contributing to the progress of the whole, is of great importance.

It is emphasised most effectively by action and ceremonial, and we pass here from instruction through the mind to the very valuable, because largely unconscious, instruction through the eye and personal action.[2] Explanations will be needed of the different postures of the congregation. We stand to welcome the entry of the priest with his attendants as representing Christ in the midst of His mystical Body; to greet Him at the Gospel, as if He were Himself speaking afresh to *us* His words of Life; to share in the triumphant assertion of our common faith in the Creed, of our thanksgiving in the *Gloria*. We might well teach our people to stand also at the *Sursum Corda*, to mark the beginning of the Canon, during the whole of which the congregation was accustomed in early days to stand, representing their share with the priest in the Church's priestly offering. We sit to listen—at the Epistle and the Sermon. We kneel, in penitence, at the Kyries, Confession, etc., and for the Blessing; we have come (less reasonably) to use kneeling as the ordinary posture of prayer, even of thanksgiving. We genuflect, or bow, at the *Incarnatus* in Creed (and Last Gospel) to express our sense of the deep humility of Christ in coming down for our sakes to be made man, and as our act of adoration to hail His Presence among us after the Consecration. So the sign of the Cross expresses, at the end of the Creed, our personal ' signature ' to the Church's

---

[1] Cf. the author's *The Church's Offering* (Mowbray, 1*s*. 6*d*.).

[2] The best general introduction to the theory of ceremonial is Bishop Frere's *Principles of Religious Ceremonial* (1928 edition: Mowbray), an admirable and most illuminating study. For instruction on the meaning of the actual ceremonies, see the list at the end of this essay.

act of Faith, the reminder of our Baptism into that faith. We sign ourselves before the Gospel on head and lips and breast, an acted prayer that we may obey the Gospel in thought and word and deed; in Absolution and Blessing to accept those gifts, which with the same sign the Priest as it were conveys to us; before receiving Communion, as a devout preparation for the Lord's gift of His sacrificial life.

So the ceremonies of the service also give their message, underlining the chief points and bringing their meaning into clearer relief. The Gospel procession from altar to nave presents the picture of Christ and His Church leaving the sanctuary to come down into the common world of men, to proclaim the Good News. The Cross leads; the lights and incense symbolise the illumination and fragrance of the Gospel message; the attendants round the deacon are the Church—laity, not clergy alone, setting forth Christ's witness in the world. The congregation hail the revelation in Christ with their triumphant " Glory be to Thee, O Lord " at its announcement. The deacon represents the Christ Himself, proclaiming the heavenly message, Christ's own words or deeds, not past only but addressed to, done amongst, His disciples in this as every age. Traditionally it is sung towards the north, the region of darkness and ignorance.

The Offertory again, too often a mere matter of the sanc-tuary to which the congregation pays no heed, deserves the fullest ceremonial we can give to show its meaning. It is the offering of the people's labour, originally made in kind, as an acknowledgment of powers and gifts God-given. Its symbolism underlies the rest of the liturgical drama. It is these offerings of the Church, unworthy at their best, which Christ in Consecration takes up into His perfect sacrifice and makes worthy; which He gives back in Communion as the vehicle of His life to be lived out by His members in the daily occupations, where they win their daily bread and give their witness to Him. Some restoration of the Offertory Procession through the Congregation, if possible (like the alms) by representatives of the people themselves, might well be attempted.[1] Its significance will in any case be explained,

[1] See Essay XIII, p. 277 below.

R

but the act is of greater teaching value than any words.

Again, the ceremonial (however it may differ in detail in different churches) during and after the Prayer of Consecration needs explantion. Attention should be drawn to the Manual Acts ordered by the Prayer Book, as repeating the actions of Christ in the Upper Room and taking us back to the very institution of the Sacrament. The Elevation is a teaching symbol of the atoning work of Christ offered as Man towards God, and of the Eucharist as the perpetual memorial before God and man of that one perfect Offering. The gong, the lights, the incense, greet the Presence of Christ the King amidst His people. The church bell unites with the worshippers in church the faithful absent through sickness or press of work, and proclaims to the world around the Church's intercession for her in her midst. The Amen of the congregation—St. Jerome describes it in earlier days as like a " roll of thunder " [1]—attests the participation in the eucharistic act of the whole Body, for whom the priest is mouthpiece. The silence that follows draws earth and heaven together in one act of common adoration of God's redeeming love. The Fraction speaks of Christ's death; the Commixture of His Resurrection; the Kiss of Peace of the unity of the brethren now to be consummated in Communion; the lifting of the Host, as the priest turns to give Communion, of Christ coming forth to feed His people; the gift to each one personally of his share in Bread and Cup, of Christ's entry into each individual soul; the kneeling side by side, of the one Body of Christ in which every soul is a member, and from which each receives the power to live and bear witness within his own sphere to the one Lord. After Communion, the whole fellowship pledges itself afresh, thus reunited to each other in the Lord, to the Godward offering of self and life in the Lord's Prayer, the prayer of the Christian family; of which some thoughts are drawn out more fully in the Prayer of Oblation or Thanksgiving which

---

[1] " Ubi sic ad similitudinem cœlestis tonitrus AMEN reboat, et vacua idolorum templa quatiuntur? "—Preface to St. Jerome's Commentary on Galatians.

follows. The Gloria again unites in thanksgiving earth with heaven, the Church below with the angels, for Incarnation, Redemption, the heavenly Kingship, the glory of the eternal Trinity. Then with the blessing the priest sends them back into the world ("lets them depart" is the rubric) [1] to carry out into daily life the power of Christ in His Body into which they have been bound up afresh in the Offering and Communion of the Eucharist. A common breakfast together, where possible, will further emphasise this aspect, and be itself an instruction in the meaning of the Church.

We may draw out more fully the teaching value of some parts of the setting of the Eucharist. Incense has been mentioned incidentally. It is not, of course, a mere elaboration. It is the world-wide and scriptural symbol of prayer, a vivid picture of the Church's offering in Christ borne up to heaven. It speaks too of the cleansing of the Church in her approach to God at the opening of the service; [2] of the honour due to Christ in His Word (at the Gospel), as in His sacramental presence (at the Consecration); of the uniting of people with priest in the eucharistic action, at the censing of the congregation after the Offertory.

The eucharistic vestments again speak of the continuity of the Church, by the simple historical fact of the priest's wearing of the same vestments as have been worn all down the ages; of his ministering as the representative of Christ, in garments which represent his putting on of Christ's own priesthood. Other interpretations, which have been put upon them, are more arbitrary, but they are not therefore without devotional value, for example, their explanation as the instruments of the Passion, or the armour of the Christian warfare. [3]

---

[1] Cf. *Ite missa est*: i.e. the Church is dismissed, from serving God in the liturgy to serve Him in home and office and factory.

[2] In the Old Testament, another idea of incense was as " a veil between the presence of God and sinful man " (*New Commentary* on Leviticus xvi. 3). Cf. Isa. vi. 5.

[3] We need to keep the distinction between *origin* and *interpretation*. *E.g.* the vestments originated as the clothes of the better-class Roman of the third and fourth centuries, continued in use for ceremonial occasions such as the celebration of the Liturgy. Interpretations (not very happily termed ' mystical '), such as those given above, came later, and appeal differently to different minds. See the interpretation quoted on p. 308, below.

Of the value of colours we have spoken already, and we need only underline what has been said in other Essays [1] of the immense importance of the really careful choosing of hymns. They may add enormously to the provision of the right setting, or mar it quite disastrously.

Finally, if our worship is to teach rightly the meaning of the fellowship of the Church, certain points in our practice in regard to Communion may need revision. There is the matter of frequency of Communion. Can we remain content with an individual rule? This is the common meeting-place of the whole family week by week; can we be content with less than a weekly rule of Communion? So our preparation will be made from a different angle. We are coming not merely to perform our individual duty, but to join in a corporate act. What is our contribution to the common offering? Best of all, such preparation will be made together on Saturday evening in church. First, the priest will outline the Church's intention for the morrow, taken from the Collect, Epistle, Gospel, etc.,[2] indicating some or all of the following:—(1) What picture of Christ, or of God, is there specially presented for out *adoration*; (2) what subject for common *contrition*, and (3) for *thanksgiving*; (4) what Christian *grace* should be particularly sought for the congregation's life of witness; (5) what subject for wider *intercession* on behalf of the Church or of the world. These should be given as briefly and clearly as possible, e.g. in a form which could be summed up as "biddings" at the Eucharist on Sunday.[3] Secondly, among prayers of preparation there will be opportunity for personal self-examination, considering sin not only as a matter of individual failing but in its effect on the witness

[1] See pp. 221 and 281–2.
[2] The Meditations on pp. 230–2 will serve as examples for expansion in a brief address.
[3] Example of intentions for the Sunday before Advent:—

(1) Adoration—God, rewarder of His faithful. (Collect.)
(2) Contrition—lack of will to serve God. (Collect.)
(3) Thanksgiving—the bounteous mercies of God, typified by the rich banquet of the Lord's Table. (Gospel.)
(4) Petition—faithful and fruitful service. (Collect.)
(5) Intercession—" justice in the earth." (Epistle.)

of the Body. An outline is given at the end of the Essay suggesting the method of approach. Even if only a few can come, a service of preparation of this sort on Saturday evening is of the greatest help to the worship of the morrow. Those who cannot come will be encouraged to make their private preparation along these lines. To allow individualism to creep in at such points is to detract from the meaning of the Eucharist as the great act of common worship. We shall find, indeed, that it becomes a touchstone by which to test our approach to a multitude of problems, a call in many cases to re-orientate details of our teaching and of our practice.[1]

3. LITURGICAL MISSIONS

We may conclude with a brief outline of a more particular and concentrated form of Instruction in Worship.[2] The method known as a Liturgical Mission is still a novelty in the Church of England, and in the stage of experiment, but it owes much to experience gained on the Continent, particularly by the Benedictine Fathers of Mont-César, Belgium. The name, though not wholly satisfactory, expresses concisely the intention. It is a ' Mission,' for its object is the quickening of religion in a parish; not so much through conversion of individuals, or of outsiders, as by a revival among the faithful of the corporate sense of union in Christ, and of the call to common witness through membership in the Church. It is ' liturgical,' because the message comes through a better understanding of the way of worship.

Such a Mission requires a background of steady teaching, preferably over several years, and a parish priest in full sympathy with the corporate ideals of worship and of Churchmanship. More immediate preparation over the three or four months preceding the chosen date will consist, partly perhaps in a series of sermons or instructions, certainly in the use of every means to stimulate interest and

---

[1] On this (as on other matters touched upon in this Essay) the author may be allowed to refer to their further treatment in his *The Sacraments and the Church* (Mowbray, 3s. 6d.).

[2] A fuller description will be found in the *Church Quarterly Review* for October 1936.

prepare the soil.[1] Some congregational practices of music for the Eucharist in which all can join will be advisable, where such settings are not in use. The servers also will be prepared for the demonstrations at the evening Instructions.

The Mission itself will cover three evenings (Thursday to Saturday) culminating in a Sung Eucharist with corporate communion on the Sunday morning. It may well prove the starting-point, immediately or after further consultation, of a regular Parish Eucharist. Its hour therefore will need careful thought, and will probably be neither 8 nor 11, but something between—9 a.m. or 9.15 has proved convenient. On the first night, the subject of Instruction will be the corporate nature of liturgical worship. This may cover twenty minutes or more. The congregation is then encouraged to join audibly in Amens and responses, both in saying and singing. To illustrate the theme, as well as to provide relief, the Gospel procession is demonstrated by the parish priest and servers in cassocks, the Missioner commenting on it as an example of a ceremony in which many people play their parts, including the congregation with their response to the Gospel. The latter part of the instruction will explain the different postures of priest and congregation, the use of vestments, ceremonial, etc. As an act of common worship, the service will conclude with some prayers and the singing of the Nicene Creed.

On Friday evening there should be already an increased sense of fellowship and expectancy. Questions may be answered. The Instruction will deal with the Eucharist. The meaning of the Offertory will be emphasised, and the demonstration will be of the Offertory as customarily performed in the particular church. Then the meaning of Consecration and Communion will be expounded, the purpose of the Parish Eucharist explained, and after final prayers, *Gloria in excelsis* sung together.

Saturday's Instruction will be on the individual's contribution. First, some words on seeking an *Intention* from

---

[1] S.P.C.K. publishes (3*d.*) under the title *A Way of Renewal*: no. 21, *Public Worship*, a scheme of study which might usefully form a basis for discussion groups, or suggest subjects for addresses.

the Church's Collect, Epistle and Gospel of the Sunday, and such intention given for the morrow. Next, the individual's preparation—what is my contribution? With this in mind, the demonstration may take the form of a model Offertory procession (as suggested above) coming from the back of the church to the altar. Then, all kneeling where they are, the Missioner will conduct in the aisle a brief preparation on the lines indicated, and the service end quietly with closing prayers.

The Eucharist of Sunday morning will thus come as the culmination of the Mission, putting into actual practice what has been learned. The service itself will follow lines already made familiar in this book, so no detailed description need be given. The Missioner, in pulpit or aisle, will lead the congregation in their part. In place of the sermon, the intentions given the previous night will be recalled, perhaps in the form of biddings, together with the usual prayers for the sick, etc. It has been proved in practice that this final act of worship and corporate Communion is felt to be the abiding experience of the Mission. The service will suitably be followed, if feasible, by a common breakfast. The ' following-up ' of such a Mission must depend on the circumstances of the parish. If a Parish Eucharist is not already established, it will very probably be demanded, and for this the parish priest must be ready. But the ' success ' of a Liturgical Mission cannot be tested so simply. Let one of the Belgian Fathers give his own experience. " Though these Liturgical Missions," he says, " are not directly evangelistic in their aim, indirectly they have a strong evangelistic influence through the raising of the spiritual temperature of the congregation, making them more sincerely Christian, devout, charitable." [1] Such a mission should leave behind a congregation not only better instructed in worship and its meaning, but more conscious of their membership in Christ's Body, and of their duty and privilege of witness to Him.

[1] *Questions liturgiques et paroissiales*, Feb. 1935, p. 33. This review is most valuable for information on the methods and progress of the Liturgical Movement in Belgium and elsewhere.

APPENDIX I: An Act of Self-Examination, for Public or Private Use

(This form is not suitable for regular use in church, but it has been found useful on special occasions. For private use, it may help to correct the over-individualism of many of the forms to be found in books of devotion.)

A. *The Christian family is called to be devoted to God.*

Hear the words of Our Saviour Christ:—

" The first of all the commandments is, Thou shalt love the Lord thy God with all thy heart, and with all thy soul, and with all thy strength." (S. Mark xii. 29, 30).

Have we put God first?

Have we sought His will—in the conduct of our daily lives?
in the seeking of His purpose for each of our own lives?

Have we recognised His claim on

our loyalty	— been ashamed of Him?
our trust	— given way to anxiety, or worry?
our worship	— failed to join in public worship?
our thought	— study and Bible-reading?
our money	— almsgiving?
our time	— private prayers?

B. *The Christian family is called to bring others nearer to Christ.*

Hear the words of our Saviour Christ:—

" As My Father hath sent me, even so send I you."
" Ye shall be witnesses unto Me." (S. John xx. 21. Acts i. 8.)

Let us examine our examples of Christian living.

Have we hindered others from coming to Christ? *In our home and among our friends* by bad temper? gossip? selfishness? gloominess? impatience? In our relation towards parents or children? employers or employees? *In our work* by dishonesty? lies? bad language? evil talk? cowardice in not owning to Christ? or in falling in with wrong ways?

C. *The Christian family is called to love of one another.*

Hear the words of our Saviour Christ:—

" By this shall all men know that ye are my disciples, if ye have love one to another." (S. John xiii. 35.)

i. Have our sins divided the Christian family? By quarrels? Is there anyone with whom we are not friends? whom we have not forgiven? (Offer God our resolution to make up any quarrel, as we ask forgiveness for ourselves.—Cf. Lord's Prayer, and Ye that do truly—). Are we touchy? sensitive? jealous? If so, is this due to pride? self-importance? conceit? Have we indulged in malicious talk? scandal? unkind criticism? Have we shown ourselves stand-offish? snobbish?

ii. Have we failed the Christian family in public worship?

" Not forsaking the assembling of ourselves together, as the manner of some is." (Hebrews x. 25).

At the Eucharist? other services? in our share of giving for Christ's work? in our joining in the duty of fasting?

D. *The Christian family depends on the spiritual health of all its members.*

Hear the words of Saint Paul:—

" If one member suffer, all the members suffer with it." (1 Cor. xii. 26).

Consider the secret sins which poison our own life, and prevent our contribution to the family being as good as it should be.

Thoughts of envy? jealousy? bitterness or revenge, in thought or feeling? Impurity in thought or act?

Any special sin on our own conscience?

(This may be followed by the saying of the Confession in the Communion Office, no Absolution being given until the Eucharist or in private Confession.)

APPENDIX II : BIBLIOGRAPHY

Several useful books have already been mentioned in the footnotes. For the priest, to provide a general background, may be suggested: Duchesne, *Christian Worship* (S.P.C.K., 15s.); Cabrol, *Liturgical Prayer, its History and Spirit* (Burns, Oates, and Washbourne, 6s.), E. Underhill, *Worship* (Nisbet, 10s. 6d.), and as a book of reference *Liturgy and Worship* (S.P.C.K. 15s.). The books of Guardini, a leader of the Liturgical Movement in Germany, are also most suggestive: *The Spirit of the Liturgy* (now reprinted in *The Church and the Catholic*, 5s.) and *Sacred Signs*, 2s. 6d. (both published by Sheed and Ward).

For detailed explanations of the actual ceremonies, especially of the Eucharist, the following may be noted (suitable for layfolk, or in tract cases): *The Congregation in Church*, an excellent general handbook (Mowbray, 2s.); for more specifically ' English ' ceremonial, two older books are still useful, V. Staley, *Ceremonial of the English Church* (Mowbray, 2s. 6d.), and T. I. Ball, *The Ritual Reason Why* (Mowbray, 2s.); for the ' Western ' or ' Roman ' ceremonial of High Mass, see K. D. Mackenzie: *The Way of the Church* (Mowbray, 2s. 6d.), and smaller tracts of the Church Literature Association, such as *A Guide to High Mass*, and *I Can't Follow the Service* (2d. each).

The following pamphlets in S.P.C.K. ' Little Books on Religion ' are good: no. 29, *The Communion Service Explained*; no. 32, *The Church Vestments*; no. 77, *Have you Understood Holy Communion?* (these three, 2d. each); no. 104, *Notes on the Holy Communion Service* (4d.). Also Crafer: *Our Prayer Book* (Mowbray, 6d.). *What we see in Church*, and *Some Catholic Customs* (Mowbray, 1d.). R. O. P. Taylor: *An Introduction to the Holy Communion Service* (S.P.C.K., 2d.). V. Staley, *Church Customs* (Mowbray, 1s. 3d.).

Among the many manuals for use at the Eucharist, *Our Bounden Duty* (Mowbray, 6d.) and *Adoremus* (S.P.C.K., 6d.), may be recommended.

XII

FROM A COUNTRY VILLAGE

By the Rev. F. R. FAIRBAIRN
Vicar of Alderminster

AND

The Rev. F. M. DOWNTON
Sometime Assistant Curate of Temple Balsall

FROM A COUNTRY VILLAGE

CONDITIONS to-day in country parishes are not what they used to be. There were places in the last century where it was not the etiquette of the village church to begin the morning service until the squire and his family had taken their places. Even in later Victorian days most country parishes of any size, having successfully confronted the charge of introducing Romish practices, gloried in their surpliced choirs; and to-day, though the village choir is still in many places looked upon in theory as essential to the well-being of the Church, almost as necessary as an Article of the Faith, yet in practice it is found that it can be a hindrance as well as a help—that, owing to the attractions of modern life, it is not as reliable an institution, nor as easy to maintain, as it was of old.

The isolation of rural districts has been rudely broken into, mentally and physically, by the coming of modern transport: country life is now invaded by town ideas. Many of our men are workers in industrial concerns in neighbouring towns, and just come home to sleep. Our children are wafted off in motor 'buses to urban schools for their education. The wireless, now installed in almost every house, is a very great influence indeed, mostly for good, but it makes people critical of local effort, and though it is used by a few as an excuse for not going to church, it calls to us to do our best, or be condemned as out of date. There are, too, temptations to the inhabitants of the country to provide 'bed and breakfast' for week-enders, which militate very much against their attendance in church on Sunday mornings. We are sometimes provided with 'mystery drives' by motor-'bus companies on summer evenings, which also tell against good congregations at Sunday Evensong.

Apart from this, people to-day have lost the corporate sense of the Church as the Family of God. Their conception of religion, so far as they have one, is individualistic: the thought of Holy Communion as a holy fellowship, in which all join together in the common meal of the Family, is almost non-existent. If we are to stem the tide of this individualistic religion still prevalent among Church-people who are not Catholic-minded, we must remind ourselves again and again that the Christian religion is a sacramental religion, that the Christian sacraments are social ceremonies, social acts: the acts and ceremonies of a society which is the Family of God. This essentially corporate character of Christianity lies in the fact that the Christian society, the Church, is the Body of Christ: that individual membership in it consists in a *relationship*, a living contact, of one with another, and with our Lord Himself, within the one Body. All this, no doubt, is obvious enough to a well-informed churchman; but it is not equally apparent to the rank and file of the Church, who for the most part own only a nominal membership in the Church.

This irresponsible attitude to the Church as a purely human institution, loyalty to which is optional, a matter of opinion, and not necessarily involved in faith in our Lord Jesus Christ, accounts for an individualistic attitude not only to Holy Communion, but also to Baptism, Confirmation, and the Sacrament of Penance, all of which concern membership in the one Body of Christ, and are essentially corporate in character. Thus it is that anything we can do to develop a responsible sense of membership in the Church, as involved in loyalty to our Lord, will help men to realise the corporate character of the Church's highest act of worship: while anything we can do to stress the corporate side of Communion, and to show its social implications by means of a family gathering held in connection with it, will help to build up the corporate consciousness of the Family of God as the Body of Christ in the parish. All the fighting forces of the faithful in the parish need to be taught and encouraged to foregather on the first day of the week, and to consecrate themselves and their time to the service of

God and His Kingdom, by uniting to make the memorial of the redemption of the world by Christ in the way which He ordained. Nothing less than the obedience of faith in this matter, at the cost of real sacrifice on our part, can avail to release the forces of redemption which are sacramentally involved in that Memorial. Here is the focus of conversion, here is the hub of reunion, here the fountain of evangelistic enterprise, here in the Father's House the foretaste of heaven on earth.

Here, too, the country priest may find a refuge and reinforcement when oppressed by the numbing sense of spiritual loneliness. He may often pine for a spiritual keenness in his flock, and fail to find it: he may feel, as William Law's Ouranius felt, that he is up against a wall of contented ignorance, and be tempted to become hopeless of being able to pierce the fog of indifference to spiritual things. But let him not lose hope. All depends on keeping his own spiritual life true and real. Hopefulness is always possible for one who prays. He must learn to eternalise the common things of life. The village priest has the great advantage not only of being able to know all his people, but of praying for them individually; he has the opportunity, if he will, of bringing them one by one to God.

He has his Church and his altar: they must be used. He can, if he will, offer the Holy Sacrifice frequently, perhaps daily, for his parish, for the Church, and for the world. However isolated he may feel, he has the privilege—nay, the duty—of joining up with the rest of the Church in the *opus Dei*—that is, of saying the daily Offices, as the Prayer Book bids him, morning and evening in his church, even if he must be alone there with God and the saints and angels. And if he calls attention to this, as the Church bids him to do, by tolling the bell " a convenient time before he begins," his people will know, even though they cannot or will not join him there, that they have a man of God among them for whom prayer and the reading of God's Word are things of importance. " My house shall be called the house of prayer." But the priest must set the example.

One other thing may be said about the country priest.

He is often pitied as being more cut off from his clerical brethren than the parish priest of the town.   But if the clergy of a truly ' rural ' deanery would foregather monthly, or at least once a quarter, for corporate Communion followed by breakfast, and place the needs of their parishes before God as a band of brothers at the altar, this loneliness might be overcome in the best and highest way.   At one time we used to meet thus and sing the Eucharist together, and after breakfast one of the brethren would conduct a meditation for the rest.   This was followed by a time of silence, and then each brought forward the needs of his own parish in short statements for united intercession. There was time after this for ruridecanal business, or for theological papers.   But the fellowship in Communion and breakfast was the foundation of the whole morning's work.

It was the writer's privilege to be for twenty-nine years Vicar of the large and scattered parish of Temple Balsall, in Warwickshire.   The parish consists of a district four miles long, and three wide, in the triangle formed by Birmingham (15 m.) Warwick (10 m.) and Coventry (7 m.)   There is no village round, or even near, the Temple, which is the parish church.   This was built in the thirteenth century as a chapel for a Preceptory of the Knights Templars, and after their dissolution came into the possession of the Knights Hospitallers.   It was restored in the seventeenth century as the Chapel of a Hospital, or Almshouse for women, and a village school.   In 1850 there was a later restoration of the church by Sir Gilbert Scott, and shortly after that, in 1863, the ecclesiastical parish was constituted, and the Master of the Hospital made Vicar of a parish of more than five thousand acres, taken out of the parish of Hampton in Arden. Consequently except for the Almshouses, the School, the Master's house, and a farmhouse with five cottages, there is no village at the Temple, as the very beautiful church and little colony are called.   It stands on the edge of the parish looking into the parish of Knowle;   and parishioners have to walk one or two miles from Fen End, two and a half from Chadwick End, and a mile and a half or even farther from Balsall Street.

These conditions all contributed to favour the establishment of one united morning service, at which the faithful could receive their Communion together, fasting, and of a common meal, at which they could meet socially once a week and refresh themselves before returning home. As a result of a Mission held in 1913 we were able to establish a sung Eucharist at 8.45 a.m. as the principal service on Sunday. Matins was said at 8 o'clock. Sometimes the Litany was sung as a kind of Introit to the Eucharist. If not so sung it was always said immediately after Matins, and was followed by an interval in which the bulk of the congregation came in.

In the service all the main elements of eucharistic worship, as included in the Prayer Book Communion Service, were represented—namely, the Preaching of the Word, the offering of the Holy Sacrifice, and the communion of the priest and people, with the addition of liturgical music and hymns. The service was sung to Merbecke, edited as to the melody by E. G. P. Wyatt, and as to the accompaniment by Francis Burgess (both published by A. R. Mowbray & Co.). The choir gradually melted away, both at the Temple and at the daughter church; but the congregation sang Merbecke's melody well in a homely and natural style, and a very little musical talent went, by the blessing of God, a long way. A hymn was sung while the priest and servers made their preparation, another after the Epistle, and a third at the Offertory. At the parish church, where the organ and singers were not too near the Sanctuary, two or even three hymns were sung after the *Agnus* during the Communion of the people. The daughter church, however, was too small for this: it proved too disturbing to the communicants. The hymn after the blessing, when the ablutions were taken, was thus the fifth, sixth, or seventh, according to the number sung during the communion of the people.

The Sermon was preceded by the giving of the notices from the pulpit, and at St. Peter's, a district church of which more will be said later, by a partly extempore Bidding Prayer, in which the celebrant and the congregation were

s

reminded of causes and persons specially needing their prayers and thanksgivings. This part of the service took about a quarter of an hour, and the whole service lasted about an hour and a quarter at the Temple, and an hour and five minutes at St. Peter's.

The Temple is an extraordinarily beautiful church, shaped like a College Chapel. It was built by the Templars at the end of the thirteenth century; as the late Sir Walter Tapper said, it must have been the work of the best architect of his time. Close to it stands Lady Katherine Leveson's Hospital, a collection of seventeenth-century Almshouses, including among them the Master's house, the whole forming a rectangular block of buildings enclosing a grass court. On the other side of the church, westwards, are some much-restored remains of the old monastic buildings, part of which has been converted into two cottages, though there still remains attached to them the old hall or refectory of the erstwhile Monastery. Since it was given to the Church in the seventeenth century by Lady Katharine Leveson, a grand-daughter of Dudley, Earl of Leicester, this property has been under the management of a body of Governors or Trustees, who are also patrons of the living.

It was in a room in the Almshouse court, adjoining the Master's house, known as the Parish Room, but originally the parish Boys' School, where many of the older men received their education, and with the schoolmaster's rostrum still *in situ*, that the Parish Breakfast was held Sunday by Sunday during eighteen years of the writer's ministry. This breakfast was self-supporting, a box being sent round during the meal for those who were able to contribute towards the expenses of the simple repast of bread and butter, marmalade and tea. There was always a balance in hand, and sometimes we were able of our super-fluity to give something for church purposes. A member of the congregation was treasurer, and kept account week by week of receipts and expenses in a book open to the in-spection of all who cared to see. Such homely things as the preparation of the breakfast and washing up afterwards had, of course, to be done. A woman in the Court did the former, and received a small remuneration out of the fund for her services, while the latter was undertaken by voluntary helpers immediately after the meal. There was some difficulty for a time during the War on account of rationing; but people brought their rations to supplement what we were able to get, and we shared with one another very happily, in spite of the temporary restrictions in food.

This village *Agape* did much to build up a really Christian fellowship among members of the congregation, and to realise the friendly and social side of life in connection with the Eucharist itself. A lady who came to live in our parish told us that through this congregational breakfast she had come to realise better in three weeks' time a genuine fellowship with the other members of the congregation than she had been able to do during four years regular attendance at another church.

It was interesting to note how the congregation sorted themselves out at the breakfast. There were five tables in the room, one being appropriated to the children, who, for economical reasons, were supplied with treacle instead of marmalade, and besmeared themselves accordingly: the boys and growing lads took possession of a smaller table at the side of the Master's rostrum—sometimes called " the Saints' Corner." On the other side of it were to be found the maidens of the congregation seated at a table specially claimed as their own—though they always welcomed the intrusion of guests of either sex. The middle-aged had a trestle-table for themselves of sufficient length to accommodate their number; while the clergy, churchwardens, and other leading members of the congregation, and visitors, occupied a central table in close proximity to the fire. Such is the courtesy of youth, and such the happy instinct for the fitness of things which prevailed in the little family which gathered there Sunday by Sunday after Holy Communion in church. Sometimes visitors would be present, both in church and at breakfast. The unselfconscious and simple humility with which they would share the family meal, and the sensitive courtesy with which the village people welcomed them, were good to see. The English villager is quick to disapprove of any failure to appreciate and allow for such social differences as we inherit from the past. He would regard any self-assertion on his own part, or on the part of his children, as no less vulgar and unchristian than a corresponding lack of good breeding and of Christian humility on the part of his social superiors. When the humility of the greater and the humility of the less thus meet and join hands at breakfast after Holy Communion in church, the Sacrament blossoms and bears beautiful fruit; a problem insoluble to the children of the world is solved happily and silently, and forgotten in the positive interests of the common meal and discussion of matters of common interest. A group of Christians who know and love one another is formed and grows gradually round the altar; the Kingdom of Heaven comes as leaven, which Mother Church, the woman of the parable, has taken and hidden in the lump of social life " till the whole is leavened " according to Christ's promise.

As has already been said, the parish is a large and scattered one, and while the western, central, and southern parts of it look to the Temple on its western border as their church (the southernmost hamlet of Chadwick End having a week-day celebration of Holy Communion, and a service on Sunday evening in a chapel of ease), the bulk of the population lies in Balsall Common (so called), on the northern and eastern boundary near Berkswell Station, on the railway between Birmingham and Coventry ; and for the last sixty years there has been a district church of St. Peter at Balsall Common, served for more than a generation by a resident curate, and now at last provided with a parsonage house. Here too a parish Eucharist, as mentioned above, has been sung at 8.30 for twenty years, and followed by breakfast in the parish room close by. Introduced without the good will of the resident curate or congregation, it had a struggle for life at first; but the next assistant priest persevered with it with results sufficient to justify its continuance ; and under his successor it has flourished vigorously, and has an average congregation of between fifty and sixty communicants a Sunday. A fifth centre of population, the hamlet of Meer

End, towards Kenilworth, looks to St. Peter's for its centre
of worship, and since 1928 has had its own Chapel of St.
Richard, which is filled with an admirable Sunday School
every Sunday, and has a sung Eucharist followed by a congregational breakfast once a month. Here too the combination prospers and bears fruit in a very good spirit of
fellowship and loyalty. Both St. Peter's and St. Richard's
are three miles distant from the Temple in different directions:
St. Peter's becoming more and more suburban, and St.
Richard's remaining thoroughly rural. Rural too remain
the parts of the parish which belong to the Temple, and send
their children to the Temple School. Their population was
in our time about six hundred, and the average number of
communicants at the Temple on Sunday was between fifty
and sixty.

Once a year, on Mothering Sunday, the sung Eucharist
at St. Peter's was suspended, and the whole parish met
together round the altar of the mother church, when there
were from ninety to a hundred communicants. At the
breakfast which followed home-made Simnel cakes were
provided, while on Christmas Day the congregation indulged
in mince-pies as a festal addition to the simple fare of
ordinary Sundays.

It should be stated that before the adoption of the 8.45 a.m.
service in 1913 several attempts had been made to bring the
Eucharist into greater prominence as the chief congregational
act of Sunday. At first we had a sung celebration at eleven
o'clock on alternate Sundays. On the great Festivals, such
as Easter day, there were generally three celebrations—
7, 8.15, and 10.30 a.m.; and as in our scattered district the
earliest was the best attended, it was often given added
dignity by being sung. But this multiplication of celebrations on the greater Festivals seemed only to divide up
the family of God needlessly, and to emphasise the individualistic conception of communion. There was a growing feeling
that the divorce between worship and communion involved
in a low Mass at eight o'clock, and a sung one at a later
hour, was not the ideal thing. Yet a congregational communion at eleven o'clock is for all practical intents and

purposes out of the question. That hour of the morning shuts out all but the leisured; it is too late for the majority of people to come fasting; and it prevents people getting home in time to prepare their Sunday dinner, an important item for those whose work precludes hot dinner on other days of the week. On the other hand, corporate worship and corporate communion at a comparatively early hour does give some extra rest to those who toil all the week, it does give the opportunity to consecrate the beginning of the Lord's Day in the highest act of Christian Worship, and it sets free the rest of the day till Evensong for reasonable Christian recreation.

Friends and sympathisers with the Parish Eucharist at Temple Balsall used to say: " This is possible in the country, where people live some distance from the church; it suits many of them, but it would not do everywhere; in a town parish it is extremely doubtful if it would catch on." Thank God, we are being disillusioned about this more and more year by year—if not day by day. The sung Eucharist with a communal breakfast following has now been established in many parishes both in town and country, perhaps now more in towns than in villages. There are, of course, difficulties in the way of its introduction in many places. People are frequently unreasonably conservative about changes in religion. The well-to-do often object to it because it interferes with their usual breakfast hour. Others cling to Matins at eleven o'clock, though the attendance at this service is not by any means what it used to be, and there are evident signs that it is becoming, under modern conditions of life, moribund. Some farmers say that Holy Communion at nine o'clock is impossible, because cows have to be milked, and in the winter other live-stock as well have to be fed, as much on Sunday mornings as on week-days. But experience shows abundantly that here, as so often, where there is a will there is a way. At Temple Balsall some farmers, and even their stockmen, came to the nine-o'clock service. One farmer who was a churchwarden lived two miles away and had a milk-walk; he himself milked his cows, delivered the milk, and then came with his wife and child in his side-car to church at nine o'clock Sunday by Sunday. A cowman on a large farm used to get up at 5 a.m., do his work and then come with his wife and family to church—the wife received the Blessed Sacrament with her baby in her arms and a little one of two years old by her side. In the parish which I now serve the same objection has been raised against the nine o'clock service; yet that hour has been found not only possible but suitable, even to those who have cows. A man who was head-gardener at a large house a mile away used to tell me that he could easily plead work as an excuse for not attending Communion at such an hour; but he always made a point of doing on Saturday what many usually put off till Sunday.

One great advantage of the congregational Communion, especially where people come with their families, is that the young become accustomed to the service from their very childhood. At the time of their Confirmation and first Communion they are no strangers to it. They are not timid and nervous on that solemn occasion in their lives, as so many are apt to be, who have never before been present at the Great Service: indeed, they learn to look forward to the time when they too, with their parents, may receive the Bread of Life and the Cup of Salvation. The Parish Eucharist which includes in its congregation the children of the parish has a lasting effect upon these little ones of Christ: it does more to train and educate the rising generation in the ways of the Church than a Children's Eucharist can— useful as that is in many ways—and more than a well-organised Catechism or Sunday School: the latter has its place, but it is not, and cannot be, the place of priority. Let the children be taught by the example of their parents to love their Father's House, to become accustomed from their earliest days to the great act of Christian worship, and they will not be found strangers to God's altar when they grow up. With us, as it is, among the older generation to-day, the men especially are often not at home in the House of God; they feel shy and awkward, ill at ease, out of their element.

When the writer's time came to leave Temple Balsall,

the Parochial Church Council passed a resolution before he left expressing their fervent hope that his successor would continue the 8.45 Sung Eucharist on Sunday, with the congregational breakfast following. After his departure, certain difficulties arose, the history of which it is not necessary to describe here. The result was that for a time there was no room available for church purposes; the Parochial Church Council held one of their regular meetings in the church; and on three Sunday mornings the congregation had their breakfast after service by the roadside. God blessed their pluck and determination with fine summer weather; and after the three Sundays they were able to hold the breakfast in the Templars' Old Hall; and so it has continued ever since.

XIII

FROM A TOWN PARISH: PRACTICAL PROBLEMS OF THE PARISH EUCHARIST

By the Rev. W. S. BAKER
Vicar of St. John's, Newcastle upon Tyne

FROM A TOWN PARISH: PRACTICAL PROBLEMS
OF THE PARISH EUCHARIST

THE Parish Eucharist was started at St. John's, Newcastle upon Tyne, on the Second Sunday in Advent, 1927. The church, which is at present served by a staff of three clergy, stands in the heart of the city, at a crossing of tram-routes, and within a hundred yards of the Central Station: by its central position it draws a congregation from a much wider circle than its own immediate neighbourhood. The parish itself consists mainly of shopping streets, offices, warehouses, factories, hotels and cinemas, housing a large number of caretakers; but on the outer fringes there still remain some streets of dwelling-houses. Fortunately there is no Mission Church to divide up the family into sections, and all alike find their centre and home in the parish church. In the nine years during which there has been a Parish Eucharist there has been a steady growth both in the number of those who attend, and also in the number of communicants, and of a "family spirit" among the worshippers. On every Sunday there are celebrations also at 7.15 a.m. and 8.0 a.m., as well as a Solemn Eucharist at 11.0 a.m., all of which at the present time justify their existence and are fulfilling a real need; but it is a striking fact that of the average two hundred and fifty communicants on a Sunday, the numbers at the Parish Eucharist have steadily grown in nine years from about sixty communicants to about one hundred and seventy. The accumulated experience of these years has taught many useful lessons, and has provided certain ways and means of meeting some of the many practical problems which arise in a town parish. As we are always reminded whenever two or three priests meet together, the problems of each parish are " peculiar " problems. To a very large extent each parish has to solve the problems of its Parish Eucharist for itself, and we cannot hope to find one solution to them all. If, however, we discuss the main general problems in the light of a particular Parish Eucharist, it may provide something in the way of suggestions and help.

Previous to the institution of the Parish Eucharist at 9.15 a.m., the arrangement of services on Sunday mornings at St. John's had been one which is common in a number of parishes—Low Masses at 7.15 and 8 a.m., a Childrens' Sung Mass at 10 a.m., High Mass at 11 a.m. After two years of steady teaching on corporate ideals of worship and Church-manship, a notice, in the form of a letter [1] signed by all the priests, was sent out to all parents and others in the parish and congregation, explaining the purpose of substituting a Parish Eucharist at 9.15 a.m. for the Children's Eucharist at 10 a.m.

[1] The text of the letter :

" To parents and others in St. John's Parish. We are writing to tell you that (beginning on Sunday ——) instead of the usual 10 a.m. Childrens' Eucharist there will, in future, be a Eucharist (with hymns) at 9.15 a.m., every Sunday.

" The reason for this alteration is that we believe that this new hour (9.15 a.m.) will be, on the whole, the most convenient for our parishioners (old and young).

" How you can help :

" 1. By letting your children come at 9.15 a.m., instead of, as formerly, at 10 a.m.

" 2. By—best of all—coming with them yourselves. (The 9.15 a.m. Eucharist will not be confined to children, and the ideal is for the whole family to worship together.)

" 3. If 7.15 or 8 a.m. is too early for you or those of your family who are confirmed, they can come at 9.15, and make their communion then, fasting. (The later hour will make extra rest on Sunday morning possible.)

" The great ideal is that the whole family—father, mother, and children—should all come together to worship God. The new hour (9.15 a.m.) now makes this really possible. All can come to worship then, while those who are confirmed can also make their communion. By this new arrangement we have done our best to suit the convenience of all.

" We most earnestly ask you to make this 9.15 a.m. Sung Eucharist the centre and strength of the life of the Church in this parish."

1. The Problem of the Children

This letter stressed the ideal of all the family—father, mother, and children—coming together to worship God. We will therefore take first the question " What about the children?" The two difficulties most generally raised against the children coming to the Parish Eucharist from their very earliest years, are the undue strain to the children themselves, and the fear of their disturbing the quiet and concentration of others. For the sake of the ideal that the whole Christian community should meet to worship God, no age limit has ever been set at St. John's, so that on occasions even babies in arms have been present. If the younger children are excluded, it will often be impossible for both father and mother to be present together every Sunday. Our experience goes to prove that far too much can be made of the two difficulties mentioned above. The very youngest are, if necessary, provided with picture books. The constant movement, the joining in the singing of the hymns, the Creed and Gloria, and other parts of the Liturgy, the usual acts of reverence and devotion, all help to hold their interest and keep them engaged. Long before they can read, you will find them joining in the singing of the Creed and Gloria. They begin to know the moments when something happens, as for instance when all kneel for the *Incarnatus* in the Creed, and bit by bit they learn what it all means. They watch the celebrant at the altar and the servers, especially when it happens to be an elder brother who is serving, or is " on the altar," as they say in Newcastle.

We have a nave altar, which is wheeled out into a position under the chancel arch, and as there are no steps from the nave to the chancel, the altar stands on a wooden base of its own, with three steps, so that the priest is visible to the majority of the congregation. This is likely to be necessary in many churches, as so often the high altar is largely hidden from the sight of many of the congregation owing to the length of the chancel, a narrow chancel arch, or a heavy screen.[1]

[1] In the case of the new Church of John Keble, Mill Hill, it is the

As far as possible we try to persuade the younger children, and those who come by themselves, to sit in the front seats, where they have a clear view of the altar, and can see all the actions of the priest and servers. Those who come with their parents sit, if they prefer it, with their family. As the people arrive, one of the priests is always near the door to welcome them, and to look out for strangers and newcomers. He can also keep a watchful eye on the seating of the children, and move any who have hidden themselves in the back seats and far corners. One or two of the grown-ups sit among the children in the front, not to ' keep them in order,' but to help the children to learn reverence by themselves offering of their best in prayer and worship to God. Anything that savours of ' bringing the Sunday School to Church ' is to be avoided, though in other ways the Parish Eucharist must be linked up as closely as possible with the Sunday Schools. A register of attendances should be kept, and when stamps are given, this should be only for attendance at both the Parish Eucharist and Sunday School.

2. THE LEADER

At the Children's Eucharist, which gave place to the Parish Eucharist, it had always been the custom, as in many churches, for one of the priests to stand in the aisle to give directions and to conduct the devotions of the children. In spite of the fact that many of those who were coming to the Parish Eucharist were fully instructed and knew exactly what to do, this custom was continued, and after nine years still proves to be of inestimable value. It was one of the duties of the primitive Deacon to give directions and to lead the devotions of the people,[1] and it has proved far more valuable to use one of the priests in this way than to have a High Mass. The possible objection that he must be disturbing to those who do not need his help, stands condemned as a selfish one, when the needs of the weaker

---

Parish Eucharist which has largely determined its plan. There are no pillars, and an unobstructed view of the altar is obtainable from every part of the interior. The choir is placed in the centre of the Church.

[1] Cf. Duchesne, *Christian Worship* (S.P.C.K., 5th edn.), p. 170.

brethren are remembered. Nor is he there to make any periods of silence impossible, but rather to prepare the people for the periods of silence, and to help to give them meaning. It is to be hoped that at the Parish Eucharist there will usually be one or two newcomers; and by directing the people when to sit, stand, or kneel, the priest in the aisle can help the uninstructed to feel that there is someone to see them through. If care is taken in the wording of the directions, not only those who have seldom been present at the Eucharist before, and the children, but many even of the older and more instructed worshippers, can be taught the purpose of a number of the things which they are called upon to do. As leader of the people's devotions, he gives them a sense of unity, links them up with the priest at the altar, and makes them into a congregation.

His exact duties are not easy to describe. They will best be seen if we describe the course of the service, which at St. John's follows the order of the Prayer Book of 1662, except that the ninefold *Kyrie* is sung in place of the Commandments.

When the celebrant, with the crucifer, two torch-bearers, and two servers, is vested and ready to enter, the leader gives out the number of the hymn. Instead of just announcing a number, he says " The hymn for the Introit is ——— "; thus suggesting the purpose and place of that particular hymn, and making the congregation familiar with the names of the various parts of the Liturgy, on which from time to time instruction is given.

At the end of the Introit, during which the celebrant and servers have completed their preparation, and the leader has distributed alms-bags to those who are to collect the alms, he says, " All kneel." This, besides telling the uninstructed what to do next, helps to bring on to their knees those who have a strong inclination to squat. After the Collect(s), he says, " All sit, and listen to the reading of the Epistle," and at the end of the Epistle he announces the number of " the hymn for the Gradual." The Gospel procession with the crucifer, torch-bearers, celebrant and servers to a place just outside the altar rails, the singing of

the Gospel, followed by the singing of the Creed, call for
no directions from the leader. At the end of the Creed he
stands facing the congregation, between the front rows of
seats, and gives out the notices for the week, and the biddings, and then gives a brief address. While it is most
important that every care should be taken to curtail the
length of the notices and the address, they have their essential
place in the Parish Eucharist. The notices are primarily
items of the Family life, and when carefully selected and
arranged can be of very real use in bringing before the
congregation their share in the wider life of the Church as
a whole, and their particular obligations in prayer and
service during the coming week. To avoid excessive length
and that mass of details as to times and places which defeats
its own end, it is usually possible to draw their attention to
a notice on the Church board, or in the magazine.

The main purpose of the address is to provide an intention
for the common prayer and worship of the morning. When
based on the Collect, Epistle, or Gospel of the Sunday, and
later worked into the Communion devotions, it stimulates
worship by directing the minds of all to the Church's intention for her members' common prayer that day. Five
minutes is quite sufficient time in which to say all that need
be said or can be listened to by a congregation which is
fasting. On festivals, when there has been a procession,
the short sermon is little more than a lengthened bidding,
making clear the common intention of the family's worship
on that day.

It needs to be emphasised that it is not easy to give a
five minutes' address. There is not a word to be wasted.
Such an address requires not less but more preparation than
one that lasts twice as long.

The leader, having finished the address, tells the people
to stand, and the celebrant returns to the altar and reads
the Offertory sentence. The instruction of the people in
the true meaning of the Offertory and of their part in it, had
emphasised the need of some definite action on their part
which should help them to realise it rather more forcefully
than by the mere singing of a hymn. For some time the first

step towards achieving this was taken by their saying one
of the following Offertory Prayers after the leader, before
the singing of the hymn and the collection of the alms.
The first, which is adapted from the Offertory Prayer in
the Scottish Liturgy, is used on festivals, and the second,
which is less liturgical in language, has a simple teaching
value:

1. " Blessed be Thou, O Lord God, for ever and ever.
   Thine, O Lord, is the greatness and the glory:
   For all that is in the heaven and in the earth is
   Thine:
   All things come of Thee,
   And of Thine own do we give Thee."

2. " By the hand of Thy priest, O Lord,
   We offer Bread to Thee, and Wine,
   To show that we give our lives
   And all that we do, to Thee.
   Accept and bless our gift,
   Together with the alms which we give."

During the saying of the prayer, we now have an Offertory
Procession. A credence table is placed at the west end of
the church, and on it two vessels containing the approximate
number of breads that will be required for the communion
of the people, and two wine cruets. When the celebrant
returns to the altar after the address, four members of the
congregation who have been chosen beforehand (if possible
a man and a woman, a boy and a girl) go to this credence
table, and while the congregation are saying the offertory
prayer, carry the people's offerings of bread and wine
through the congregation to the altar rail, where the
offerings are received by the servers and handed to the
celebrant for presentation at the altar. Such a procession
helps the people to realise the significance of the Offertory,
by giving it a visible dramatic form. It restores the act of
offering to its true importance, and marks it as the foundation
of the whole eucharistic action. It has the additional
value of giving a share in the action of the worship to a

T

greater number of the laity, who need not all be of the male sex.

From the Offertory to the Communion there is little that calls for any special mention. For the sake of the younger members of the congregation, for whom the unbroken period of kneeling would be too long, all stand for the *Sursum corda*, and remain standing until the end of the *Benedictus*. This also helps to mark the beginning of the central section of the service, the Consecration, and to recreate alertness. Before leading the people in the Confession, and again just before the prayer of Consecration, the leader in the fewest possible words draws the attention of all to what they are doing. " Let us together confess our sins to God," " Let us keep quiet and still in mind and body, that we may welcome Our Lord present with us in this Sacrament, as He promised, to accept and bless our offering." What is said varies from Sunday to Sunday, and has proved a real help, especially to the children and uninstructed, in understanding and devotion. After the Consecration the leader conducts the Communion devotions, working into them thoughts appropriate to the season or festival, or those suggested by the Collect, Epistle, or Gospel of the Sunday, which have been previously drawn out in the short sermon. Part of the time is spent in silent worship, and this is prevented from being a meaningless pause, with fidgeting and shuffling on the part of the children, by the leader suggesting some simple line of thought.

When the celebrant has made his communion and turns to give communion to the servers, the leader tells the congregation to stand for the singing of the *Agnus Dei*. During the communion of the people, hymns are sung, which are intended primarily for those who are unconfirmed. Whenever instruction on the Parish Eucharist is given, it is made clear to communicants that they are not expected to stand and sing these hymns during the time before and after making their communion, and it is clearly understood that they are free to use the time for prayer and devotion in the way which seems best to them. The practical difficulty of avoiding the long queue of waiting communicants is one which we have not yet succeeded in solving at St. John's, owing to the geography of the church; but in some places it has been found possible to regulate their approach to the altar, by someone standing in the centre aisle facing the altar, and moving back a few rows at a time, only those in front of him leaving their places.

At the conclusion of the service after the final hymn, when the celebrant and servers have left the altar, all kneel, and the leader and congregation say together the following prayer, so that having offered themselves as a family to their Lord, and received the gift of His Body and Blood, they may go out to serve Him as members of His Body in their different spheres of life:

" Receive, Almighty Father, this Holy Sacrifice, which Thou hast graciously allowed us to offer to Thee, by the hands of Thy priest. Grant us grace to offer to Thee all through this day and the coming week our thoughts, words, and deeds; and may Thy Holy Spirit, by His strengthening grace, make us more fit for Thy service, through Jesus Christ our Lord.

> The Lord be with you.
> And with thy spirit.
> Let us depart in peace.
> In the name of the Lord. Amen."

The main purpose of this rather lengthy description of the service has been to give a clear account of the duties, and, it is to be hoped, the great value of the Leader. It is difficult to avoid giving the impression that he must be all the time intruding himself, but whether he be priest or layman, this will not be the case if he remembers that he is only a link between the congregation and the priest at the altar. When a Parish Eucharist is first started, certain directions as to kneeling and standing have to be given, which later become unnecessary, and can be dropped. There comes a time when the spontaneous action of the congregation gives all the direction that is necessary at such points in the service. But our experience seems to us to have proved that the function of the Leader, as of the Deacon in earlier days, does not become unnecessary as time goes on.

3. MUSIC

We must now turn to the question of music.   The Parish
Eucharist, being the assembly of the Christian Community
for the worship of God, in which it realises its character as
the mystical Body of Christ, must therefore have a corporate
character throughout.   Those present are not there as mere
listeners, but as active participants, so that the singing by
all the congregation of Kyrie, Creed, Sanctus, Agnus, and
Gloria is essential.   There are now quite a number of good
simple settings of the Mass, really strong and solemn, which
can be sung in unison throughout, and soon win their way
into the hearts of a congregation.[1]   A sense of responsibility, which greatly strengthens their singing, is created in
a congregation, if it is possible to dispense with a choir for
the Parish Eucharist.   It requires a certain amount of effort
to sing when you are fasting, and the presence of a choir
in the chancel, who can be relied upon to carry on when
you grow tired, is a temptation which few congregations
can resist.

For the nine years that there has been a Parish Eucharist
at St. John's, we have sung the Mass to Merbecke, and so
far have not felt any need of a change.   The music so truly
expresses the spirit of the Liturgy, that there is no more
question of growing tired of it than of the words to which it
is set.   Most of the members of the choir are indeed present,
not as a choir, but as ordinary members of the Family, sitting
in the congregation, and those who are confirmed making
their communion.   They bring their breakfast with them,
and have it in the vestry before the High Mass at 11 a.m.
An assistant organist, who takes over the playing of the
communion hymns after he has made his communion,
enables the organist to make his communion too.

At those churches where on a Sunday morning there is
no sung service after the Parish Eucharist, the problem of
the choir is a more difficult one.   No parish priest would

---

[1] *E.g.* Merbecke (Novello, ed. Basil Harwood); Missa de Angelis
(Faith Press); Martin Shaw (Modal—Curwen); Martin Shaw (Folk—
(Curwen); Geoffrey Shaw (Novello).

want to give the impression to the choir that he considered
them unnecessary, or thought little of their painstaking
work. But if the members of the choir have been taught to
think of themselves first and foremost as members of God's
Family who give their service to the Family by singing,
and not first and foremost as "choir-boys" or "choirmen,"
belonging to that particular group in the parish, then there
should be little difficulty in persuading them to leave their
choir stalls in the chancel, and to sit in the nave with the
rest of the Family. They can then give far more effective
support to the singing, especially when seated near the back
rather than to the front. But there can be no question that
in the end the best congregational singing is achieved when
there is no choir on which to rely, and the members of the
choir are present just as members of the congregation.

The choosing of hymns is as important as the choice of the
right setting for the sung parts of the Mass, and every care
must be taken to avoid being haphazard. It is not just a
matter of avoiding what is bad and unworthy, whether in
words or tunes, but of choosing those which truly express the
spirit of the Liturgy, and are of the right type for the particular points in the service where they occur. This does
not imply that the selection can only be made from those
hymns which are included in the Holy Communion section
in our hymn books. Each of the five or more hymns has
its own contribution to make to the right setting for worship,
and a very wide choice is possible. The Introit strikes the
note of the service. On festivals, and during seasons such
as Advent and Lent, there is little difficulty in finding the
right hymn; on other occasions, the Collect and scripture
readings of the day provide guidance and help. The first
hymn generally needs to be fairly long, because, in spite of
frequent exhortation to punctuality, many still continue to
arrive late. The Gradual should be short, and, if possible,
seasonal; during the long Trinity season, the choice can
quite well be limited to two or three well-known and familiar
hymns, such as "Author of life divine," "Blest are the pure
in heart," "Come let us join our cheerful songs." The
number of definitely Offertorial hymns is small, though

one, "We pray thee, heavenly Father" (Stuckey Coles), when sung to the tune "Meirionydd," is supreme in words and music, and bears frequent repetition.[1]   The hymn during the Offertory can also most usefully fit in with the subject of the short sermon which has preceded it.   With the hymns at the Communion care should be taken always to have at least one Godward hymn, and to avoid having only what may be called "Jesus-hymns," or those which are mainly individualistic, self-centred, and self-contemplating. The two verses of "Wherefore, O Father" (E.H. 335) and of "Father, see Thy children bending at Thy throne" (E.H. 308) give an epitome of what we most want our hymns at the Communion to express; and while the "Jesus-hymns" have their place, we need to beware of leaving out the Godward offering of life and self.   In some churches E.H. 335 or the first two verses of E.H. 302 are sung after the Prayer of Consecration and as it were in continuation and conclusion of it, to give the people an added sense of their co-operation with the celebrant in the act of consecration.[2] The final Post-Communion hymn will generally strike the note of praise and thanksgiving.

The possible use of a psalm or psalms in place of one or more of the hymns, needs to be remembered.[3]   The truncated forms of the old Propers, as printed in the *English Hymnal*, are not satisfactory for the use of the average congregation at a Parish Eucharist, but the use of a whole psalm as an Introit, for which we have the precedent of the Prayer Book of 1549, or for the Gradual, should not be too difficult an achievement in many parishes.

4. BREAKFAST

The Breakfast which follows our Parish Eucharist at St. John's can scarcely be described by so dignified a name as a Parish Breakfast.   We have no parish hall, and the only

---

[1] The reference is to the version of this hymn in the *English Hymnal*, not that in *Hymns A. & M.*   Another excellent Offertory hymn is E.H. 521, "O Lord of heaven and earth and sea."

[2] Sometimes at St. John's the Leader says the Prayer of Oblation at this point.

[3] Hebert, *Liturgy and Society*, pp. 72 ff., 214 ff.

available place is the choir vestry, which is small even for its proper purpose, and far too confined to allow anything in the nature of an orderly meal. During the summer, the problem of overcrowding is partly solved by using a part of the churchyard just outside the vestry door, where some old pews have been placed round three sides of a small square.[1] The people bring their own food, and with the aid of one gas ring, tea is provided at a penny a cup. The meal never begins until 10.20 a.m., and at 10.45 a.m. the patient organist at last puts his foot down, and insists upon the vestry reverting to its proper function, so that the choir can be ready for the High Mass at 11 a.m.

Even under these difficult conditions this breakfast has a very high value and importance. Following as it does immediately upon the Eucharist, in which all have partaken of the Bread of Life, it links the common actions of every day with the worship of God, our Heavenly Father, who gives us our daily bread—" Life blends into worship, worship irradiates and energises life." The breakfast is itself an expression of the meaning of the Church as the Family of God, giving the supreme experience of human life, the joy of Christian fellowship; " the gladness and richness of our common life as it was meant to be." It is also a witness and an aid to Fasting Communion. Without the breakfast many of those who come to the Parish Eucharist, and make their communion fasting, would be unable to do so. There would be no breakfast for them at home, when they return late in the morning, without serious inconvenience to themselves and to others. In countless ways it fosters the family spirit in Church life. For it brings together people who otherwise would know little or nothing of each other, although for a number of years they might be communicants at the same altar; many who come as strangers to the Eucharist are in this way given a welcome and a chance of getting to know other members of the Family; clergy and people have a unique opportunity of access to each other for the hundred and one purposes of parish life.

[1] There is a certain oddity in the fact that this picnic breakfast takes place in view of the street within two minutes' walk of the Central Station.

5. Two Difficulties

Two difficulties, which I have heard raised against having a Parish Eucharist, call for consideration: 1. " Adults will not, children cannot, fast until 10 o'clock." 2. " If people attend the Parish Eucharist properly, its length will become unmanageable."

1. As regards children, experience does not bear this out. The years during which fainting is most common are from fifteen to seventeen, though even that is a very rare occurrence at St. John's, and I cannot remember a single case of a younger communicant fainting during the four years that I have been there. It is true that the majority of our children go to bed at a very much later hour on the Saturday night than is generally considered suitable for a young child's bedtime, and share in the family supper just before doing so. Although not to be commended as a solution of this supposed difficulty, it is a prevailing habit of family life, not, I imagine, peculiar to Tyneside, which in our case helps to prevent the difficulty from arising.

Apropos of children fasting, it came out once that one or two of our children, who were the only members of their families to practise their religion, were having what they called " an unreal breakfast " before coming to Mass and making their communion. The unreal breakfast meant a scrap of bread, or any other morsel which could be discovered, still left on the table from supper the night before. When this came to light, it called for a sermon on fasting communion the following Sunday, pointing out that breakfasts, real and unreal, equally broke the fast. " Unreal " was an interesting adjective, which showed that the children had at least realised that a rule of the Church did exist of making their communion fasting.

The problem, in the case both of children and of adults, is a matter of teaching more than of anything else. In a parish where the Fast before Communion is consistently taught, and is understood to be a rule, the congregation at nine o'clock will come fasting then as naturally as at an earlier hour. Where it is neither taught, nor expected, nor generally practised, it is probable that the communicants at eight o'clock will have broken their fast with the customary cup of tea. (It is to be remembered that the exact hour of the Parish Eucharist must be adapted in different parishes to the habits—in this case the breakfast habits—of the people. At St. John's the majority of the congregation would not naturally be breakfasting even as early as ten o'clock on a Sunday morning.) With us the Fast is taught as an act of willing loyalty to the Church's mind, and of an easily understood bodily preparation for the Sacrament, rather than on rigorist lines. We do not believe the objection to the Parish Eucharist commonly raised by those who shrink on this ground from altering the tradition of eight o'clock communion, is in fact a real one.

2. " If people attend the Parish Eucharist properly, its length will become unmanageable." When that happy thing has happened, we shall have to deal with it. At the present time it is unlikely to be an immediately pressing problem here at home. I have seen a letter from Central Africa, where this very difficulty is having to be faced. In a certain district which has a population of some 4,000 people in all, 430 are hearers, 280 catechumens, 3,000 Christians —of whom about 1,000 are baptised but not confirmed —and the remaining handful are heathen. Of the 2,000 confirmed Christians, about 300 are either away, out of church for various offences, or slack, so that the total number of regular communicants is 1,700. The church will hold at a pinch 1,200, and the staff consists of two priests, one European, and one African, one of whom is frequently away, and a deacon. The average attendance on a Sunday is in the neighbourhood of 2,000, and as the church cannot hold them all, on Sundays and great festivals there are two main Masses, the earlier one being always High Mass. This is attended by the adults, and the average communion is 500, and could be more: for a large number more would, with only a little encouragement, make their communions weekly, but the priests dare not encourage them to do so. If they did so, the number of communicants would be anything from 1200 to 1500, of whom at least

1,000 would be at the High Mass. 1,000 communicants
take about one and a quarter hours for three ministers to
communicate. " The difficulties that I have tried to outline," says the writer of the letter, " are very formidable, as
they would be in England if the confirmed people in our
parishes came to their communions as often and as regularly
as they do in Central Africa."

If, when people come to Communion in hundreds, we
seek to solve the difficulty by separating communion from
the Mass, and giving them communion from the reserved
sacrament, then indeed the success of the Parish Mass has
defeated itself.   The true line of solution would be to increase
the number of ministers, by ordaining lay deacons, or perhaps
subdeacons authorised to assist at the Communion by
administering the chalice.   Also some plan might be worked
out, whereby after one long communion hymn the celebrant
should finish the service at the altar, while the other ministers
still go on distributing communion; and let the later communicants have their thanksgiving separately, perhaps in
batches.

But these are dreams of the future for us in England,[1]
and we must not let them make us forget that the length of
the Parish Eucharist is an important point which needs
practical thought and handling.   The number of our
communicants seems pitiably small when we think of
Central Africa.   With an average of 170 communicants,
and three ministers to give communion, our Parish Eucharist
takes from an hour to sixty-five minutes.   On great festivals
when there is a Procession, and there are about 200 communicants, it takes little longer, as time is saved by substituting a lengthened bidding and intention for the short
sermon.   There must, however, be no waste of time or
unnecessary intervals, and punctuality in starting is most
important.   Minutes here and there can be saved by bringing
a hymn to an end when the action at the altar is completed,
as for instance at the Offertory, and by ending the final hymn

---

[1] At the same time, it is true that already to-day many a single-
handed priest in new housing areas and elsewhere would be greatly
helped if there were a lay-deacon to assist at the Communion.

when the celebrant and servers have left the altar. This calls for intelligence on the part of the organist, as this should only be done when the sense of the words allows it. While bearing in mind what has been said above about the regrettable queue which is so often to be seen at the Communion, it is important that the people should not prolong the time by not being ready to fill the places at the rail.

Neither the priest's own private devotions before his communion, nor the corporate devotions of the people must be hurried, and the time allowed for the latter depends upon the time taken over the former, but the priest is the instrument and servant of his people, and must therefore be reasonable over the time that he takes.

The service ought certainly not to last longer than an hour and a quarter, and, while avoiding anything in the nature of a scramble and rush, our aim should be an hour.

Much that might have been said has of necessity been left unsaid. In no two parishes will the problems be quite the same, but the aim of the Parish Eucharist will everywhere be the same. It is expressed in the following words written on the Parish Eucharist at St. John's by a former member of the staff:

" The Eucharist both expresses membership in the Church, and nourishes it. Our ideal Eucharist must then be a meeting of the whole local congregation of the faithful. It must proclaim the unity of the fellowship: its common self-offering: its united consecration by Christ: its renewed unity in the common receiving together of the Holy Food. To not a few the 9.15 has brought a fresh vision of all these profoundly important Christian truths. It seeks at least to set them forth—not just in speech, but in a visible form to see and share in. It is for these truths of Christian theology that it stands, and they are truths vital to full Christian experience and worthy Christian life."

XIV

THE CHURCH IN THE WORLD

By the Rev. CHARLES H. SMYTH

Senior Assistant Curate at St. Giles' with St. Peter's, Cambridge

THE CHURCH IN THE WORLD

1. The Nature and Purpose of the Church

THERE is an initial difficulty regarding the use of these words ' Church ' and ' World,' and it is imposed by the complexity of meaning that attaches to them. When we speak of ' the World,' we may be thinking simply of man's natural environment without reference to the problem whether it is good or evil, friendly or unfriendly; ' the world ' in a purely neutral sense. Or we may mean ' the world ' as ultimately good because, however much distorted and perverted and overlaid by human sin, it is still God's world, the world which He created and saw that it was good, the world that is enriched by His gifts and illuminated by His glory, the world in which all things are returning to perfection, the world in which Christ is King. Or finally we may mean ' the World ' as a hostile power, antagonistic to the purposes of its Creator and contemptuous of His authority; human society, wise in its own conceits, organising itself apart from and in despite of God. Again, when we speak of the Church, we may mean either the *Civitas Dei*, transcending the limits of this world and even of humanity, comprising within its membership the holy angels, the faithful dead, and the elect on earth: or simply the Church on earth, " the open known Church," [1] a visible society within which there are tares mingled with the wheat, and without which there is wheat mingled with the tares. " And let this City of Gods remember, that even amongst her enemies, there are some concealed, that shall one day be her Citizens: nor let her thinke it a fruitlesse labour to beare their hate untill she heare their confession;

[1] Archbishop Cranmer, *Answer to Smith's Preface*, in *Works* [P.S.], Vol. I, p. 377.

as shee hath also (as long as shee is in this pilgrimage of this world) some that are partakers of the same sacraments with her, that shall not be partakers of the Saints glories with her, who are partly knowne, and partly unknowne. . . . For the two cities (of the predestinate and the reprobate) are in this world, confused together and commixt, untill the generall judgement make a separation. . . ." [1] For St. Augustine in his *De Civitate Dei*, the City of God, or, rather, " that part of it which sojourns on the earth and lives by faith," is represented by, and for all practical purposes identified with, the visible Church. But this is simply a working identification. The line of demarcation between the righteous and the reprobate, the saved and the lost, does not by any means coincide exactly with the line of demarcation between the Christians and the non-Christians, between the Church and the World.[2] "*Nam sunt quidam in*

---

[1] *Saint Augustine, of the Citie of God . . . Englished by* J. H[ealey].— 2nd ed. (1620), pp. 44–45 (*Booke I*, chap. 34).

[2] A frank recognition of this would save a good deal of popular confusion, especially over the meaning of the word ' Christian.' There is a classic example of such confusion in the Notes for Instructors at the end of *Scouting for Boys*, where the Chief Scout alludes to " the *practical* Christianity "—viz., manly self-reliance and unselfishness—" which (although they are Buddhists in theory) distinguishes the Burmese in their daily life " (*op. cit.*, 16th ed., 1932, p. 304). That is, perhaps, a *reductio ad absurdum*. One might as reasonably speak of ' the *practical* Buddhism which (although they are Christians in theory) distinguishes the English vegetarians in their domestic habits.' Surely it is time that we recognised that the word ' Christian ' is, like the word ' Buddhist ' or ' Mohammedan,' a technical term with a technical and therefore limited meaning. Christianity is neither a religious philosophy nor a code of social ethics nor an emotional tinge: and the primary distinguishing mark of the Christian as compared with the non-Christian is not the fact that he is a good man and a good citizen, decent, moral, kindly, tolerant, public-spirited, and so forth, but the fact that he is visibly a member of the visible Church of Christ. (Cf. Bishop Gore, *The Religion of the Church*, passim.) The difficulty is that nowadays in our own country, although to ' go to church ' is to defy social convention and to lay oneself open to the charge (which the Englishman dreads more than almost any other) of eccentricity, yet the prestige of Christianity in the abstract still stands extraordinarily high, so that to tell a man that he is not a Christian would be regarded as even more insulting than to tell him that he is not a gentleman: and it would be a delicate task to persuade the average Englishman (who is a theist of a sort, believing in Something or Somebody that can most recognisably be described as ' God,' and combining with this a certain amount of admiration or respect for Jesus Christ and some acquaintance with His teachings, or at least with what is popularly regarded as the general spirit of His teachings, and an emotional tender-

Ecclesia nomine et re, ut boni Catholici ; quidam nomine nec re, ut præcisi ; quidam nomine tantum ; quidam re tantum." [1]

The Church is therefore to be defined not so much in terms of membership as rather in terms of activity, and of an activity which is only mediately her own.

ARTICLE XIX. *Of the Church*

The visible Church of Christ is a congregation of faithful men (*cœtus fidelium*), in the which the pure Word of God is preached, and the Sacraments be duly ministered according to Christ's ordinance in all those things that of necessity are requisite unto the same.[2] . . .

Nothing is said in the XXXIX Articles of the Church of England concerning an Invisible Church. The very use of the word ' visible ' indeed reminds us of its limitations. But where the formularies of a more radical Protestantism refer specifically to the Invisible Church, and speak of the true Church as invisible,[3] the Anglican Articles are silent. Like the New Testament writings, they are concerned only with that visible society which was instituted by our Lord

---

ness for *Abide with me*) that ' practical Christianity,' as distinct from ' practical goodness ' or ' practical benevolence,' begins with practising membership of the Christian Church. We have therefore to emphasise, with St. Augustine, that the distinction between Christians and non-Christians is not to be confused with the distinction between good people and bad people, or between the elect and the reprobate, or (in more popular language) between those who are ' going to Heaven ' and those who are ' going to Hell ': it is simply the technical distinction between those who do, and those who do not, visibly belong to the visible Church of Christ, and to some particular organised part of it.

[1] Gratian, *Decret.* 2 Pars, Causa xxxiii., Quæst. 3. de Poenit. dist. i., cap. 70.   Cited by Bishop Ridley, *Works* [P.S.], p. 127.   (" For some are in the Church in name and in reality, as good Catholics; some neither in name nor in reality, as cut off and separated from it; some only in name;   some only in reality.")

[2] A third note, or mark, of the Church—' the authority of the keys duly used '—is specified in the XI Articles of 1559 and in the 2nd part of the Homily for Whitsunday; as also in the Form and Manner of Ordering of Priests in the Book of Common Prayer.   Cf. E. Tyrrell Green, *The Thirty-nine Articles and the Age of the Reformation*, p. 130.

[3] Tyrrell Green, *op. cit.*, p. 129.   Cf. also E. J. Bicknell, *A Theological Introduction to the XXXIX Articles*,[2] p. 302: on this conception of ' the Invisible Church of all true believers ' Charles Marson has a characteristic passage (" It is intangible and indeterminate. . . . It apparently must not intrude upon the visible world or tithe the visible pig," etc.), vide *God's Co-operative Society* (1914), p. 5.

U

Himself. "The Church must be visible because Christ was incarnate" (Khomiakov) [1] : and the objective evidential value of its visibility is one of the dominant themes in St. Augustine's apologetic. "What do we see which the disciples saw not? The Church throughout all nations. What do we see not which they saw? Christ present in the flesh. As they saw Him and believed concerning the Body; so do we see the Body—let us believe concerning the Head. . . . The sight of Christ helped them to believe the future Church; the sight of the Church helps us to believe that Christ is risen. Their faith was made complete, and ours is made complete also. Their faith was made complete by the sight of the Head, ours is made complete from the sight of the Body." [2]

But of even greater significance is the distinction between the Nineteenth Article (and the Confession of Augsburg, Part I, Art. VII,[3] with which it is allied) and Art. XII of the Saxon Confession of 1551, drawn up by Melanchthon: "*Dicimus igitur Ecclesiam visibilem in hac vita cœtum esse amplectentium Evangelium Christi, et recte utentium sacramentis*" ("We say therefore that the Church visible in this life is the congregation of those who embrace the Gospel of Christ, and rightly use the Sacraments").[4] According to the latter definition, the Church is a society of certain persons who do certain things: according to the former, the Church is primarily a society in which certain things are done. The Anglican Articles speak of the preaching of God's Word and the ministration of His Sacraments: the Saxon Confession speaks of men's response to this Divine initiative. By so doing, it does not sufficiently guard against the first of the two major heresies concerning the Church: that, namely, which regards the Church as a Voluntary Association among other voluntary associations, "a voluntary

---

[1] Cf. Möhler's *Symbolik*, Vol. II, p. 7, quoted in Bishop Forbes' *Explanation of the XXXIX Articles*,[3] pp. 265 ff.

[2] *Sermon* LXVI (CXI), § 6. Quoted in J. N. Figgis, C.R., *The Political Aspects of S. Augustine's 'City of God'* (1921), p. 30.

[3] "*Est autem ecclesia congregatio sanctorum, in qua evangelium recte docetur, et recte administrantur sacramenta.*" Tyrrell Green, p. 127.

[4] *Ibid.*, p. 128.

Society of Men, joining themselves together of their own accord, in order to the publick worshipping of God, in such a manner as they judge acceptable to him, and effectual to the Salvation of their Souls " (Locke) [1]: in other words, " a devotional club which those who are so disposed are at liberty to join." [2]

On the contrary, the Church is by its very nature an *involuntary* society, not constituted by the religious preferences of men, but created by the will of God. It differs from any aggregation of like-minded persons drawn together by a community of culture, of opinions, and of tastes. It is, by contrast, a congregation of unlike-minded persons such as would never have dreamed of constituting themselves into one body, but whom the Word of God Himself has gathered into oneness and community by His ordering of history and circumstance, and by His rule over the personal and domestic life of each man, woman and child. (*Ye have not chosen Me, but I have chosen you, and ordained you, that ye should go and bring forth fruit, and that your fruit should remain.*) It is not in a self-imagined inward unity of the like-minded and the like-conditioned (which is the creation of our own wills and tastes), but in the outward conformity of the unlike-minded and the unlike-conditioned (which is the social creation of the common Father of them all) that we discover the valid mark of the Catholic Church.[3] For the first truth about the Church is its essential *givenness*. " The Church stands a visible institution in history from the first chapter of the Acts of the Apostles onward, awaiting the conversion of individuals to Christ. The individual converts did not combine to form the Church. It was there before them." [4] " The Christians at Antioch did not

[1] *A Letter concerning Toleration* (2nd ed., 1690), p. 13. Cf. farther Sir Leslie Stephen, *History of English Thought in the Eighteenth Century*,[3] Vol. II., ch. X., § 25 (p. 150).

[2] *Report of the Archbishops' Commission on the Relations between Church and State* (1935), Vol. I, p. 7.

[3] Cf. G. W. E. Russell, *Henry Cary Shuttleworth* (1903), pp. 129–30 (Shuttleworth on the nature of a Parish). This passage is obviously suggestive with regard (*a*) to the problem of Intercommunion, (*b*) to the Christian conception of Marriage and the Family.

[4] Bishop Gore, *The Religion of the Church* (1916), p. 39. Cf. Archbishop Temple's sermon preached at the consecration of Truro Cathedral,

exclaim: ' Go to; we are scattered; union is strength; let us organise ourselves into a Church.' " The Church was there before them, and they were baptised into it, and embraced that Way of life, continuing steadfast in the four fundamental things: the Apostles' doctrine and fellowship, and the breaking of bread, and prayer. There is here no question of men ' joining themselves together of their own accord.' The Church is an ἐκκλησία called together by God Himself. It is more than a ' Fellowship.' [1] It is a Body, not of men's construction, but of God's creation.

Nevertheless, the modern secular State is bound, from its own standpoint, to regard the Church as if it were a voluntary association, because it is not based on legal compulsion. In other words, the State can hardly avoid treating the Church as a sect.

This also is anticipated by John Locke, who, in his *Letters on Toleration* (1689–92), and elsewhere in his writings, maintains, not only that " the Care of Souls is not committed to the Civil Magistrate," but also that the State has no more interest in a Church than in " a club for claret," and is no more bound to protect religion than is the East India Company. It should accordingly confine itself to its proper function, which is the promotion of " the temporal good and outward prosperity of the society ": that is to say (in Hooker's scornful phrase), it has " no other end and purpose but only to fat up men like hogs, and to see that they have their mast." [2] We may thus observe that from this heresy concerning the nature and purpose of the

---

quoted in Bicknell, *op. cit.*, pp. 302–3. " Men talk sometimes as if a Church could be constituted simply by Christians coming together and uniting themselves into one body for the purpose. Men speak as if Christians came first and the Church after: as if the origin of the Church was in the wills of the individual Christians who composed it. But on the contrary, throughout the teaching of the Apostles, we see that it is the Church that comes first and the members of it afterwards. . . . Everywhere men are called in: they do not come in and make the Church by coming."

[1] The word is never used in this sense in the New Testament: κοινωνία—communion, fellowship, intercourse—is an attribute, not a title, of the Church.

[2] *Ecclesiastical Polity*, VIII. iii. (ed. R. A. Houk, p. 189): *Works*, ed. Keble [7], vol. iii., p. 363.

Church, Locke has also fallen into heresy concerning the nature and purpose of the State.

For the powers that be are ordained of God, and they are the ministers of God to men for good. The State, as Aristotle taught, possesses a moral character and a moral purpose—namely, the promotion of the good life for all its citizens. It is, as the Fathers maintained, no part of the natural order, because it is the consequence of sin, but it is also a divinely appointed remedy against sin: it is both punitive and curative. But from the Aristotelian position it is no far cry to the second of the major heresies concerning the Church—that, namely, which regards it as a State Department, and, *ex hypothesi,* in a democratic State, the organ of the religious sentiment of the democracy: "A National Church means a Church teaching the religion which the nation holds, and not that which it ought to hold." [1]

If Locke may be considered as a representative exponent of the first of these two heresies, Robespierre may be taken as a representative exponent of the second. In his speech on the Civil Constitution of the Clergy (1790), he declared that " Priests, in the social order, are really magistrates set aside for the maintenance and service of public worship. From this simple axiom are derived all the principles which govern the question. The first of these principles is that all public functions are instituted by Society and have for their purpose the order and welfare of Society. It follows that no social function can exist which is not useful. Hence all those benefices and ecclesiastical establishments which serve no end should disappear; only bishops and parochial clergy should be preserved in France. The second principle is that ecclesiastical officials, since they are instituted for the welfare of the people, should be nominated by the

---

[1] George Harwood, *Disestablishment: or, a Defence of the Principle of a National Church* (1876), p. 175, cf. pp. 247, 381: cf. also the serious contention of Sir Thomas Inskip, in the Prayer Book debates of 1928, that it is the function of our leaders " to bring the doctrines of the Church of England into accord with the doctrines of the people " (Hansard, *Parl. Deb.*, vol. 218, col. 1311). A very crude illustration of this point of view is to be found in Robert Blatchford, *Saki's Bowl*, pp. 287-300, esp. p. 292.

people. The third principle is that, since the clergy are instituted for the good of Society, the amount of their stipends ought to be subordinated to the general welfare." [1] From this point of view, the clergy are simply the ecclesiastical officials of the democratic State.

It will be noted that these two heresies, despite their radical divergence, have much in common. They are at one in regarding the Church as a human institution, in ignoring its divine origin and character, and in denying its essential ' givenness.' In a word, they both derive from an initial failure to comprehend its meaning and significance as *Corpus Christi Mysticum*.

2. Church and State

Under normal circumstances, the challenge of the World to the Church finds its expression in the challenge of a culture based upon different values, upon values that are non-Christian or only partially Christian, or even upon genuinely Christian values which have become detached from the theological context from which they take their meaning, like the few clear details in a photograph that is out of focus. This is the challenge of the World in its most seductive and insidious form. It is manifest (and is remarked by non-Christian idealists, sardonically no doubt, but also with the bitter, if illogical, resentment of men who feel themselves betrayed) wherever a Church has accommodated itself to the political and social order and has adapted itself to worldly aims and ends. But it is also manifest wherever we find Christian preachers whose preaching is not controlled and disciplined by theology, and therefore is become anthropological (for they are talking about man rather than about God). The preachers who preach Communism or Fascism or Socialism or Liberalism or Conservatism; the preachers who preach Pacifism or Internationalism or Humanitarianism; the preachers who preach Idealism or Philosophy or Natural Ethics; the preachers who go down to public schools and preach what Dr. Cyril Norwood,

[1] Translation from R. Somerset Ward, *Maximilien Robespierre: a Study in Deterioration*, p. 289.

with a fatuous admiration, calls "just solid Service, and
no more " [1]: these are they from the sounding-boards of
whose pulpits echo, not the word of prophecy, but the
sophisms of contemporary culture, which are the natural
and appropriate vehicle of the challenge of the World to
the Church. For it is not the function of the preacher to
expound some contemporary ideology in religious language,
but to proclaim the Word of God and to weigh and measure
all contemporary ideologies (in so far as they are relevant)
by that criterion. The purpose of a sermon is not to relieve
the boredom of the congregation by introducing into what
must otherwise be a singularly tedious performance an
interlude which everybody can understand and enjoy (and
at the end of which they can, at a pinch, go out), a discourse
about the topics in which they are interested, couched in
the phraseology to which they are accustomed. The purpose of a sermon is, on the contrary, to declare the righteousness of God, and thereby to minister to the salvation of
souls and the edification of the Body of Christ. The
moment that the Church's message becomes a mere adapta-
tion or refinement of the message of contemporary culture,
it becomes apparent that the babble of the World has
silenced her prophetic voice.

But the circumstances of contemporary Europe are not
normal: and upon the Continent the challenge of the
World to the Church is the challenge not so much of a
culture [2] as rather of a rival Church, the ἐκκλησία of
Man, which finds its embodiment in the State. To the
Divine plan for the redemption of all mankind is opposed
a nationalist, secular programme of redemption [3]: for

---

[1] Cyril Norwood, *The English Tradition of Education* (1929), p. 123
and *passim*.

[2] " When I hear talk about culture, I want to draw my revolver."—
Adolf Hitler (quoted by George Seldes, *Sawdust Cæsar*, p. 341).

[3] The Spanish dictator, General Primo de Rivera, after his visit
to Mussolini in Nov. 1923, said: " On Mussolinism has been formed a
creed, a doctrine of redemption, which is drawing to it an army of re-
cruits throughout the world " (Seldes, *op. cit.*, p. 260).—" In this connection the insertion in the deaths column of a local German newspaper :
' He died in the faith of his redeemer Adolf Hitler,' is not without
interest." C. E. M. Joad in *Fords and Bridges*, Feb. 1936, p. 4.—Cf.
also almost any Russian propaganda film.

Totalitarianism is soteriological in essence, and the Dictator, Duce, Führer, is quite literally the New Messiah in a sense in which the King never was, even at the beginning of the sixteenth century: he is a successful secular Messiah of the type so eagerly desiderated by the Jews of the first century of our era, and therefore it is well-nigh impossible for him to pay fealty and homage to that Messiah whom they delivered up to Pilate to be crucified because His Kingdom was not of this world.

It is at this point therefore that we are confronted by the problem of the nature and purpose of the State. On the one hand, we have been reminded that the powers that be are ordained of God, and that the State is an appointed instrument of His purpose. On the other hand, we have been speaking of the ' secular ' State and of its ' secular ' programme of redemption. In current usage, the word ' secular ' is employed as the antithesis of ' spiritual.' But against this usage the Christian is bound to register a protest. To employ the word ' secular ' in this sense is as much an abuse of language as to employ the word ' laïque ' as meaning, not ' lay,' but ' anti-clerical.' [1] The true sense in which the State is secular and the Church is not, is that the State (as symbolising the *Civitas terrena*) adheres to the order of Time, but the Church (as symbolising the *Civitas Dei*) adheres to the order of Eternity.

In saying this, there is no need to take any narrower view of the State than that which is expressed by Burke in his *Reflections on the French Revolution*. " Society is indeed a contract. Subordinate contracts for objects of mere occasional interest may be dissolved at pleasure—but the state ought not to be considered as nothing better than a partnership agreement in a trade of pepper and coffee, callico or tobacco, or some other such low concern, to be taken up for a little temporary interest, and to be dissolved by the fancy of the parties. It is to be looked on with other reverence; because it is not a partnership in things subservient only to the gross animal existence of a temporary

---

[1] Cf. J. N. Figgis, C.R., *Churches in the Modern State* (1913), App. 1, pp. 181-3.

and perishable nature. It is a partnership in all science; a partnership in all art; a partnership in every virtue, and in all perfection. As the ends of such a partnership cannot be obtained in many generations, it becomes a partnership not only between those who are living, but between those who are living, those who are dead, and those who are to be born. Each contract of each particular state is but a clause in the great primæval contract of eternal society, linking the lower with the higher natures, connecting the visible and invisible world according to a fixed compact sanctioned by the inviolable oath which holds all physical and all moral natures, each in their appointed place." [1]

Nevertheless, Leviathan is mortal. And the supreme blasphemy takes place when the State "sitteth in the temple of God, setting itself forth as God"; namely, by arrogating to itself, in deeds if not in words, ' a self-contained finality,' *eine in sich ruhende Endlichkeit* (Tillich). For it stands to reason that that which is mortal cannot be final. Possibly in that statement lies the crux of the perennial conflict, the immemorial antagonism, between the Church and the World.

The State concerns itself rightly with its members as temporal persons so long as it recognises that they are not only temporal persons. The Church concerns herself rightly with her members as souls capable of eternal life so long as she remembers that this concern imposes on her the care not only of their souls but also of their bodies.[2] She is bound to the task "of interfering or, (as irreligious men will say,) meddling with the world." [3] The whole

---

[1] *Reflections on the Revolution in France* (1790), pp. 143-4.

[2] "They that are snared and entangled in the extreme penury of things needful for the body, cannot set their minds upon Thee, O Lord, as they ought to do. . . ." From Queen Elizabeth's private Prayer Book of 1578, tr. Ludovicus Vives: quoted at length by C. Marson, *God's Co-operative Society*, p. 100. Cf. St. Clement of Alexandria, *Stromata*, IV. cap. v. 21 (*Opera*, ed. Stählin, Vol. II, p. 257): "The same consideration applies to poverty. This, too, compels the soul to withdraw its interest from things that are needful, from contemplation, I mean, and sinless purity. It drives the man, who has not entirely dedicated himself to God through love, to spend his time over ways and means" (translation from H. B. Tollinton, *Clement of Alexandria*, Vol. II, p. 299).

[3] J. H. Newman, *The Arians of the Fourth Century* (1833), p. 278.

field of human life and labour lies beneath her scrutiny and is the subject of her unceasing vigilance. Without infringing the God-given prerogatives of the State, she has commission and authority to take cognisance of every public issue. The value of a National Establishment of religion is that it signifies an explicit recognition of this authority: " It is not to make the Church political, but to make the State religious." [1]   But, whether Established or Disestablished, " the Church abhors being shut up in the sacristy." [2]   And, precisely because she is insisting all the time upon the reality and universal relevance of super-natural values, being as she is upon this earth a Pilgrim company, in the world but not of the world, serving her generation faithfully, but always pointing steadfastly beyond the temporal order to the encircling horizons of eternity, therefore the witness and the influence of the Church con-stitute an indispensable corrective to the action of the State. She holds the temporal policies of the temporal society to the touchstone of the supernatural, the eternal, and the universal. She safeguards all that is good in human freedom by the fact that her very existence is a denial that the State is absolute, because the only Absolute is God. And therefore the Church is what the State can never be— Totalitarian—because she is the Body of Christ, τὸ πλήρωμα τοῦ τὰ πάντα ἐν πᾶσιν πληρουμένου, the fulness of Him that filleth all in all.

But, recognising this, and perceiving also that her witness consists far less in what she says, in the specific pronounce-ments that she utters in specific situations, than in what she veritably is, she is immediately compelled to ponder the

[1] Speech of Bishop Phillpotts of Exeter in the House of Lords, 22 March, 1832: quoted in R. N. Shutte, *Life of Bishop Phillpotts*, p. 360. Cf. Bishop Westcott, *Social Aspects of Christianity* (1887), pp. 75–6: " If the nation is, as we hold, a living whole, its constitution will be in-complete if it has no organ for the development and for the expression of its spiritual powers; if it has not, in other words, a national Church. . . . A national Church alone can consecrate the whole life of the people."

[2] *Osservatore Romano*, 23 Dec., 1927: quoted by Dr. Adolf Keller, *Church and State on the European Continent* (1936), p. 231.   Cf. art., ' Mucking In,' in *Christendom: a Journal of Christian Sociology*, Dec. 1935, Vol. V., pp. 295–303.

meaning of her mysterious title—*Corpus Christi*—and, by a natural association, to ponder it, her Bible in her hand, within the context of the Holy Eucharist.

3. CORPUS CHRISTI

The Abbot Herwegen of Maria Laach, in a memorable pamphlet on *Christian Art and Mystery*,[1] published six years ago, traces the decline of mediæval religious painting in Europe through its treatment of one of the outstanding themes of Christian art, namely, the Last Supper. In Byzantine art, for all its stiffness and conventionality, it is the *sacramental* character of the Last Supper that is visibly set forth, the historical setting and the human, psychological interest of the incident being purely secondary: the attention of the beholder is riveted to the sacramental mystery. Giotto still preserves a superficial correspondence with the Byzantine treatment of the subject. But there is a change. For him, the Last Supper is essentially the last reunion of Jesus with His disciples: the interest is primarily historical and sentimental: the sacramental theme is muffled and obscured. Finally, in the justly celebrated fresco of Leonardo da Vinci, the objective character of the rite is wholly lost: the interest is purely psychological, and the Drama of the Eucharist is submerged in the painter's sense for the dramatic: the emphasis is simply on the question, ' Lord, is it I? ' And with this precipitation of the human, psychological interest from the sacramental theme, the door at once is opened to triviality and superstition. The eye of the spectator wanders from the central Figure and indulges in the singularly futile effort of identifying individual Apostles: and in front of Judas the salt-cellar is seen to have been overturned and the salt spilled upon the table.[2] In fact, despite the sacredness of the subject, it is not religious art: it is a Problem Picture in the best Royal Academy tradition.

If this analysis be correct, it suggests something of pro-

---

[1] *Christliche Kunst und Mysterium.* I am indebted for this reference to the Rev. Dr. J. H. Srawley, Chancellor of Lincoln.
[2] Herbert Thurston, S.J., *Superstition* (1933), p. 107.

found importance for our understanding of these words, *Corpus Christi*.

Suppose that you were to pick up a book entitled *The Body of Christ*: you could not be certain what it was about until you had discovered whether the writer was an adherent of the Western or of the Eastern Church. If he belonged to the Western tradition, you would expect the book to treat of the Blessed Sacrament of the Altar: if, on the other hand, he belonged to the Eastern tradition, you could as safely assume that you had in your hands a book about the Church. The Feast of Corpus Christi by its very nature comprises both these themes: it is the festival of the Body of Christ in the most holy Sacrament of the Altar, and it is the festival of the Body of Christ throughout the world. To us, indeed, this use of the word 'body' as a collective noun—as when we speak of 'an ecclesiastical body,' or of 'a body of men'—is the most ordinary and familiar thing. But, as the Bishop of Derby has demonstrated in his essay in *Mysterium Christi*,[1] the metaphor is of purely Christian origin. When St. Paul told the Corinthian Christians that they were 'a body,' he was using the word σῶμα, 'body,' in a sense hitherto unknown in Greek. And Dr. Rawlinson proceeds to argue that it was from the sharing in the Body of Christ in the Holy Communion that the Church apprehended her own unity in the Body of Christ. To St. Paul, the unity of the Church is sacramental: the scattered Christian communities, with all their diversities of outlook and of circumstance, are One before the altar, are One within the sacrament of the Body and the Blood. And are we not still fumbling after that whenever we speak of our divisions as 'communions'—'the Anglican Communion,' or 'the Orthodox Communion'—phrases which seem to challenge with the authority of the New Testament that other and less happy phrase, 'the Roman obedience.' Not that way lies the road to unity. But "we that are many are one loaf, one body, for we all partake of the same loaf" (I Cor. x. 17): and with this compare the well-known

[1] A. E. J. Rawlinson, *Corpus Christi*, in *Mysterium Christi*, ed. G. K. A. Bell and Adolf Deissmann (1930), pp. 225–44.

passage from the *Didache* (ix. 3–4)—" We give thanks to
Thee, our Father, for the life and the knowledge which
Thou hast made known to us through Jesus Thy Servant.
To Thee be the glory for ever.   As this bread that is broken
was once scattered upon the mountains, and being gathered
together became one, so may Thy Church be gathered
together from the ends of the earth into Thy Kingdom."
Mark that it is not some abstract spiritual unity of which
St. Paul is speaking to his Corinthian converts, of an union
of human sympathies, of human opinions, of human senti-
ments of piety and fellowship, such as is sometimes taken
for a sufficient basis for intercommunion in small self-
constituted groups of more or less like-minded Christians
belonging to separate denominations [1]: it is a concrete,
ordered, bodily unity in Christ Jesus.   And this is sufficiently
indicated by the fact that when St. Paul introduced this
new and revolutionary metaphor into current speech, he
never spoke of the Church as ' *a* body of *Christians*,' but only
as ' *the* Body of *Christ*.'

So this conception of the Body of Christ, whether by it
we mean the Sacrament or the Church, is strikingly objective
and impersonal.   It is here that the point of Abbot Herwegen's criticism of da Vinci becomes self-evident.   And
yet, as members in particular of the One Body, we still
retain our own particular identities.   We remain, not only
Christian individuals (which expresses our relation to the
world), but also individual Christians (which expresses our
relation to the Church).   We, who are many, indeed are
One: yet we, who are One, are also many.   How then,
within the unity of the Body of Christ, is this strange paradox
to be resolved?

The Eucharistic rite itself is the solution.   Think for one
moment of the Offertory.   What is it that we offer?   Bread
and wine: the coarsest and the cheapest of the good things
of God in the world into which Christ came.   But that
which is represented by the bread and wine upon the altar,
that which we offer through the medium of these common

---

[1] Cf. A. M. Ramsey, *The Gospel and the Catholic Church* (1936), ch. XIV.,
esp. pp. 223, 224–6.

symbols, is in truth our very selves, our souls and bodies, our public and our private lives, our hours of solitude and of society, of labour and of recreation, church life, family life, social life, business life, all the crumbs of which our several existences are compacted, to be gathered up and pressed together into the One Loaf, to be blessed, and broken, and given back to us again, no longer common bread, but Christ's own Body, that we may pass on to our brethren that which we have received, in all the crumbs of which our several existences are compacted, our hours of labour and of recreation, of solitude and of society, church life, family life, social life, business life, our public and our private lives, ourselves, our souls and bodies. . . .

The world does not see this sacramental bread upon our altars, because it will not come to church. Yet God has provided a Host for the world—Corpus Christi—the Body of Christ—the Church: gathered by God Himself into this sacramental oneness and community, sanctified, hallowed, broken, offered in sacrifice for the redemption of humanity enslaved, a reasonable, holy, and lively sacrifice, a sacrifice acceptable to God. For there is no escaping from this sacrificial purpose. But what do we mean by the word ' sacrifice '? In the common idiom of our daily speech, we talk of ' making sacrifices,' of ' giving to the maximum of our ability,' and so forth. But here the initiative is in the hands of God. Here, in the power of this most holy Sacrament, it is not we who give, but we who are given: not we who make sacrifices, but we who are made a sacrifice.

For this sacramental rite is not something self-contained and self-sufficing. It is no *in sich ruhende Endlichkeit*. The Blessed Sacrament of the Altar, the most comfortable Sacrament of the Body and Blood of Christ, has no intrinsic validity of a final sort: it is a Means, and not an End. Here God's act meets man's need, and both the divine action and the human need become supremely manifest and articulate at this point of contact and of intersection. The Sacrament does not proclaim Itself: it proclaims the redemption of mankind, and sets against all our activities the mark of death: it speaks the wisdom of God in a mystery. And as no single aspect of this Sacrament can legitimately be detached from all its other aspects and, as it were, enjoyed in isolation, so also this Sacrament itself cannot legitimately be detached and isolated from the Work of God in its entirety.

And what is true of Corpus Christi in the Blessed Sacrament of the Altar is true also of that other Corpus Christi which is the Church of God. When we are talking about God's action and man's need, then we are speaking of the Church. But when we begin to talk about the Church, then we are talking about something which is not the Church—about some human institution, some ecclesiastical corporation, some humanitarian association, some devotional club—about something which may be very edifying, very admirable, very impressive, very helpful, but about something which is other than *Corpus Christi*, a broken Body offered in sacrifice to God in Christ for the redemption of the world, " to make all men see what is the dispensation (οἰκονομία) of the mystery which from all ages hath been hid in God who created all things; to the intent that now unto the principalities and the powers in the heavenly places might be made known *through the Church* the manifold wisdom of God " (Eph. iii. 9–10). " But we have this treasure in earthen vessels, that the exceeding greatness of the power may be of God, and not from ourselves; we are hard pressed on every side, yet not straitened; perplexed, yet not unto despair; hunted, yet not forsaken; smitten down, yet not destroyed; always bearing about in the body the dying [*lit.* putting to death] of Jesus (πάντοτε τὴν νέκρωσιν τοῦ Ἰησοῦ ἐν τῷ σώματι περιφέροντες), that the life also of Jesus may be manifested in our body. For we which live are always delivered unto death for Jesus' sake, that the life also of Jesus may be manifested in our mortal flesh. So then death worketh in us, but life in you " (II Cor. iv. 7–12).

When therefore the priest, on whom this duty is laid upon each several occasion not by his own volition and desire, but by the Body of needful men and women of which he is the organ and the representative, vests in the sacristy for the holy Mass, he knows that "the *Amysse* . . . signifies the Veil, with the which the *Jews* cover'd the Face of *Christ*, when they buffeted him in time of his Passion," and cried, ' Prophesy, who is it that smote Thee? ' " The *Albe* signifyeth the white Garment, wherewith *Herod* cloath'd *Christ*, in Mockery, when he sent him to *Pilate* . . . The *Girdle* . . . signifies the Scourge with which *Christ* was scourg'd. . . . The *Stole* . . . signifieth the Ropes or Bonds that *Christ* was bound with to the Pillar, when he was scourged. . . . The *Overvesture*, or *Chesible* . . . signifies the Purple-Mantle that *Pilate's* Soldiers put upon *Christ*, after that they had scourg'd him." [1] And as the priest, garbed in these Gospel vestments, enters the sanctuary, stripped of his own identity as an individual Christian man, he enters as the *Dramatis Persona*, in the character of our great High Priest, offering to Almighty God His Body— *Corpus Christi*—a sacrifice for the world.

> *For the Son of Man was not crucified once for all,*
> *The blood of the Martyrs not shed once for all,*
> *The lives of the Saints not given once for all :*
> *But the Son of Man is crucified always*
> *And there shall be Martyrs and Saints.*
> *And if blood of Martyrs is to flow on the steps*
> *We must first build the steps ;*
> *And if the Temple is to be cast down*
> *We must first build the Temple.*[2]

---

[1] *Ceremonies to be us'd in the Church of England, together with an Explanation of the Meaning and Significancy of them* (c. 1540): printed from a MS. in Biblioth. Cotton. (Cleop. E. 5., fol. 259) in Jeremy Collier, *An Ecclesiastical History of Great Britain* (1714), Part II, Book III (Vol. II, p. 194): ed. T. Lathbury, Vol. V, pp. 110–111. Cf. A. E. Baker, *These Holy Mysteries* (1936), pp. 134, 139–40, to which I owe this reference.

[2] T. S. Eliot, *The Rock : a Pageant Play* (1934), p. 42.

A SELECT INDEX OF SUBJECTS

PRINTED AND BOUND IN GREAT BRITAIN BY
RICHARD CLAY & SONS, LIMITED,
BUNGAY, SUFFOLK.